OUR SUBVERSIVE VOICE

McGill-Queen's Studies in Protest, Power, and Resistance

Series editor: Sarah Marsden

Protest, civil resistance, and political violence have rarely been more visible. Nor have they ever involved such a complex web of identities, geographies, and ideologies. This series expands the theoretical and empirical boundaries of research on political conflict to examine the origins, cultures, and practices of resistance. From grassroots activists and those engaged in everyday forms of resistance to social movements to violent militant networks, it considers the full range of actors and the strategies they use to provoke change. The series provides a forum for interdisciplinary work that engages with politics, sociology, anthropology, history, psychology, religious studies, and philosophy. Its ambition is to deepen understanding of the systems of power people encounter and the creative, violent, peaceful, extraordinary, and everyday ways they try to resist, subvert, and overthrow them.

1 New Media and Revolution
Resistance and Dissent in Pre-uprising Syria
Billie Jeanne Brownlee

2 Games of Discontent
Protests, Boycotts, and Politics at the 1968 Mexico Olympics
Harry Blutstein

3 Organizing Equality
Dispatches from a Global Struggle
Edited by Alison Hearn, James Compton, Nick Dyer-Witheford, and Amanda F. Grzyb

4 The Failure of Remain
Anti-Brexit Activism in the United Kingdom
Adam Fagan and Stijn van Kessel

5 The Participation Paradox
Between Bottom-Up and Top-Down Development in South Africa
Luke Sinwell

6 Citizens, Civil Society, and Activism under the EPRDF Regime in Ethiopia
An Analysis from Below
Edited by Camille Pellerin and Logan Cochrane

7 Intercommunal Warfare and Ethnic Peacemaking
The Dynamics of Urban Violence in Central Asia
Joldon Kutmanaliev

8 Our Subversive Voice
The History and Politics of English Protest Songs, 1600–2020
John Street, Oskar Cox Jensen, Alan Finlayson, Angela McShane, and Matthew Worley

OUR SUBVERSIVE VOICE

THE HISTORY AND POLITICS OF ENGLISH PROTEST SONGS 1600–2020

John Street, Oskar Cox Jensen, Alan Finlayson,
Angela McShane, and Matthew Worley

McGill-Queen's University Press
Montreal & Kingston • London • Chicago

ISBN 978-0-2280-2372-2 (paper)
ISBN 978-0-2280-2401-9 (ePDF)
ISBN 978-0-2280-2402-6 (ePUB)

Legal deposit first quarter 2025
Bibliothèque nationale du Québec

Printed in Canada on acid-free paper that is 100% ancient forest free (100% post-consumer recycled), processed chlorine free

McGill-Queen's University Press in Montreal is on land which long served as a site of meeting and exchange amongst Indigenous Peoples, including the Haudenosaunee and Anishinabeg nations. In Kingston it is situated on the territory of the Haudenosaunee and Anishinaabek. We acknowledge and thank the diverse Indigenous Peoples whose footsteps have marked these territories on which peoples of the world now gather.

Library and Archives Canada Cataloguing in Publication

Title: Our subversive voice 1600–2020 : the history and politics of English protest songs / John Street, Oskar Cox Jensen, Alan Finlayson, Angela McShand, and Matthew Worley.
Names: Street, John, 1952– author | Cox Jensen, Oskar, 1988– author | Finlayson, Alan, author | McShane, Angela, 1959– author | Worley, Matthew, author
Series: McGill-Queen's studies in protest, power, and resistance ; 8.
Description: Series statement: McGill-Queen's studies in protest, power, and resistance ; 8 | Includes bibliographical references and index.
Identifiers: Canadiana (print) 20240476042 | Canadiana (ebook) 2024047922X | ISBN 9780228023722 (softcover) | ISBN 9780228024026 (EPUB) | ISBN 9780228024019 (EPDF)
Subjects: LCSH: Protest songs—Great Britain—History and criticism. | LCSH: Music—Political aspects—Great Britain—History.
Classification: LCC ML3917.G7 S92 2025 | DDC 782.421/5920941—dc23

This book was designed and typeset by Lara Minja in Dante MT Pro 11 pt/14.5 pt. Copyediting by Eleanor Gasparik.

To all those who, at risk of being drowned out by 'his master's voice', protested – with words and music – and helped us all to find 'our subversive voice'

CONTENTS

Figures

Acknowledgements

Writing this book has been a team effort, but the team is much larger than the five names listed on the cover.

We owe a special debt to Helen Stokes, who joined our project for its second year. She was a joy to work with; her imagination and ingenuity brought the research vividly to life. She created and organised exhibitions in libraries, at Latitude Festival and at Cecil Sharp House. The 'beer mat' she devised for each of the songs and the stylish booklets she produced for our events were works of genius.

Our website, which accompanies the book, was designed by Mat Martin of Mat Martin Studio. His skill and vision will be evident to anyone who visits oursubversivevoice.com. He persuaded us to drop our rather conventional ambitions and produced a site that, as we write, has attracted some fifty-five thousand unique visitors.

That site has also been enriched by other members of our vastly extended team. We consulted many experts in compiling our long list of 750 protest songs, and the shortlist of 250. They were very generous with their thoughts ('don't include songs that just whinge') and opinions ('Noël Coward isn't a protest singer!'). They, though, are not to blame for the final selection. For a list of those who are spared culpability, go to: https://oursubversivevoice.com/about/.

We owe thanks, too, to the people who kindly agreed to be interviewed: Ren Aldridge of Petrol Girls, Billy Bragg, John Foreman (a.k.a. The Broadsheet King), Simon Frith, Sue Gilmurray, Jake Glanville, Maggie Holland, Steve Ignorant, Mike Jones, Kimwei, Marek Kohn, Neil Lanham, Sam Lee, Jay McAllister of Beans on Toast, Alison Morgan, Alice Nutter and Boff Whalley of Chumbawamba, Dave Randall, and Peggy Seeger.

We incurred further debts to those who contributed to the 'Other Voices' section of the website: Uri Agnon, Håvard Haugland Bamle,

Pam Bishop, Tim Brinkhurst (a.k.a. Timothy London), Stewart Duncan, Julia Hamilton, Ariel Hessayon, Noriko Manabe, Mat Martin, Marta Michalska, and Keith Negus.

Those who came to a workshop that we hosted at the end of our project gave generously of their time and their insights. We learned much that day from Jeremy Gilbert, William 'Lez' Henry, Jonathan Hicks, Sarah Hill, Mike Jones, Nicola Kearey and Ian Carter of Stick In the Wheel, Keith Negus, Mark Philp, Steve Poole, Joad Raymond, Lucy Robinson, and Stuart White. A special mention is owed to Ian Newman of Notre Dame University, who not only contributed to the event but also helped to fund it.

None of this would have been possible without the financial support of the UK's Arts and Humanities Research Council (Grant no. R207070) and without the help of the University of East Anglia's Research Office – especially Erin Wright, Hannah Chroston, and Megan Rudrun. We also benefitted from a writing workshop hosted by Newcastle University.

Cathy Davies helped us to make contact with the wider world. Neil Lanham and John Foreman gave us valuable material from their personal archives. We also benefitted immensely from the time and expertise of librarians and archivists at the BBC archives, Caversham; the British Library; the Pepys Library, Magdalene College, University of Cambridge; the Goldsmiths archive, University of London; the Ewan MacColl and Peggy Seeger Archive, Ruskin College, University of Oxford; the Vaughan Williams Memorial Library, Cecil Sharp House; Baker Library, Harvard University; and Somerset Archives and Local Studies.

One of the particular joys of the research for this book was being able to display some of the results and to talk about them. For this we depended on the kindness of librarians at Mile Cross, Coleman Road and UEA libraries in Norwich; and on the skill of photographers who helped to illustrate our exhibitions and their accompanying booklets: Andi Sapey, Brian Shuel, and Ann Nicholls.

Among the highlights – for us – of the project were the concerts that we were able to stage. The first was at the Norwich Arts Centre (NAC), at which Steve Ignorant, formerly of Crass, both spoke and performed. Thanks to Jona Hoffman for helping arrange this. The last event was at

Cecil Sharp House, when Andy Watts and the brilliant Carnival Band performed songs from our list of 250. A special mention is owed to Hannah James, who stepped in at the last moment to sing 'Brazen Hussies' when the great Viv Ellis, who also contributed generously to the project, was laid low by ill health. Katy Spicer of the English Folk Dance and Song Society, Bradley Glasspoole at the NAC, and the staff at both venues were unfailingly helpful.

One of our greatest debts is owed to those who provided our greatest surprise. When we submitted our grant application, we had promised to organise a couple of protest songwriting workshops. It was not a very imaginative or exciting proposal … until we took the idea to Simon Floyd, director of Norwich's theatre group The Common Lot (Principles: 'Everyone must benefit'; 'All contributions are equally valued'). Simon, together with Duncan Joseph, Siobhan O'Connor, and Charlie Caine, among many others, turned our damp squib of an idea into a 75-minute show that was performed to over three thousand people in Norwich and at Latitude Festival, where we also had the help of Jennifer Shaw, Beth Derks-van Damme, Aimee Dexter, and George Cooke, and the support of Laura Bates of the Everyday Sexism Project.

Finally, and very importantly, we are beholden to the work of McGill-Queen's University Press: to Richard Baggaley, who commissioned us; to Jonathan Crago, who became our editor; to Kathleen Fraser, who oversaw production; to Eleanor Gasparik, who did wonders as our copy editor; and to all the other MQUP people who helped along the way. They may have been the last recruits to the team, but the results of their considerable efforts are before you now.

Authors' Note

THE OUR SUBVERSIVE VOICE WEBSITE

As part of the research for this book, we created a website at oursubversivevoice.com. And in writing the book, we have used the site as a companion to it. Whenever we discuss a particular protest song, we provide a link to its location on the website, where you will find a brief description and, where available, a recording of the song. We hope that readers will also visit the site out of curiosity. You will be greeted by a randomised ordering of 750 protest songs from across the period 1600–2020. Of these, we have highlighted 250 songs, for which we give more extensive information. The list is searchable and filterable. The website also offers interviews with performers and others, case studies on particular themes, and specialist contributions. Readers will find their own paths through this thicket – and will no doubt see things that we have missed. Comments and suggestions are welcomed via the site.

OUR SUBVERSIVE VOICE

INTRODUCTION

In 1603, King James I of England sells knighthoods. In 1679, parliament attempts to pass an act excluding the Catholic James, Duke of York, from the throne. In 1787, the Society for Effecting the Abolition of the Slave Trade is founded. In 1795, Prime Minister William Pitt the Younger introduces two acts to restrict freedom of speech and association. In 1819, at a rally demanding reform of parliamentary representation, eighteen people are killed and hundreds injured by the charging yeomanry. In 1906, the first suffragette is arrested and imprisoned in Holloway. In 1950, at a former RAF AIrfield in Aldermaston, Britain, begins to develop nuclear weapons. In 1974, the Labour government initiates a social contract agreement with the trade unions. In 1984, striking miners are confronted by the police at Orgreave in Yorkshire. In 2016, the United Kingdom votes to leave the European Union. In 2020, George Floyd is killed by a police officer on a Minneapolis street in United States, and a crowd topples the statute of slave trader Edward Colston into Bristol Harbour.

At first glance, such events may seem to have little in common. But they all prompted the composition of at least one protest song: 'Come all you Farmers out of the Countrey' (1603); 'The Ballad of the Cloak' (1679); 'The African' (1788); 'Lock Jaws' (1795); 'Song of Slaughter' (1820); 'March of the Women' (1911); 'The H-Bomb's Thunder' (1958); 'Smash the Social Contract' (1979); 'Orgreave' (1994); 'Fuck Brexit' (2017); 'Wildfires' (2020) and 'Good Morning Mr Colston' (2022).[1] Indeed, almost every political event of any significance for England and its people over the last five centuries has protest songs associated with it. What role these songs played in political history is one of the main topics of this book. Another is the question of how, as a form of political communication and expression, songs – as distinct from speeches, newspapers, pamphlets, placards, blogs, livery, banners, and caricatures – 'speak' about politics, as words, voices, melodies, rhythms, and performances. And finally, the book explores which people and what processes account for the creation and dissemination of those songs.

Performing protest songs has never been a risk-free activity. In 1643, a singer was shot by troops policing the five-thousand-strong 'women's peace march' and in 1681, Stephen Colledge was hanged for sedition for performing the song 'A Ra-ree Show'.[2] Nearly four hundred years later, London's Metropolitan Police continue to restrict the performance of grime and drill music, using the lyrics of songs as evidence of criminal intent. In 2018, as the barrister Keir Monteith reports, the Met obtained a 'gang' injunction against the musicians Skengdo and AM, 'which among other things prevented the duo from performing music that incited violence. In 2019, they performed an old song called "Attempted 1.0" and as a result were taken to court. The judge imposed a nine-month sentence suspended for two years'.[3]

Despite the risks attached to songs of protest, their history follows the history of political dissent itself, and the story of the protest song might begin in almost any year. 'Protest', as we understand it today, may have become part of the language of politics only in the nineteenth century, but long before then, expressions of dissent, acts of rebellion and sedition, and other subversive behaviour that went under the label of 'riot' or 'tumult' were all associated with song. This use of song – to give voice to complaints and demands, and to organise those making them – is our topic. And one of our central arguments is that the protest song did not begin, as is widely supposed, in the twentieth century, but many centuries earlier. We choose to begin in the seventeenth century, not because this marks the first recorded incident of the protest song, but because it marks the beginning of the song industry in England, the reproduction and sale of songs in the marketplace. *Our Subversive Voice* is a record of this long history of political protest in song, of its creation and dissemination, and of its language and form as a medium of political communication and expression.

Other accounts of the protest song only rarely grant it this extensive heritage. It is commonly assumed that the protest song is a post–World War II phenomenon, tied to the folk revival and to the rise of anti-war protests in the 1950s and 1960s in the United States and the United Kingdom. While it is true that this period and these countries saw a flourishing of the protest song, and indeed the coining of the term itself, neither etymology nor history confines it to these particular times or places.[4] The protest song has been a key part of political activity in many countries and at many times. Hence one of the central claims of this book is that protest songs are a vital – if overlooked – part of the repertoire of political communication. And that the long history of protest songs is part of contemporary music culture too. The singer and songwriter Billy Bragg remarked that his songs about the 1984–85 miners' strike were inspired by the political unrest of the seventeenth century: 'I was now part of a tradition that stretched back to the Diggers and that historical perspective opened up in front of me'.[5]

In recognising the protest song's long history, we are acknowledging its political importance. It does not deserve to be used simply as an easy symbol of political dissent, a passing footnote to the 'real' business of activism. Equally, it is not to be dismissed as mere 'propaganda' – the enemy of creative art. Certainly, there have always been those who have regarded the protest song as unworthy of serious musical or political attention. In the 1960s, the magazine *Little Sandy Review* devoted an entire issue to attacking the protest song, which the editors called 'the nightmare of our folk art', accusing protest singers of being the equivalent of 'The Muck Rakers of the 1930s, the television commercial with its asinine jingles, the pep fest, the Sousa march, the football cheer'.[6] More recently, music and media scholar David Hesmondhalgh has argued that, while the protest song may be 'powerful, moving, and even inspiring', it forms 'a relatively minor part of the music of the world'.[7] While noting that music can contribute politically, he claims that 'music is not good … at establishing facts, or the truthfulness of one account over another … or at explaining or articulating belief systems, or even individual beliefs'.[8] Our book challenges these claims, and contends that the protest song not only warrants a more significant place in the history of music and politics but also has contributed to political action in many more ways than is typically supposed by its critics.

Besides establishing the protest song's long history and its political importance, *Our Subversive Voice* gives full recognition to its place in *English* history and politics. In doing this, we are seeking not simply to correct the tendency to treat it primarily as a US phenomenon but to draw attention to the political context in which protest songs appear. Like political communication more generally, they are attempts to understand and change the world. One of the earliest songs we consider, 'Well Met Jockie Whether Away', from 1604, argues that, to its detriment, the English court, under the new Scottish king, James I, has been taken over by Scots. Issues of who belongs to the polity, who defines the nation, are a persistent theme of protest songs, and are voiced in examples such as 'Alas Said the Papist' (1640), 'Britannia Excisa' (1733), 'Daughters of England' (1908), Sister Audrey's 'English Girl' (1982), and Bob Vylan's 'We Live Here' (2020). Who or what defines the community is the concern of Ewan MacColl's strictures about what constitutes the 'English' folk tradition, just as it is the concern of Maggie Holland's 'A Place Called England' (1999).[9] Understanding that 'place' and its time is key to understanding what a protest song is saying and doing.

England is important to our study not only as a site of struggle over rights and identity claims. It is also significant because of England's particular history and how this shaped, and was shaped by, song. Our study begins as London's ballad trade develops into a vibrant and specialised popular music industry, producing thousands of songs and serving nationwide markets from the 1590s onwards.[10] It ends with an industry that is global and digital, concentrated in a small number of transnational companies and platforms.[11]

While England's borders remain unchanged throughout the history we recount, its reach expands massively as it becomes a maritime power, creating an empire and a trade in slavery. All of these establish the conditions for, and the fault lines within, the rise of English protest songs, songs that are not necessarily written or performed by the English or about England alone, but which speak to the politics of the place from which they emerge. Hence, our website and the examples we discuss in this book include songs by the Manic Street Preachers (Wales), Van Morrison (Northern Ireland), Claude Joseph Rouget de Lisle (France), Peggy Seeger (United States), and Junior Marvin (Jamaica). Similarly, while many of the songs speak about issues that affect England specifically, others adopt a wider perspective.[12] There are songs that relate to global causes (such as anti-imperialism and climate change) and to issues that affect other countries (the partition of Poland and the Vietnam War). They remain, though, the product of their context: the politics of England.

In telling the story of English protest songs from 1600 to the present day, *Our Subversive Voice* does not recount a simple or straightforward tale. While there are common themes – disdain for the political class being one, poverty and hunger being another, and concern for the environment a third – there is much variation as new issues and concerns arise. In the early era, songs featuring the monarchy are commonplace; latterly, they are much rarer. Many of the protests in the later period come from the political left, but by no means all. The right, too, has its own repertoire – for example, Dominic Frisby's pro-Brexit '17 Million Fuck Offs' (2019). More importantly, the long history of the protest song calls into question the reductionism of left–right categories. The political complaints and demands to which songs have given voice have been, like the songs themselves, freighted with ambiguities and complexities that are not helpfully resolved into simple binaries. Or put another way: the protest song, like political communication more generally, admits to many different meanings and messages.

So while it is important to tell this history, to establish the persisting presence of the protest song, that is not the only or even the main task of this book. Protest songs, we argue, are a form of political communication, to be included alongside, if not conflated with, speeches, sermons, pamphlets, parliamentary debates, banners, cockades, videos, caricatures, and press commentary. Songs disseminate political ideas, highlight issues, and argue for causes, just as do these other forms of political communication. You would not know this, however, if you relied on most political science accounts of political communication.[13] Music is noticeable only by its absence. Our argument is not simply that students of political communication should add the protest song to their list of media in which politics is communicated, but rather that the protest song raises important questions as to what exactly is entailed in the communication of politics. What songs *do* is not the same as what a speech, pamphlet, or banner does. They do not provide just another means of delivering a political 'message'; they are a form of political activism.

We are not suggesting that the protest song has been entirely neglected. It may have been overlooked by scholars of political communication, but it has received attention from scholars of music.[14] Much has been written on the protest song and protest music, drawing attention to the variety of topics with which it has engaged: from R. Serge Denisoff and Richard Peterson's *The Sounds of Social Change* in 1972 to Ian Peddie's collection *The Resisting Muse: Popular Music and Social Protest* in 2006, Dorian Lynskey's *33 Revolutions Per Minute* in 2010, and Noriko Manabe's *The Revolution Will Not Be Televised: Protest Music after Fukushima* in 2015.[15] There is also now a large body of research on the relationship between social and political movements and music, begun in earnest by Ron Eyerman and Andrew Jamison's *Music and Social Movements: Mobilizing Traditions in the Twentieth Century* in 1998, and followed by many others.[16]

Our Subversive Voice highlights the protest song as a significant form of political communication, placing it at the intersection of political, historical, and music studies. While research on political communication has become increasingly attuned to the 'mediatization of politics' and to the new platforms and styles that this creates,[17] little or no space has been found for music – as opposed to film and television entertainment.[18] Songs may not be the equivalent of a manifesto or policy document, they might not occupy the time and attention accorded to a political speech by news media, but they may, we argue, still convey political ideas or mobilise political action, and reach many more people.[19] Indeed, it is likely that more public attention is paid to songs than to the news. They are part of the language in which politics is communicated and ideas formed. Perhaps more than any other type of political communication, they can constitute audiences as a 'people', singing together, dancing together, acting together. How and when songs do this is, of course, no simple matter, and an issue to which we devote much of our later discussion. Suffice it to say that it is a matter of not just the lyrics but also the voice, not just the melody but also the rhythm.

Claiming that protest songs should be regarded as part of political communication is but a first move. It highlights the focus of this book yet says nothing about how we approach our task. Political communication is, after all, more than the words uttered or written. It is also about how they are delivered or phrased, and about how they are heard and read. They are the results of performances and production systems. They depend on multiple agents and networks. So it is with protest songs. Thus, *Our Subversive Voice* is about the *processes* by which a protest song is made, distributed, communicated, and received – and sometimes repressed.

The story we tell of how protest songs have been made, distributed, and sung begins as the market in music begins. Some of the earliest songs we consider – such as 'Come all you Farmers out of the Countrey' (1603) and 'Well Met Jockie Whether Away' (1604) – were produced privately and restrictively circulated among the elite whose interests they expressed. These are to be contrasted with the ballads of the same period that were produced for the popular retail market. The first *commercial* song that we mention is 'Times Alteration: Or, The Old Mans rehearsall', written by a very well-known professional writer and published between 1628 and 1631. As if to announce the commercialisation of song, its publisher was the subject of a rights dispute.[20] But more importantly, these examples indicate that song had become a regular vehicle for popular protest.

In focusing on the protest song process, we raise far more questions than we answer. This seems right. In placing the protest song in the company of political communication more generally, our concerns are the same as those of other students of political communication. What is being communicated, by what means, to whom, and with what effect? And just as the literature on political communication abounds with competing theories about, and answers to, these questions, so too does our enquiry into the protest song. But there is method in our approach. We want to make protest songs the object of debate and argument, and to challenge those who would write them off as time-bound propaganda or a poor substitute for news. For us, the protest song should rightly be seen as a means by which political ideas are explored and expressed, by which political claims (and the right to make them) are asserted in musical form. As such, it is not to be dismissed as trivial or superficial, but rather as demanding the same rigorous analysis as that accorded other forms of political communication. But to do justice to our argument, we need to be clear about the subject of our study. So, what do we mean by a 'protest song'?

DEFINING THE PROTEST SONG

In opening the protest song to close scrutiny and to accord it significance, we have had to make a number of definitional and theoretical assumptions (and set some limits). In doing so, we were aware of the dangers of anachronism caused by, as Eric Drott puts it in a survey of protest music studies, 'a promiscuous extension of the term's sphere of application', while, on the other hand, wanting to shake 'loose some of the ingrained assumptions about what protest musicking can and does consist of'.[21] We found ourselves asking whether all political songs are protest songs, whether they have to address governments or other sites of political authority, and whether a protest song has to sound angry. Many songs are about romantic love sought, found, and lost. Can we assume that none of them qualify as protest songs? The answer to the latter question may seem obvious until we consider that demonstrating love for the monarch was a key feature of political language and critique in the seventeenth and eighteenth centuries, while deciding if a song was seditious – placing its producers and performers in jeopardy of prosecution – was judged partly on affective criteria, as we show in chapter 6.

In defining the protest song we consulted fifty-five experts, one of whom helpfully responded with the suggestion that we exclude songs that merely 'whinge'. By this they meant songs that do no more than complain about the state of the world without actually proposing that anything can or should be done about it. Such songs may well be political, at least insofar as they refer to more than feelings of romantic love or loneliness. But this is not enough to make them protest songs.

We argue that a protest song, like protest itself, is intent upon political change – of ideas, attitudes, or actions. It may be directed at formal sources of political authority (governments and constitutions), but it can also target other locations or types of power (capitalism, patriarchy, the church). Often, especially in the contemporary period, songs are a means by which citizens address each other, upbraiding or praising them for their sympathy, support, or solidarity with some cause or other. To protest is to envisage (the possibility of) change, to insist that something should be done (or not done). For this reason, many of the songs associated with UK punk of the late 1970s were political in some more or less explicit sense, expressing deeply felt and widely shared anger, frustration, and despair at what the Sex Pistols memorably called 'England's Dreaming'.[22] But while musical, fashion, and performance style carried powerful meanings, punk's lyrics only rarely indicated what, if anything, could be done to alleviate that anger, frustration, and despair.

SELECTING PROTEST SONGS

Those same experts who helped us define the protest song also helped in selecting the songs that were the focus of our research and of this book. Their expertise ranged across disciplines and across the centuries. Together we produced a list of 750 songs, of which 250 were highlighted as warranting special attention. Our aim was to ensure that all periods of history were included as well as the multiple styles and topics of the protest song.[23]

If this is beginning to sound almost pseudo-scientific, rest assured: it isn't. The history of song is in part a history of ephemera, and no dataset can claim to be reliably representative of a body of works so subject to erasure – whether by deliberate suppression, commercial lack of interest, material degradation, or other forms of neglect. Many of the most potent songs of protest, improvised during action or carefully crafted sub rosa, may never have been written down, remaining in the fugitive realm of tongue, ear, and air.

Aware that any claim to statistical rigour would thus be impossible from the outset, our methodology in assembling these 750 songs is not scientifically defensible. Historical vicissitude not only means many songs are no longer extant but also skews the archive. As researchers, we are much more likely to encounter songs preserved in prominent and accessible databases and publications than those preserved only in minor record offices or obscure private collections. Within an archive such as the English Broadside Ballad Archive (EBBA) or the Bodleian Library's ballad archive,[24] no amount of digitisation and cataloguing can redress the imbalances caused by the preferences and practices of the original collectors – antiquarians and enthusiasts such as Samuel Pepys, John Bagford, Walter Harding, or

Charles Harding Firth.[25] And whereas the era before sound recording possesses these partial, text-searchable archives, manageable in size (besides the great number of other sources we consulted), the more recent past lacks comparable institutional repositories, leaving us more reliant upon journalism, individual scholars, and our own musical experiences (which, we need hardly add, contain any number of gaping and predictable lacunae).

When choosing 250 songs from the 750 for extensive close reading (and listening), we have sought to redress – within reason – the massive chronological disparities that have overpopulated certain periods of the 750. This is not a purely telescopic imbalance: the twenty-first century and the 1980s are hugely overrepresented in the 750 as are the 1790s and 1810s; the seventeenth century has far richer pickings than the eighteenth century before 1789; and the period 1918–45 is perhaps the leanest of all. Our criteria for selection may leave us open to accusations of tokenism in including a mere handful of reactionary, nationalist, or far-right protest songs – though we might argue that, so far as we can tell, these have always been exceptional in the more recent historical record. All 750 songs can be found on our website (oursubversivevoice.com).

While we have tried to check, broaden, counterbalance, and second-guess in creating our list of protest songs, we acknowledge that this remains a fallible and subjective endeavour.[26] It is, though, a necessary one. It allows us to offer the first long history of English protest songs and to give due attention to the particularities of that history; to explore the genesis of individual protest songs; to understand the circumstances that allowed for their distribution, circulation, and use; and to appreciate how they engaged with the politics of their time. These are the subjects of subsequent chapters.

THE BOOK AND ITS ARGUMENT

We approach our study of English protest songs in several different ways. We include a chronological account, but we also consider the protest song as political rhetoric and political performance, and as the product of political processes. This means that the same song may appear in various places, analysed in contrasting ways. Case studies in the later chapters reveal the intimate details of how songs are made to communicate and how they are created and distributed – and indeed, how they are repressed. These case studies also serve to highlight both continuity and change in the lives of English protest songs. We hope that, as a result, a full picture emerges of the multiple dimensions of the history and politics of English protest songs.

In chapter 1 we use our definition of the protest song to trace the history of this form of political communication from 1600 to the present day.[27] This allows us to demonstrate the persistent presence of the protest song, whilst also enabling us to ask questions about what shapes its form. Is it a product of changes in the world, and in particular the political order? This is the argument advanced by Peter Manuel, who explains the rise and decline of the protest song in terms of changes to domestic and international politics. For Manuel, the protest song flourished in the period 1950–70 because the political movements of that period were hospitable to the protest song in a way that the current world, and the new social movements that inhabit it, are not.[28] There is, not surprisingly, some close correlation between political change and the concerns of the protest song, but of course, correlation is not causation. Our narrative reveals a more complex story in which the shifting focus of the protest song is not determined by political change – and indeed might, on occasion, work in exactly the opposite direction.

Our approach is of necessity an interdisciplinary one. We represent historical expertise in the different periods that we cover, and we draw upon a range of disciplines and skills – most obviously political and music studies – and within them specialisms in political rhetoric and political communication. Working together has, we hope, enabled us to escape the problem of much previous research on protest songs, what Drott labels 'inert seriality' or 'atomized interventions that are only connected by a rough similarity of theme or focus'.[29]

Politics

Our argument depends upon a particular conception of the theory and practice of politics. Definitions of the 'political' are, after all, about much more than the meaning of a word. They are about how the world is to be understood, and about the possibilities it represents. Few would confine the term 'politics' solely to the business of government and to those who aspire to run government. We share with music scholar James Garratt the view that studies of the relationship between music and politics too often 'address just one aspect of the political' and define politics in 'wilfully narrow terms'.[30] Equally, to claim that 'everything is political' runs the risk of emptying the term of meaning. Better, then, to think of the scope of politics as itself one of the things that people struggle over, including in song. More broadly, they also struggle to give meaning and value to our common existence. Politics involves everything to do with establishing who 'we' are and what 'we' want from the lives we lead. It is about who is included in – and excluded from – that 'we', and what follows from membership (or its denial). Politics, in this sense, is an exercise in creativity, of 're-presenting' the world, as F.R. Ankersmit suggests.[31] The protest song serves this end by asserting, demanding, and creating political voices.

Chapter 2 develops this account of politics to show how the song engages with politics (and vice versa). It suggests that protest songs can be understood as political thought, taking one of two forms: political ideology or political theory. Songs, we contend, make claims and arguments, developing propositions about the exercise of power and the distribution of rewards and resources, about ideas of freedom, equality, and justice. They are especially concerned with, and especially good at, *moral* kinds of political evaluation, representing events and persons in ways that show them to be departing from common moral standards. This approach to the protest song sees music as having the potential to educate listeners, to allow them to deliberate, and to mobilise them.

We do not, of course, assume that all protest songs do this, or do so successfully. Just as other forms of political communication fail so too do protest songs. One of our key questions is what it is that protest songs *do* politically. Central to our account of the protest song as political theory and political thought is the relationship that the song has with its political context. Political thinking, as Quentin Skinner and other historians have argued, is always located within a specific setting. 'I argue that, if we are to write the history of ideas in a properly historical style', writes Skinner, 'we need to situate the texts we study within such intellectual contexts and frameworks of discourse as to enable us to recognise what their authors are *doing* in writing them'.[32] In making this case, Skinner speaks of the need to understand the 'performativity of texts'. We take the same approach to the protest song.

In chapter 3, we treat the protest song as political rhetoric and oratory, looking at how the lyrics and the music seek to constitute the audience and then to persuade and to mobilise them. In doing so, it is important to appreciate what we mean when we describe a song as a text. As Garratt notes: 'At its extremes, music as political expression morphs into speech or into brute, disruptive noise. While talking and singing have become increasingly compartmentalised within the West in modernity, the middle ground of rhetorically heightened, ritualised speech retains its potency'.[33] While there are similarities between the political song and the political speech, they are different in many ways, and one theme of this book is the distinctive character of the song as a means of political communication.

Songs as Products

A protest song does not spring into existence fully formed. As with all political communication, it has to be produced, distributed, and seen, read, or (usually but not necessarily) heard. This depends on the available technology, and on the systems of production and distribution. It also depends on the skills and resources of the performers and those who work with them, and on the skills and resources of their audiences. Any appreciation of the politics and history of the protest song must take account of these elements and see how the song does, and does not, differ from other media in which political ideas are communicated.

Our study begins in 1600 because, as we have noted, this marks the transition towards a large-scale popular music industry, based in London, that served an ever-increasing and socially broad national market for song. Songs were published in anthologies and in newsbooks (and, from the eighteenth century, in newspapers), but most were printed on single sheets known as broadside ballads and sold from shops and stalls or by singers and hawkers in marketplaces, on streets, and in alehouses, taverns, and inns. From 1624, the ballad trade was effectively divided between and capitalized by a company of publishers. They bought up rights to tried-and-tested best-selling songs and independent speculative publishers who specialized in locating and producing fashionable new songs.[34] The latter group (mostly booksellers) produced topical and political single-sheet songs for the retail market, including several of our protest songs – see, for example, 'The Whig Rampant' (1682) and 'A New IRISH Song; OF Lil-li bur Lero' (1689), which are the subjects of case studies in chapters 4 and 5.[35] A third group of producers (mostly printers) emerged from the 1640s and were commissioned by activists to print songs for political campaigns. Often given away gratis to target groups in the first instance, these song sheets were published in roman type and looked very different from popular retail ballads (which, until the 1680s, were typically published in gothic or 'blackletter' type). Several of our protest songs were surreptitiously produced by such politically dedicated or commissioned printers – for example, 'The Sea Martyrs' (1691) and 'A Ra-ree Show' (1681).[36]

By the eighteenth century, a new group of specialist music printers had joined the retail trade, and while London remained the most important centre of production, the ending of the Stationers' Company's printing monopoly in 1695 opened the door for regional producers to become active in the popular song market.[37] Until the mid-nineteenth century, this trade was dependent on and restricted by the capacities of the hand press and handmade paper. However, the scale of production was revolutionised by two new technologies: machine-made paper (*c.*1801) and the rolling press (*c.*1847), which introduced true mass production at low cost.

Subsequently, other forms of production and distribution have also shaped the history and form of the protest song – including developments in musical instruments, microphone and amplification technology, recording facilities, broadcasting institutions, record labels, and streaming platforms. In this sense, the history of the protest song is also the history of the market in songs and in the technologies of production and distribution, although it is not only a consequence of these factors. Changes in technology can modify both the form of the protest song and access to it, whether for creators or audiences. They can alter the creative and distributive possibilities. They can also affect attempts to control the protest song. Protest songs have always been censored, as we show in chapter 6, but the reasons for this and the means of exercising control have changed with time and technology. However, our account is not a deterministic one. The protest song is not simply a by-product of commercial and technological change.

One implication of producing songs as marketable goods is that demand for the product also has to be created. For the song to have exchange value, there must be an audience that has resources, skills, and tastes to access and value it. Therefore, our history of English protest songs is a history of audiences as well as of market forces and technology. In the case of the protest song, that audience is almost always associated in some way with a social, religious, or political ideology, movement, or cause. To this extent, the history and politics of the protest song are also the history and politics of those movements and their use of song in communicating their cause and mobilising their supporters.

A further element in our approach to the protest song as product is the performer or creator. Neither publishers, record companies, nor streaming platforms are solely responsible for the content that they produce, just as audiences *as audiences* do not, for the most part, generate the products they consume. Even in the case of marchers singing primarily to themselves, their songs were invariably penned by individuals, who were often not present during the demonstrations. While there may have been a tendency within much writing on music to overstate the importance of the artist, we could not make sense of the protest song without reference to those who wrote and performed them.

Finally, while many of the songs and songwriters that we discuss are implicated in some way with the world of commerce, there is within protest music – as with music in general – an amateur tradition, found in the activist groups, community choirs, religious groups, and theatre companies that create and perform protest songs, but are not motivated by, or implicated in, their sale. For example, 'Brazen Hussies' (1983) by the Greenham Common Women's Peace Camp owes little or nothing to commerce or to technology.

Singers as Political Activists

Singers of protest songs are important as political actors as well as performers. One of the implications of our account of politics – and the place of political communication within it – is that attention needs to be directed at who they are 'for'. In the late-modern era, protest singers and songwriters, like politicians, are often presented, or present themselves, as speaking for their audience or as bearing witness to a cause.[38] They may not always make this explicit, or be fully aware of what they are doing, but it is implied by their use of music for political ends. They are making a claim to 'represent' a cause or a people, and as such to be taken seriously.[39]

This musical imitation of representative democracy is a relatively recent development, but throughout the period we study, the performance of song takes on a political guise. In the seventeenth and early eighteenth centuries, singers lived dangerously. Many were whipped and imprisoned. Their performance was seen as a defiance of authority. In the nineteenth century, the protest song had a different, and less fraught, relationship to politics. It was often communally sung, and so there was no discernible distinction between audience and singer. And what was sung was, likely, a non-commercial song written by an absent or unknown composer. Nonetheless, a representative claim was still being made; it was just performed in a different way. The communal singing could be seen, as historian and political scientist Benedict Anderson argues, as evoking the 'imagined community' of a nation or, in this case, a class.[40]

How the claim to represent is made, authenticated, and legitimated in musical performance is the subject of chapter 4. This follows the argument developed in chapter 3 that songs are to be understood as forms of rhetoric, and that this rhetoric is contained both in lyrics and in sound. Our approach incorporates the role of performance in conveying meaning and encouraging action. In analysing how protest songs are performed, we concentrate on the specific question of representation, and of how songs, singing, and staging perform the claim to represent or speak for a cause and a people. This, after all, is central to what a protest song is doing. It is 'speaking out' and 'calling' for action. Such speech acts have to be seen as 'credible' or 'legitimate' to engender a response. The question is how this happens. What, in musical discourse and practice, constitutes the legitimacy or credibility of the claim?

We argue that many dimensions of performance are implicated. One of the most obvious, at least in recent decades, is genre. Genres differ in the degree to which they allow or encourage performers to communicate politically.[41] Hip hop, folk, and reggae, for example, are contemporary genres in which political comment is accepted or expected, but protest is not confined to these musical templates.[42] There are examples of this on our list of 250, just as there are in that most familiar of pop events, the Eurovision Song Contest.[43] But also apparent is that the idea of 'genre' makes little or no sense when applied to ballads of the seventeenth century or for much of the period we cover. Balladeers and music hall performers drew upon styles and modes of address from the theatre or from communal singing performances borrowed from religious traditions.[44] Even now, claiming the right to speak politically is not just a matter of genre. Appearance and gesture can also do some of the authenticating or legitimating work. Dressing like your audience can help to create some sense of shared identity, which can in turn help to ground a claim to political representation. Such an impression can be generated, too, by the way performances and performers are mediated by journalists and others, who make connections between performances and politics. There are, of course, many other stylistic and discursive links to be made between music and claims to political representation. Chapter 4 offers an insight into how the performance of the protest song supports and sustains its claim to speak for people and causes.

The Protest Song Process

Our approach to the study of the protest song stresses the need to understand its history and politics as a text, a performance, and a product. There is a fourth important aspect: process. This describes how the text, performance, and product come to be connected. Bob Dylan once said of his music: 'These songs didn't come out of thin air. I didn't just make them up out of whole cloth … It all came out of traditional music: traditional folk music, traditional rock and roll, and traditional big-band swing orchestra music'.[45] For us, the protest song is not simply the result of a process of learning and borrowing from other musical traditions – although that is clearly part of the story we tell – but also of dependencies upon a range of actors and institutions. Rather than thin air, protest songs are the result of a network of material and organisational resources, which can both facilitate and thwart them.

Chapters 5 and 6 provide examples of the processes that have given rise to protest songs. The first traces the organisations and individuals that have enabled protest song to be created, distributed, and heard: the trade unions that founded folk clubs; the churches and societies that created choirs; the local authorities that provided spaces for singing; the trade producers, political parties and social movements that supplied the causes. The second looks at the other, negative side of this process: the authorities – from trade guilds to moral guardians, police forces to broadcasters, governments to streaming services – that, by various direct and indirect means, censored and regulated the protest song process, to the extent of imprisoning and even killing those responsible for protest songs in the seventeenth and early eighteenth centuries. Later, the punishment was less draconian. In the 1940s and 1950s, the BBC, through its many layers of committees, compiled a list of 'banned songs'. These were prohibited for many different reasons – for being excessively 'sentimental', or for advertising commercial products, or for failing to treat classical music with due respect. And some were refused airplay for their politics (such as Paul McCartney's 'Give Ireland Back to the Irish' in 1972).

These two chapters furnish the last elements of our approach to understanding the history and politics of the protest song. The protest song is a form of political communication and, as such, needs to be analysed as political thought and theory as well as musical performance. It must also be understood as the result of a process of creation, distribution, and consumption, and of regulation or control.

What Protest Songs Do (and Do Not Do)

One of the reasons people give for criticising or dismissing protest songs is that they do not achieve anything. Certainly, the question of the effect of protest songs is raised more than any other when we present our research.

Protest songs, critics assume, are sung to and heard by those who already share the sentiments being expressed. They are, at best, boringly predictable and, at worst, propaganda. There are, of course, protest songs that deserve such criticism, but not all. There are love songs too that are cloyingly sentimental or predictable, but this is no grounds for condemning all songs about love. Similarly, we would not dismiss all forms of political communication just because some of it fails to engage or enlighten its audience. We do not expect every political speech or newspaper headline to change how people see the world, so why should we expect it of a song. But as with some speeches and headlines, many protest songs do important political work.

Protest songs contain and communicate political ideas and arguments. Understanding a protest song means looking at what it says, how it says it, where it says it, to whom it says it, and in what context it says it. And certainly, there is much anecdotal evidence of how songs have made a difference – tales of how The Smiths' 'Meat Is Murder' (1985) converted people to vegetarianism, or how The Special AKA's 'Free Nelson Mandela' (1984) introduced fans to the injustices of apartheid South Africa. It is worth noting that these are also examples – common across the centuries – of songs that, by virtue of being successful in the marketplace, certainly did reach beyond an audience of the already-converted. But while such stories of the impact of particular songs should not be discounted, they cannot be treated as systemic, scientific evidence of the impact of any given song. Such evidence, it can be argued, is impossible to obtain. No natural or laboratory experiment can test for this kind of effect and control for all the others. More plausible perhaps is the suggestion that protest songs form part of a much broader political discourse, composed of all manner of media and all manner of political ideas.

This is how we view and treat the protest song here: as one part – an important but neglected part – of political communication and of the circulation of political ideas, feelings, and vocabularies. It is, as we say in chapter 2, a case of politics 'in the wild'. Protest music is vernacular political and ethical thought. It is the sound of politics from below.

In what follows, we provide the evidence for our case, tracing the long history of English protest songs, exploring the styles and devices that have

I.1 • The Common Lot performing at their *Songs of Hope and Protest* show, Cow Hill, Norwich, in 2022.

been used to persuade those who hear them, and recounting the processes that have brought them into existence. Our book traces the intersection of political, musical, and commercial culture to produce a powerful – perhaps the most powerful – form of political communication.

In 2022, we collaborated with The Common Lot theatre company in Norwich. Together we devised a show called *Songs of Hope and Protest*. It drew from our list, but it also led to the writing of new examples. This was the chorus of one of those 'Song of Protest':

> So we sing our song of hope and protest
> And it's justice that we fight for
> We'll keep singing on 'til the one per cent notice
> That the rest of us won't take it anymore.[46]

The song's creation, performance, and enthusiastic reception recall the larger and longer story that this book recounts.

1

PROTEST (AND) SONG'S LONG HISTORY

1976. Neil Innes – musician, comedian, songwriter for Monty Python – performs a sketch on his friend Eric Idle's BBC Two show *Rutland Weekend Television* (1975–76) spoofing the same channel's *The Old Grey Whistle Test* (1971–88).[1] Innes introduces his song in a diffident English accent with the memorable lines: 'Er, this next number is a protest song ... Er, I've suffered for my music – and now it's your turn'. The song's lyrics are deliberately opaque and asinine, delivered in a cod-American drawl that rises to an explicit Bob Dylan impression for the chorus. If they have a message, it is self-defeating: markers of capitalist consumerism and self-interest are more prominent than the hollow line, 'We're marching for freedom today, hey'. But the words are less significant than the other targets of Innes's knowing satire: his monotonous acoustic guitar playing, the bathetic harmonica solos, his appearance (double denim, cap, and shades) – and the full thirty seconds he spends deliberately failing to retune a discordant high-E string that repeatedly delays the song's start.

1995. Hugh Laurie – actor, comedian, blues singer-to-be – performs a sketch on his and Stephen Fry's BBC One show *A Bit of Fry & Laurie* (1989–95).[2] First aired on 1993's *Comic Relief* – and also opening with a fumbled introduction delivered in received pronunciation – the song reproduces the Dylan-parodying tropes of accent, acoustic guitar, and harmonica. A full-band incarnation allows for still more American signifiers, all of them white and male. Here, the lyrical and musical scaffolding is more coherent, a message of a world in dire need of rescue – the singer has the answer – the musical logic builds to its culmination: 'All we gotta do is ... [inaudible]'. The chorus reiterates, 'We gotta [inaudible]', followed by platitudes – 'every woman every man', 'time after time'. In other versions, the song ends with a repeated 'All we gotta do is ...', delivered crescendo, at the crucial point of which Laurie pulls a panicked face before dipping his head to his harmonica, the semantic replaced with the ineffable.[3]

Two skits, some twenty years apart, offering an essentially unchanged reading of 'the protest song' as ineffectual, annoying, hypocritical, and stylistically defined by the 1960s output of a handful of US performers, primarily Bob Dylan. Effectively, they contrast a caricatured American naive sincerity with a knowing English cynicism. Yet the period of English history these parodies bookend – roughly corresponding to the governing Conservative Party's embrace of Thatcherism – is responsible for perhaps the single most fertile episode in English protest song, across many musical genres, of which the acoustic singer-songwriter is among the *least* prevalent.

Still more significantly, the chronological implications, that 'protest song' is both an invention of the boomer generation and frozen in time as a musically recognisable genre, are testament to a collective memorialisation that separates the 'post-war' (a label that itself epitomises the phenomenon) from all history before that date, effectively discarding the former period. For although the term 'protest song' is unknown until 1953[4] (with the exception of a single 'Protestlied für Schleswig-Holstein' from 1848[5]), songs of explicit political protest in many cultures, particularly that of England, date back at least to the early-modern era (*c.*1500–1700), if not before.

This chapter both elaborates and interrogates this much longer chronology of at least five centuries, envisaging this *longue durée* as both two and three eras, before examining three songs – from 1647, 1832, and 2017 – as exemplary of the key cultural, historical, and socio-political aspects of this chronology. The resulting conception of English protest song and its long history is, perhaps, just a little more intriguing than Innes and Laurie would have us believe.

QUESTIONS OF CHRONOLOGY

Though the printed song sheet had been around for roughly a century by 1600,[6] our chronology begins in the 1590s for two key reasons. First, London's exponentially growing popular music trade began to be more professionalised and specialised. Second, controls over the print trade in general and the ballad trade in particular were codified and intensified. These developments heralded a new era of accessible and widely circulated song, marking a significant change from earlier phenomena, such as a body of mid-sixteenth-century songs recorded only in manuscript form that protested the dissolution of the monasteries and launched ad hominem attacks on Thomas Cromwell.[7]

Strictly speaking, the first commercially published protest song of our period should have been Thomas Deloney's 1596 ballad 'A Complaint of the Great Want and Scarcity of Corn'. A highly effective song written by one of the first truly professional and celebrity ballad writers of our period, it led, on the one hand, to Deloney's imprisonment and the destruction of his songs and, on the other hand, to ameliorative action regarding the provision of food by the governing authorities (see 'The Subversive Voice of Early Modern Hunger').[8] However, destruction of song sheets – whether by governments, consumers, fire, or worms – means that survival rates of commercial ballads are very poor for the first forty years of our period. No instance of Deloney's ballad survives. Hence, in a bid to have examples from every decade, our first two extant protest songs for 1600–10 were privately produced in manuscript, and circulated among a small social elite. They protested the unpopular personal union of the English and Scottish kingdoms under James I and VI (1603–25).

Thanks to the vagaries of survival, therefore, our historical narrative begins in reaction to the influx of Scots to the English court and James I's financially motivated cultivation of a new gentry class. But from the 1620s, the survival of commercially produced and distributed songs widens out the issues being protested, encompassing the socio-economic (consumption, sumptuary laws, gender relations), European diplomacy, and even the consequences of selfish parenting ('The Lamentation of Mr Page's Wife of Plymouth', 1624). From the 1630s, songs of protest were dominated by issues such as threats to Protestantism, whether at home or abroad; the ravages of plague; shortages of food; and the intense political protests that led up to civil war, regicide, republican government, restoration, plots, crises, and 'glorious' revolution. Crucially, many of these songs accompanied forms of embodied direct action beyond singing, ranging from street marches to petitioning, some of which became violent and bloody.

Within the vast corpus of political song these conflicts generated, a high number might be classified as protests, by royalists, parliamentarians, Diggers, Williamites, Jacobites, and different denominational factions. Indeed, a passing knowledge of English 'high' political history will supply the context for many songs in the centuries that followed: from the pro-Stuart Jacobite rebellions to agricultural enclosure, the French Revolution to the Peterloo Massacre of 1819, Chartism and socialism to the suffragettes, hunger marchers to Oswald Mosley's fascists and their 1980s revivalists (the far right had its protest songs too), the atom bomb and Vietnam to the Falklands and Iraq wars, the miners' strike and the Brixton riots of the early to mid-1980s to Brexit in 2016 and the COVID lockdowns from 2020.

It would be far too simplistic, however, to present a simple correlation between an event-centred, almost picture-book version of English political history and the story of protest song. As later chapters analyse in considerable detail, the relationship between the conditions for protest songwriting and the production of protest songs is a complex one. It can safely be assumed that at all times during these centuries, *political* songs have been continually written and sung. Indeed, political songs probably form the primary object of study for historic song specialists of all periods.[9] Thinking chronologically, it may be more profitable at this stage to consider how the political conditions of English society, and the balance of power relations within it, have determined which of those political songs may be considered as songs of *protest*. This definition is not just a pedant's attempt to categorise but also a way of tracing the transhistorical shifts in the currents of political discourse and power, and its communication.

We might begin etymologically, by considering the terms employed by historical actors themselves. There is a key reason for the prevalence of the Innes-Laurie stereotype of the protest song – and, just as importantly in those examples, of the protest *singer*. Though applicable across time and context, that label has been claimed by very few except singer-songwriters in the Woody Guthrie–Bob Dylan–Joan Baez or, perhaps in the UK, the Ewan MacColl–Billy Bragg–Grace Petrie tradition. Even within these few decades, Joan Armatrading, for instance, who has multiple songs on our list, has repeatedly rejected the label of protest singer.

As Mark Philp notes, the term 'protest', like 'politician' and 'politics', is highly contingent upon historical circumstance.[10] The idea of a legal written 'protest' predates our period – hence, of course, 'Protestant' – whereas the modern idea of *a* protest, involving collective action and public demonstration within the law, dates only from the 1850s, with its associated verb following two decades later.[11] While it would take even a century longer to link songs to that specific action in the English language, it is not actually historically insensitive to describe much earlier songs – written, published, performed especially by individuals – as protest songs. As early as 1550, one could 'protest' *against* something in public, orally as well as in writing.[12] At the start of our period, such songs were sometimes titled as a 'complaint' or occasionally 'lamentation', as part of a wider lexicon of titular labels (remonstration, exhortation, and so on). These words had much less passive connotations than they do today. Before the Enlightenment-era concept of public opinion was established, such assertions of a dissenting voice in public were an extraordinary action to take (see below).

Indeed, the personal stakes involved in authoring, publishing, or singing a certain kind of political song have often marked these songs as noteworthy protests: a combination of a song's lyrical content with its conditions of production, dissemination, and performance. As the first model of periodisation elaborated below makes clear, the majority of such songs written before the realm of public discourse became a relatively 'safe space' for the articulation of political dissent halfway through our period were likely to be seen as illegitimate. In this earlier period, the songwriters risked legal persecution that might result in anything from fines to execution (see chapter 6). This legal jeopardy persisted into the nineteenth century, though short-term imprisonment was the worst that might befall a post-Waterloo radical or Chartist writer such as Samuel Bamford or Thomas Cooper.[13] In the early twentieth century, suffragettes might be imprisoned for direct action, but their songs went uncensored; in later decades, broadcasters such as the BBC might issue bans against songs, but their writers were free to consider this a badge of honour (see chapter 6).

James Garratt, among others, argues that protest has historically been a relatively niche subset of political song and music.[14] This is correct, and especially in the seventeenth to nineteenth centuries, the majority of English songs with content that could be considered political were far from subversive. They tended instead to endorse the status quo, predominantly by Othering enemies of the state (Catholics, Irish rebels, Napoleon, Russia ...) and by fêting the Crown, constitution, established Church, armed forces, and the nation's seafarers in general.[15] Beyond its lyrical content, a protest song should come from a place of (at least perceived) underdog status in terms of political power relations, as well as standing outside the mainstream of consensual political discourse. Thus, for instance, only a minority of the many thousands of election ballads across the long eighteenth century may be classed as protest songs (for example, those that protested the result of individual votes, alleging corruption, error, or injustice).[16] The seventeenth century, witnessing as it did a series of regime changes and extreme political instability, is inevitably the most heightened period for protest song production. Until the Bill of Rights 1689, which fixed the rights of parliaments to meet, this was the era when the 'high' political arena of government, Church, and party or faction was one wherein dissent was often classed as sedition or treason and the whole country was, willingly or not, engaged in the political ferment.

Throughout this period – and at least until the pro-shoemaker ballad 'The Gentlecraft's Complaint' of 1714 – those terms 'lamentation' and 'complaint', adopted self-consciously, were mostly associated with songs of socio-economic protest, conceptually associated with the culture of petitioning so prevalent in the early-modern era (and characteristic of bottom-up calls for redress well into the nineteenth century). The terms continued to be used after this date until at least 1856, but swiftly became far less common. With the exception of a handful of 'Laments' in the years after Waterloo that protested economic downturns in certain trades, they were generally used in a more knowing fashion, to give an affective titular weight to songs protesting issues of all kinds. These included the American War of Independence ('Britannia's Lamentation On the Devastation [of] War', *c.*1778), abolitionism ('The Negro's Complaint', 1788), naval mutinies ('The Saylor's Complaint', 1797), and violence in the workhouse ('The Women Flogger's Lament of Marylebone Workhouse!', 1856). Though extremely rare, the persistence of such titles indicates a continued perception not of a musical genre as such, but of a recognisable tradition of a particular form of songwriting that sought to make a political intervention from a subordinate and aggrieved perspective.

Even in the seventeenth century, however, most protest songs pretended to no such distinct formal identity. The idea of song 'genres' in the modern sense is a very recent and overwhelmingly musical rather than lyrical development. Throughout these centuries, writers of protest songs have couched their efforts in a wide range of musical idioms, from the theatrical to the sacred, the anthem to the cabaret ditty, work song to art song – as well as (whatever the implications of the Innes-Laurie stereotype) in modern genres from rap to reggae, disco to dub, punk to prog. In this contemporary era of genre, some musical styles have seen a predisposition to the expression of countercultural political sentiments, most famously punk, but also of course folk, reggae, and multiple subgenres of Black urban music. 'Heavier' genres such as metal, hard rock, and prog might even be taken musically to constitute a form of protest against the mainstream (see again, punk) and naturally to harbour expressions of protest. Counterintuitively, however, the explicit engagements with the wider political process of the sort with which we are concerned are *less*, rather than more, likely to be found in these genres. An overt political statement is much more significant in a high-charting pop song with radio play than it is in a self-consciously niche genre of song – and also perhaps more likely to constitute a deliberate political act rather than a conventional (for the genre) expression of alienation or disillusionment. We are aware this argument may seem unpalatable, and even – taken to extremes – dismissive of certain musical subcultures. Rest assured we do consider 'War Pigs' to be a protest song. The point is that, by creating a deliberately (even wilfully) narrow definition of protest, we seek to highlight the songs that go the furthest to engage a wider audience or effect political change. Rather than looking for an enduring historical self-consciousness of a practice or a song type that knew or, worse, *assumed* itself to *be* protest song, we might do better to examine the vast and motley array of songs that *we* consider to be protest songs, and see if, taken as a rudimentary transhistorical corpus, they admit of patterns or periodisations that are historically significant.

1600–2020 CONSIDERED AS TWO ERAS

Taking our cue from the discussion above, we might wish to conceive of two long eras of protest song – and protest singer – that cleave on the basis of the political situation and personal stakes. In the earlier era, most sung dissent was not officially tolerated and could have serious, even fatal, legal repercussions. In the later era, protest song, however subversive, has generally been deemed an acceptable part of political discourse. In the latter, songwriters may have been imprisoned, but not *solely* for their songwriting, and not for very long. Songs may have been denied a platform by broadcasters or tour promoters, but their sale and performance have rarely been prohibited absolutely. We might describe these as the illegitimate and legitimate eras of protest song. Though rudimentary, this periodisation allows us to make some sense of the changing nature of our long history.

As Bruce Smith observed more than twenty years ago, ballad culture in seventeenth-century England was inherently subversive, irrespective of the songs' contents, because it extended the spatial and social realm of active political discourse beyond the limited sphere prescribed for it by the established authorities: 'A voice projects the singer into the acoustic space around him, as the singer takes her place in a speech community, so the ballad ranges outward to grasp authority figures and draw them by force into the singer's song. To *ballad* is to make a political gesture ... From the standpoint of authorities, ballads were dangerous not only for *what* they might say but for *how* they might say it. To ballet [i.e., the etymological root of the verb 'to ballad'] a subject was to commandeer the subject'.[17]

This perspective has never entirely gone away. However, the extension of the electoral franchise in the nineteenth and twentieth centuries legitimised participation in political discourse among ordinary and working-class subjects and citizens. Earlier still, the development of what Jürgen Habermas so influentially conceptualised as the public sphere – in which quotidian spaces beyond courts and parliaments, such as coffee houses, taverns, even streets and squares, and their equivalents in print, became recognised sites of political communication and critical expression – may be argued to have transformed the status of protest song, from fundamentally illegitimate to legitimate.[18]

We need not pursue the many critiques and revisions of Habermas's thesis to make the generalised point that you could freely say more things in more places in the England of the 1780s than the England of the 1680s (see chapter 6 for a full discussion of censorship and repression). Nor can we view these developments in isolation from the profound demographic changes of the nascent Industrial Revolution and associated phenomena from the mid-eighteenth century onwards, resulting in population growth and the development of an increasingly educated and self-aware urban and even rural working class. This is by no means a simple or even an entirely linear narrative. But viewed at the macro level, there is a clear rationale for conceiving of two distinct eras in which protest song has operated in England.

By this rationale, we would expect our protest songwriters to reflect the following conditions as the first era ended and the second began: increasingly plebeian, self-confident, acknowledged, and active in the sites of this new public discourse. At which point, enter the Birmingham publican John Freeth, who began publishing his own collections of political and protest songs in the early 1770s. As we discuss in chapter 5, Freeth embodied the new era, from his geographical location in a rising industrial centre to his role as a pub landlord. From this point onwards, we can begin to assemble an illustrious roll call of similar figures, almost a who's who of English radical history in the long nineteenth century. To name but a few: Edward Rushton, James Montgomery, Samuel Bamford, Eliza Flower, Ebenezer Elliott, Thomas Cooper, Eliza Cook, Ned Corvan, William Morris, Edith Nesbit, Ethel Smyth, Ewan MacColl, Aldwyn Roberts a.k.a. Lord Kitchener, and any number of living artists. Freeth, however, was something of an outlier. Protected by his reputation as a pillar of society in an already quite radical midlands city, he was relatively sheltered from the (often physical) intimidation and prosecutions that continued to oppress the last Jacobites, 1790s Jacobins, and would-be Luddites prior to the conclusion of the Napoleonic Wars in 1815. Particularly in the 1790s, writers were once again being arrested and prosecuted due to their songs. But in 1819 and 1820, in response to the Peterloo Massacre and the Queen Caroline Affair, an unprecedented number of protest songs were published with impunity: the political landscape had undeniably altered with the end of the wars. It is at *this* date then, 1815 rather than 1770 – almost precisely halfway through our chronology – that we might be most tempted to draw a line and speak of two distinguishable eras of protest song and protest songwriters.

In the latter era it is significant that, notwithstanding the continued lack of self-proclaimed 'protest songwriters', we *do* witness the rise of what we would now call activists: political or moral campaigners who turned to songwriting as a core part of their activism. This was true of reactionaries and loyalists as well as of radicals. Hannah More is perhaps the foremost example of the latter in the 1780–1800s,[19] while even Tory minister George Canning appears to have tried his hand at writing a song in the loyalist cause: 'The Pilot That Weathered the Storm' (1802), in praise of William Pitt the Younger.[20] Before the age of recording in particular, song was a customary part of political discourse, essential to parliamentary elections, political dinners, club culture, marches, assemblies, journalism – in brief: political activity of all kinds, except regulated debate within the Houses of Parliament themselves,[21] and songwriting featured prominently among the output of activists.

Set against this clear emergence of 'legitimate' activist-songwriters, we must admit that, though the conditions in the earlier era were much less conducive and though it seems anachronistic to talk of self-identifying 'activists' in the first 150 years of our chronology, it is nonetheless evident that even when the voicing of protest in song was proscribed by law, people persisted in doing so, sometimes quite openly. Given the practice of what Nace calls 'co-composition',[22] it is harder to generalise about the songwriters of the earlier era – yet even here, we can reach some definite conclusions. Some were certainly authors of whole ballads: Martin Parker (*fl.* 1624–*c.*1656) and Laurence Price (*fl.* 1624–*c.*1667) were extremely prolific 'celebrity' ballad-writers, leading exponents of their art, whose output in these turbulent decades inevitably included several notable songs that we would consider to be protests. Some writers were tradesmen or lowly farmers, such as Irish cobbler Richard Rigby (*fl. c.*1640–*c.*1695) and west country husbandman Laurence White (*fl.* 1670s). Other known writers were men of property writing from political or theological conviction – landed gentlemen, such as Thomas, 1st Marquess of Wharton (1648–1715) and his brother Henry Wharton (1650–1689); bishops, such as Richard Corbett; academic divines, such as Walter Pope (*c.*1627–1714); and radical preachers, such as Henry Walker (1638–1660). Yet most political and protest songs – many of which were lengthened into ballads – were written by 'professional' poet-playwrights, such as Thomas Jordan (1614–1685), Thomas D'Urfey (1653–1723), and Matthew Taubman (*fl.* 1680s).

These biographies should help dispel any ahistorical notions of 'the folk' in the earlier era, or an immediate association of anonymous song production with a collective or popular voice. It is not until the era ushered in by Freeth (and perhaps prefigured by the anonymous authors of the *Charnwood Opera*, *c.*1751, a subaltern rural dramatization of an anti-enclosure uprising)[23] that we consistently begin to identify protest songs with a markedly plebeian social origin. That said, it is foolhardy to generalise about songwriters' social status in any era. Freeth himself had periods of poverty in his youth, but his decades as a songwriter saw him propertied and semi-respectable. The centuries that follow evidence the growth and self-fashioning of the working class as a political force, but also feature protest songs penned by relatively elite writers, from poet William Cowper to socialist intellectual William Morris to playwright Noël Coward to composer Cornelius Cardew.

Across both eras, the vast majority of known writers have been relatively privileged in their schooling, with a demonstrable knowledge of the classics, for example, in the first era – an era also distinguished for containing no *known* writers of protest song who were not male, heterosexual, and white. In fact, we have not been able to identify an English protest song written by women before *c.*1800 (and by named women before the 1830s); by an acknowledged queer writer before 1886; or by a global majority writer before 1953.[24] All these dates are centuries later than the first English songs *of any kind* produced by writers with these identities, a consideration suggesting that the absence of female, queer, or global majority protest songwriters before these dates is due to more than lack of opportunity. It hints at an element of constitutive social censorship: that writers were either reluctant to put, or prevented from putting, their names to songs of protest (see, for example, the discussion of emancipated eighteenth-century Black composer, songwriter, and grocer Ignatius Sancho in chapter 5). Considered geographically rather than socially, there was a marked preponderance in southerners, especially from London, in the earlier era, corresponding to the concentration of both the print trade and the country's wealth. Mapping on as it does to the Industrial Revolution, it is unsurprising to see an increase in midlands and northern song from the 1770s onwards. Areas without a major industrial centre, such as the east and southwest of England, remain relatively quiet throughout.

Instructive as these findings are, the two-era model has one increasingly clear limitation: in the considerations above, protest songwriters appear more often as illustrative of wider historical phenomena, helping to bring trends into focus, than as themselves affording a useful category of enquiry. Perhaps the greatest benefit of this two-part periodisation has been to refocus attention from the 'canonical' decades of the 1950s–1980s, by making clear not only that protest song has a much longer history but also that its stakes were much higher in earlier centuries.

The legitimacy of asserting a subaltern political voice may broadly be said, then, to have shifted significantly halfway through our period. Yet more significant still might be the ways in which the assertion of that voice in song has changed over time, and how the structuring and performance of that voice has related to both political communication and political organisation. We might, in short, advance a more profitable model to encapsulate the *longue durée* of English protest song by listening to what these voices are saying and how they have said it: by turning from composers to content.

A song, protest or otherwise, is by definition a composite medium, most usually broken down into two essentials: music and lyrics. As David Atkinson has argued convincingly, this separability into constituent parts reflects centuries of actual practice.[25] The conventional mode of composing an 'art song' has always been for a composer to set an existing poetic text to new music, and the middling songs produced by professional writers for the theatres, pleasure gardens, music halls, and drawing rooms of centuries past have often been created by a composer and lyricist in collaboration. However, the default mode of 'vernacular' songwriting has always been to take an existing tune and give it new lyrics, a process known as contrafactum. Until approximately the 1950s, most of our protest songs have conformed to this latter type, whether originating as a commercial street ballad, a courtier's or politician's invective, or a labourers' anthem. The majority shift to a practice of simultaneous musical and lyrical composition reflects not the switch to recorded music but the rise of rock 'n' roll and subsequent genres derived chiefly from the Black Atlantic. In both these periods – the long and the recent – there have been exceptions to this generalisation, with new tunes for protest songs being written in significant numbers from the 1830s onwards, and some recent songs adhering to the old practice of rewriting an existing tune. These patterns conform to what is known of song culture in general – suggesting that protest songwriting has always remained closely tied to its broader cultural context – with perhaps a more marked prevalence of *meaningful* contrafactum where the tune is chosen for an intentional political effect, for example as parody or satire, than is the case in that broader culture.

It is of course impossible to insist too much upon such generalisations in what is clearly an ephemeral medium. We can speak only of the corpus we have assembled, never of a totality of historical protest songs. Yet on at least two significant and closely correlating criteria, our songs may be divided into three distinct historical eras, which do much to advance our understanding of both song and political protest in England.

1600–2020 CONSIDERED AS THREE ERAS

The three eras are 1600–1789, 1789–1945, and 1945–2020 – all (over)familiar and recognisable within Western history, so much so that we may as well give in and call them the early modern, modern, and contemporary (we draw the line at 'post-war' for the third, given the near-constant state of war across all three eras). These periodisations apply both to the content of the songs' lyrics and to their application in musical performance.

Taking the first of these: it is in the nature of songs, especially protest songs, to speak to several issues at once. Yet, partly because of our selection process, focusing on songs that sought to intervene in particular political issues, it has proved possible (though still wholly subjective) to analyse our 750 songs at the macro level, assessing their thematic preoccupations. Make no mistake: this was no scientifically viable, quantitative exercise. This was simply an attempt to screw certain lenses into our analysis, the better to bring into focus certain trends over our *longue durée*, and see how far these three periodisations reflected changes in the content of the songs. Ultimately, most songs seemed to foreground one of nine primary concerns – from 'The Powte's Complainte' (1619) for the environment to Billy Bragg's 'It Says Here' (1984) for the media. Four of these categories (including the preceding two) appear only sporadically across the whole time period, and together constitute a small minority of the total. Two issues, meanwhile, are historically ever-present: the violent themes of war, peace, and empire; and the impact of social and economic change – in other words, the political evils to which people react in all times and places, whatever their ideology and awareness. This continuity may appear predictable, yet it is not unimportant. It suggests that, irrespective of the particular political conditions, some of which we previously used to divide our timeline into two eras – what is permitted as free speech, who has access to the means of songwriting production, what form of government is in power, which new political ideologies are prevalent, and so on – what amounts to a 'tradition' of protest has endured, that has consistently decried the use of violence, the effects of war, developments in industry and capitalism, and used similar discursive means to protest these. This is indicative not of a passive but of a *profound* continuity in both English politics and its systems of communication.

If we nuance the issue of violence – of war, peace, and empire – and subject them to a closer subjective scrutiny, two major anomalies emerge. Firstly, we have not found any songs protesting international affairs in a 'disinterested' fashion until after 1815, the year of Waterloo and the end of the Napoleonic Wars – a crucial date marking a major shift in England (or rather Britain's) role upon the world stage. Before this date, the conduct of other nations, or their internal affairs, only comes in for protest when there is a direct connection to English interests – normally through war, territorial dispute, or religious difference, such as during the Thirty Years' War (1618–48). After this date, however, we see English songwriters addressing political concerns that have no specific domestic bearing – exemplified by songs like 'Hymn of the Polish Exiles' (1833) and 'Freedom for Palestine' (2011). It is tempting to reflect, here, upon how particular these trends might be to the British experience: a close spiritual and economic entanglement in affairs on the European mainland but geographically divided; an early and enthusiastic imperialist power but only dominant and a global superpower in the nineteenth century; from that point on, closely implicated in and aware of geopolitical and anti-colonial struggles in every part of the globe.

Secondly, during the near century between 1890 and 1980, the state's leader, the government, its ministries and institutions, and the justice system all come in for far less criticism in song than before and after. Neville Chamberlain and Anthony Eden, for example, play no part in our story, and it is only with Margaret Thatcher's premiership that things return to what we might call the historical norm. The late 1970s sees the emergence of the police force, rather than the military, as the focus of songs protesting state violence, from dub poet Linton Kwesi Johnson's album *Dread Beat an' Blood* (1978) to punk band Chelsea's 'Government' (1979). Clearly, those ninety years were hardly free of suitable targets for protest – from appeasement and the Suez Crisis to any number of personal political scandals, to military atrocities everywhere from Kenya to India to Northern Ireland – and it is intriguing that we have found no songs protesting these topics. We are not necessarily stating that such songs did not exist and were not sung, but rather that we are observing a relative obscurity and ephemerality that is itself suggestive.

There is no obvious political reason for this uncharacteristically long silence, spanning as it does many of the most significant episodes in both the struggle for electoral enfranchisement and the history of the British Empire and armed forces. While absence is always much harder to account for than presence, we might conjecture that the answer lies somewhere in the history of song, rather than the history of politics. It reminds us that England's 'golden age' of contemporary protest song was not the 1960s, but the 1980s. It also calls into question what subjects could conventionally be protested in the forms and spaces of song dominant across this near century – the music hall, 'light music', the 'folk revival', and so on.

As a corollary to this point, it is also notable that songs that relate specifically to *constitutional* questions – the franchise, the form of government, upper chamber, head of state, established Church, written constitution, and other such topics that are vociferously protested in all eras up to the 1980s – fall off entirely from this point onwards. They form practically no part of protest song discourse in the past fifty years. Even in the late 1970s and 1980s, these topics seem to have become increasingly the preserve of committed anarcho-punk bands such as Crass, Conflict, and Discharge, rather than issues aired in the musical mainstream. Increasingly, these might be seen as inappropriate or 'unfashionable' subjects for songwriters (think of the eye-rolling that might typically greet complaints about 'the system' from sincere young punks or hippies). However, this dwindling also seems indicative of a redistribution in the political energy of reformers and radicals in general, shifting from a focus on the head to the body of English politics. Rather than protest being framed (to varying degrees of accuracy) as bottom-up, there has been a clear shift to peer-to-peer protest, a phenomenon discussed in detail across the next two chapters.[26]

Returning to our most distant reading, the real narrative of long-term change is revealed by shifts in the two most prevalent preoccupations of our chosen protest songs: the high political realm; and civil-social rights and the social contract. It is in the shifting prominence of these two themes, from a dominant high politics at the start of our period to the pre-eminence of civil and social issues more recently, that the logic for our three-era periodisation is most clearly endorsed. In the early-modern era to 1789, the political process is the focus of more than half the total of our songs, and civil rights accounts for just a sixth. In the modern era (1789–1945), the two are equally balanced. In the contemporary, the pendulum has swung: civil rights are out in front at well over a third of the total, and the political process has shrunk to an eighth, comparable to themes of war and peace or the impact of socio-economic change.

Considered at the macro level, the energies of protest songwriters thus appear to track narratives familiar to us from both political and intellectual history. The pivotal moment is demonstrably the end of the eighteenth century. When confronted with the evidence of our 750 songs, it is impossible to deny the seismic impact of the late Enlightenment and French Revolution upon English protest, redefining debate around the rights of man. Given how much of the modern period is concerned with the 'high' politics of franchise reform and representation, it is all the more striking how this period sees civil rights and the social contract attain equal footing with these pressing issues – and suggests that English protest songs, writ large, were perhaps more influenced by Jean-Jacques Rousseau than by Thomas Hobbes and John Locke. It may also be indicative of the relative turmoil and stakes of English politics before and after the late eighteenth century. While no one would characterise the era of Jacobins, Chartists, and suffragettes as calm, it is undeniable that the 'highest' stakes of absolute power, and the subordination of almost all other issues to the root factor of who wielded it, were most prominent in the early-modern era. These centuries saw two successful revolutions and numerous failed attempts at regime change, and questions of religious authority became matters of ultimate import in this world as well as the next.

By contrast, the contemporary era seems muted. England's purportedly universal if antiquated form of democracy has seen little real challenge, and the target of political protest has evidently moved from a generally consensual *system* to the realm of the social. Perhaps, with certain battles won and others (republicanism, socialism, fascism – or at least, fascism as a formally recognised form of government) off the table, an age of idealism in song has given way to one of pragmatism. Recent songs are much likelier than those of the modern era to stay close to home and pinpoint specifically delineated grievances than they are to proselytise for systems change on the grand scale – the environment being the obvious yet correspondingly niche area of exception.

This form of distant reading is clearly profitable, but it is equally clearly *just* reading: it treats songs as written texts only. A consideration of their specific properties as songs, however – musical works to be made, disseminated, performed, and heard by bodies operating in time and space – produces our most revelatory version of the three-era periodisation. The eras are the same as before, but rather than representing a continuum of some themes and a dramatic shift in focus from the constitutional to the social, they create (like so many songs themselves) an *ABA* chronology. The early-modern and contemporary eras closely resemble each other, and the modern forms the exception.

Our first and third eras are dominated by protest songs that both operate within the parameters of the established, commercial music industry and talk *to* an audience. Their voice and their mode of performance is generally that of an individual performer seeking to instruct, persuade, critique. Even if they feature refrains or choruses that also invite communal, audience participation, these are subordinated to verses containing the main rhetorical content.

In the era to 1789, the typical protest song (from our list) is a strophic street ballad, published by a commercial printer and both sold and, in the first instance, performed by a solo street ballad-singer. If the author is known (which is not typical), they are more than likely someone used to writing in this medium, for immediate remuneration. In the era from 1945, allowing for technological innovation, the picture is much the same, except that the songs are no longer anonymous. They are still written by commercial artists as part of a wider oeuvre, published by record labels, and consumed in both recorded and live environments where there is a clear division between performer and audience. In both eras, though the rhetoric of the song may seek to deny the distinction between the two, the generic conditions still impose themselves: one voice speaking to many ears.

In between, however, this continuity is disrupted. Though still written, necessarily, by individuals – who are increasingly being identified – the modern-era songs are more typically less concerned with talking to than with giving voice to the collective. They are typically authored and disseminated in non-professional circumstances: unpaid writers, subsidised publication, orchestrated distribution, and often curation within dedicated songbooks. Typically, these are songs for communal rendition: hymns, anthems, and marches more than ballads or pop songs. The 'we' they often envoice is meant to be realised literally in the moment of performance, sung by a multitude, in unison or harmony, rather than by a single voice.[27] And of course, this maps directly onto the (self)-organisation of the working class that is the dominant political narrative of the era[28] – one inextricable from the musical organisation of working-class voices in singing societies, choirs, bands, and via the Tonic Sol-fa movement and its competitors.[29] The era of the monster meeting, the strike, the march, and, above all, the union is the era of the *collective*, non-commercial protest song. The reversion to the single-voiced commercial model in the third era is in some ways eloquent of the decline of English socialism and the triumph of capitalism. There were organised protests, marches, demonstrations, and workers' collectives both before and after the modern era. But the evidence of our songs indicates a clear link between the *heyday* of collective organisation, and the articulation of collective forms of protest in song.

This practice is epitomised by Joseph Mainzer's hugely influential 1841 publication *Singing for the Million*, published in London. Mainzer was a singing-master from Trier who had been forced out of his homeland due to his radical politics.[30] Moving via Brussels to Paris, he developed a system of adult singing classes aimed at labourers, based on the more accessible Tonic Sol-fa principle rather than standard musical notation (think of 'Do-Re-Mi' from *The Sound of Music*). These were soon shut down by the Parisian authorities, precipitating Mainzer's relocation to London, where he recommenced his education programme in combination with publishing. Mainzer's own songs were not explicit protests – 'Independence' (1843) just scrapes on to our longlist – but he exemplifies the symbiosis between collectivist politics and collective singing. Self-expression and self-organisation were essential to both, and the development of bottom-up, often choral mass singing marched hand in hand with that of unionisation, strikes, and demonstrations.

Changes in the form and performance context of protest songs also related to changes in their rhetorical identities. At its most reductive, the modern era might be characterised as the age of 'we', succeeding the early-modern era's 'I-you' model: the populace in the collective protest song envoice themselves, constituting a lyrical and legitimised 'we', rather than being appealed to as an audience or spoken on behalf of by the single-voiced orator-narrator of earlier ballads. In the contemporary, democratic era, the potency and importance of that 'we' continues to be recognised. However, where present, it is more often in tension with the literal circumstances of a professional musician appealing to a crowd, so that the songs most often recognised as 'authentic' and embodying a collectivity are instead perhaps likelier to make use of an 'I' that is individual, yet may be heard as standing in for the listener's own identity.[31] In the era of recorded music, a bedroom-based or headphones listener is likelier to identify with the 'I' than the 'we', whereas the latter's profundity when intoned by a thousand densely packed bodies assembled for a single purpose is hard to overstate.

The predominantly commercial conditions of the first and third eras reinforce the sense of a soapbox-style politics in play, less applicable to the co-created interim. And where commercial street ballads persisted into the modern era, so too did the related rhetorical mode. Likewise, some contemporary genres that valorise the communal experience and focus on singalong choruses are more likely to retain the rhetorical hallmarks of the modern era. This sort of collaborative expression is epitomised in its purest form by short, repetitive slogans and chants, the force of which is at least as much in how they serve to bind their singers together as in the words they express. By contrast, the highly individualised and extensive lyrical forms of much contemporary rap and hip-hop music lend themselves to protest songs that, in their wordplay, allusions, elaborate arguments, and dense patterning, resemble the broadside ballads of the seventeenth century much more closely than they do anything in between. We might summarise this entire phenomenon in the simple proposition that the interrelation of political and musical *participation* has been the primary vehicle for the changes in political and musical *form* that give us our three eras.

Naturally there are exceptions to this three-era pattern, but this is the point of a distant perspective: to perceive the larger trend, which in this case is overwhelming. It is all the more interesting because it suggests something about the political agency of protest songwriters and singers that is distinct from the wider commercial and musical conditions within which they operated. Far from diminishing in the modern era, the popular music industry flourished: musical literacy and formal competence spread across the nineteenth century and new technologies made it ever cheaper and easier to disseminate commercial songs en masse, both notated and un-notated – and, in the last decades of the era, as records. Rather than tending to work either for a particular printer, if at the level of the street (or a theatre, if more elevated), commercial songwriters began to operate more like other independent authors. Their number and output increased enormously. The turn to collective, non-commercial protest songs does not, therefore, map on to the mainstream current of song production, but instead ties to the specifically political character of the era: one of self-improvement, self-recognition, mobilisation, solidarity, and idealism.

There is consonance here with the emergence of the self-aware 'activist' as propounded in the two-era model – but also a clearer sense that such persons figured more prominently in the modern than in the contemporary era. It is true that in the mid-twentieth century, artist-activists like Ewan MacColl sought to sustain the relevance and impact of non-commercial protest song, especially through the reframing and politicisation of 'folk music', as discussed in chapter 5. Even today, there are plenty of activists writing non-commercial protest songs.[32] But their impact on both their own peers and the historical record is vastly diminished in comparison to the modern period. The protest songs that have managed to 'cut through' since 1945 have typically been those amplified by commercial conditions: a major label, a celebrity artist, a touring schedule, or a radio play.

With these considerations, our distant reading and long chronology is coming ever closer to the specific historical realities with which the rest of the book is concerned. To exemplify the abstracted narratives and claims made above, this chapter concludes with the tangible example of three songs. They are considered comparatively in terms of nine aspects of their role as, in themselves, cultural and political forces.

THREE SONGS, NINE ASPECTS

Three songs that typify the 'headline' characteristics of each era – early modern, modern, contemporary – are 'The Good Fellowes [*sic*] Complaint' (1647), 'The Gathering of the Unions' (1832), and 'Question Time' (2017). The first is an anonymously authored commercial broadside ballad, ten verses long and taking anywhere up to fifteen minutes to sing. It is written to the tune of 'Old Simon the King' (here given under the variant title 'Ragged and torn and true') and subtitled, in typically early-modern syntax, 'Who being much grieved strong Licquor should [rise]/ In paying a Farthing a Pot for Excise'. It protests the new parliamentary excise being levelled on ale and beer and accompanied a number of riots in opposition to this much-resented new tax. The second song is one of a number of lyrics written by the influential reformer Harriet Martineau and set to music by her close friend (at the time) Eliza Flower, in one of the era's most fruitful songwriting partnerships. Three verses long with a two-line chorus, it is subtitled 'March and Song' and was frequently sung by assemblies of up to one hundred thousand protestors on occasions such as the 7 May 1832 'monster meeting' of unions at Newhall Hill, Birmingham.[33] Its pious lyrics envoice the singers' unity, legitimacy, and goals. The third song is a co-write by rapper Dave and producer Fraser T. Smith, featuring as the lead single from the former's second EP *Game Over*; its six intricate verses last just over seven minutes. Written in the wake of London's 2017 Grenfell Tower fire (in which seventy-two residents lost their lives) and Brexit, the song holds Prime Minister Theresa May to account and also challenges both her predecessor and the leader of the opposition, as the lyrics range across a number of connected, state-of-the-nation issues (see chapter 2 for an extended discussion).

A comparative analysis of the three songs might be broken down into nine criteria, organised into three conceptual groupings: actors, forces, and contexts.

Actors

Among the 'actors', we logically begin with the songs' writers. 'The Good Fellowes Complaint' is anonymous, placing it within a long tradition of commercial writers employed without acknowledgement by known publishers – in this case, the so-called 'Presbyterian printer' and bookseller John Hammond (*fl. c.* 1614–1652).[34] We can only speculate as to the lyricist – a stalwart of the ballad trade? an out-of-work theatrical writer (theatres had been closed in 1642)?– and can only say with confidence that they were literate and competent. In some cases, anonymous lyrics display an awareness of classical allusion and precedent that indicates a grammar-school education: the tone of this song is more demotic, appealing to a succession of tradespeople on grounds of well-reasoned self-interest, with no need to advance a more allusive or indirect argument. As for its composer, the question is immaterial: the ballad-sheet states its tune as 'Ra[g]ged and Torne and True' – an earlier name for the tune most famously known as 'Old Simon the King', a street stalwart until the end of the eighteenth century.[35] The regular metre and long duration of this tune's verses, as well as its popularity, made it an ideal choice for a lyricist working to a tight deadline.

'The Gathering of the Unions' is a more transparent affair in its creation, at least to historians. Its lyrics were penned by Martineau, a committed political activist, thinker, and writer, working in the context of successive reform bills and a heated national debate on the electoral franchise. These were set to music by her friend Flower, in one of a significant number of non-commercial collaborations in the name of a specific political cause. The records make this clear, yet the pair's names were not generally attached to the song, and many since have been unaware of its authorship. Indeed, the most famous account of its performance comes from Martineau's own *History of England* in which she makes no claim to its writing. This deliberate act may have stemmed in part from a desire to frame it as a song 'of the people' rather than an artful composition, its words elegantly patterned, its music harmonically sophisticated, the product of two relatively elite, metropolitan young women.

'Question Time' too is a co-write, but a professional one, between this commercial record's producer and its performer – distinguishing it from its predecessors, whose writers had no part in their (purely 'live') performances. Dave, born David Orobosa Omoregie, was a then-teenage rising star of British rap, bound for success and fame, but whose songs, such as this one, also stemmed from political conviction – something by no means incompatible with sales in a genre and at a time when 'authenticity', already noted as a potential factor in 'Gathering''s anonymity, could be a key part of a singer's brand identity. Its producer-singer authorship, however, moves us back towards 'The Good Fellowes Complaint', where the only individual we can tie to the song is not its author, but its publisher.

Already, we are considering our second type of 'actor' – the songs' producers. We have already identified Hammond as 'The Good Fellowes Complaint''s printer and publisher, the man responsible in law for its content and responsible financially for its typesetting and printing as part of the commercial ballad trade. Hammond was no specialist, only venturing into the usually highly circumscribed ballad trade in the 1640s when the disruption of the Civil Wars had effectively deregulated the market.[36] Hammond was typical of the era in his rather ambiguous approach to both politics and professional conduct. He was an obstreperous member of the official Stationers' Company. He had been repeatedly arrested for operating illegal presses in the 1620s; had complained (along with many others) that poor printers were not well treated by the company; and was once imprisoned for the manufacturing of fraudulent farthings. He was committed to the parliamentarian cause (he was nicknamed the 'Presbyterian Printer') and printed pamphlets on behalf of parliamentary authorities but was still willing to publish a song protesting parliamentary measures.[37]

Martineau and Flower were distanced from these commercial considerations, though their champion (and Flower's guardian), William Johnson Fox, was not just the Unitarian minister of South Place (and later an MP) but also a journalist, the editor of the *Monthly Repository*, and closely involved in the production of Flower's political songs, some with lyrics by Martineau, others with lyrics by Johnson himself. When printed and sold directly, these were subsidised. However, it was characteristic of not-for-profit protest songs like 'Gathering' that they were not the property of a single publisher but appeared, with or without notation, in a great number of political organs: pamphlets, songbooks, journals, and newspapers. We are talking here of a legion of co-producers of the song, and for most of the nineteenth century it enjoyed reprints in radical songbooks in particular, often transcribed into Tonic Sol-fa notation.[38]

'Question Time', by contrast, returns us to the world of commercial production familiar from the early-modern era, though with the added dimension of the recorded sonic object. Smith, along with several other music producers on 2017's *Game Over* EP, including 169, who co-produced the song in question, was not producing a blueprint for performance, but the definitive incarnation of Dave's own performance. We are in a different world here, where these extra, non-textual dimensions to the song product necessitate the involvement of specialist parties. But, unusually for the contemporary era of commercial song, this was an independent release, without the involvement of a record label, another factor in its perceived credibility and demonstrable freedom of expression.

Finally, we must consider the songs' singers and audiences. The recorded dimension of 'Question Time', with all the conventions of the medium, places focus on Dave as singer. It is his delivery we listen to, within a genre that privileges an individual artist's command of flow, phrasing, cadence, intonation. This is not to preclude the possibility of listeners also singing the song, of young and often Black listeners honing their own vocal skills by practice and imitation. But the complexity and intricacy of the song's vocal renders this a specialist and hyperconscious activity. One cannot 'sing along' to 'Question Time' without concentrating on the process. In general, there is a far clearer divide between the singer – Dave, a celebrated artist, whose recording is fixed in time and space – and the listeners: purchasers of the physical or digital product, or streamers of the song for free. When thinking through the place of protest song in the history political communication, it is here that the historical rupture of recorded music is key – in the separating out of a known and chronologically located singer from an unstable and evolving audience.

There is something of this division in 'The Good Fellowes Complaint', in a world where a solo ballad-singer performing to a receptive crowd of potential purchasers was the default mode of a song's first performance. There is still that separation, that hierarchy: the one and the many. Ballad culture worked by purchasers (who might obtain the ballad directly from Hammond's shop in Holborn, London, or at a country fair or market thanks to long-range distribution by itinerant chapmen, or from professional, licensed ballad-singers) then reproducing the song themselves, taking on that role of singer. And while for some street sellers, voice and delivery served only to deliver the essence of a song with which they had no real connection, for some professional ballad-singers, that song would be performed with a clear sense of ownership of a song and its message (or at least their interpretation of it) – thus furthering the sense of an authoritative voice addressing a collective 'audience'. Yet, in this respect, there remained more in common between the first and third eras of protest song than the second, when the singers and audiences of songs like 'Gathering' were in large part identical, a crowd of voices singing to themselves. Martineau's account of its performance goes beyond this, incorporating the soldiers stationed nearby who, on that day in 1832, 'must have listened from within their barracks with a longing to be on the hill'.[39]

Certainly, there existed the potential for these songs to work upon a non-participatory audience, primarily these forces of law and order mobilised to observe, police, or brutally repress the protests of radicals, reformers, Chartists, socialists, and so on. Yet the crowd envoicing itself was the essential *point* of such songs. It served not only to raise morale and coordinate physical movement but also to impress upon the singer-listeners the reality of their own politically constituted validity; to be the sonic instantiation of their collective, legitimate voice in this struggle for enfranchisement. 'Gathering''s lyrics are wholly bent to demonstrating this new political reality, the refrain running: 'And hark! we raise from sea to sea, / The sacred watchword, Liberty!'

In singing those lines to themselves, the demonstrators bore witness to their becoming true.

Forces

We have already touched on perhaps the most historically transformative force involved in these songs: technological innovation. Conceptually, all three represent the difference between our overall era and what went before: they are enabled by technologies of mass replication, rather than being reliant on the hand and voice of one individual at a time. 'The Good Fellowes Complaint' is typical of our songs up until around 1940 in that it existed – and still endures – by means of print: the mechanical hand-operated letterpress; the industrial (though still handmade) production of cheap linen-pulp-based paper rather than earlier vellum or parchment; metal type; cheap ink; the woodblock. This is a familiar story from the Reformation onwards and needs little rehearsing. 'Gathering' is much the same but benefits from the mechanisation of wood-pulp-paper production at the start of the nineteenth century, and stands on the cusp of several innovations, in areas like lithography and engraving, and the steam-powered rolling or rotary press of the 1840s. The latter would soon allow for still cheaper production at huge scale allied to more freedom and expression in a song's print incarnation, from the increased affordability of colour illustration, to an explosion in font choices, to the greater viability of reproducing musical notation at a low cost. This last combined with 'technologies' of pedagogy that expanded musical literacy among the self-improving working classes of Victorian England. These self-improving classes were of course themselves conditioned by such macro-level phenomena as a surge in population and urbanisation and the increasing availability of leisure time and disposable income among the urban proletariat. Meanwhile, the railway would soon radically expand the reach of a particular song publisher's output, so that John Harkness of Preston would soon be sending his topical ballads down to London on the first train of the day.[40]

Nonetheless, until the advent of cheaply reproduced and disseminated recording technologies in the early to mid-twentieth century, there endured a default synergy of printed song sheet (usually lyrics only) with embodied musical performance. While musical recording was a nineteenth-century invention, it did not play a transformative role in song, on the scale of the printing press, until well into the twentieth century. Thereafter its implications for how we conceptualise commercial song in relation to protest, voice, and 'the people' are enormous. 'Question Time' is a product of this technology, but its independent publication and reliance upon streaming platforms mark another great technological shift of the new millennium. Ironically, it is one in which the scope for piracy and unauthorised reproduction is something of a return to the historical norm following the unusual control of the means of musical reproduction by sanctioned rights holders in the second half of the twentieth century.

Inevitably, technology leads us to consider the role of markets, and to reiterate the importance of a commercial public to the writing and production of songs like both 'The Good Fellowes Complaint' and 'Question Time'. Their example, along with that of hundreds of others, should impress upon us the fact that most protest songs, especially in our first and third eras, do not operate in some exclusively political realm, or circulate only among political activists. They operate within existing frameworks of musical production and consumption. Thus, the commercial song market provides the conditions for many protest songs – these two included. For ballads such as 'The Good Fellowes Complaint', this market consisted of individuals engaged in everyday activities, encountered in shops, on the city streets, and secondarily at markets and fairs or in public houses, and assembled for occasions such as public executions or festivals. In all respects this was a *mass* market: not the very poorest – as a song sheet usually cost a halfpenny or penny – but including most social ranks from labourers upwards, both men and women, and both children and adults. The majority came from the lower and middling ranks of society, and possessed enough literacy to make their purchase of the written text worthwhile.

If anything, the market for 'Question Time' was and is, in theory, more diverse still, especially in terms of ethnicity, albeit with a strong demographic slant towards the young and urban. The market forces in play for a ballad were primarily the impetus of the printer and the persuasive skills of individual ballad-singers. 'Question Time', however, belongs to a medium that can benefit from a more concerted promotional campaign (see below), though of course not in this case including a publishing company. 'Gathering' was quite another matter. Its market, standing outside commercial conditions and formed of groups, unions, congregations, and activists, was propelled by print organs modelled on commercial journalism and bookselling. Yet, it was sustained by private and collectivist fundraising in a manner characteristic of political songs (not just protest songs) ever since the vast promulgation of loyalist and reactionary material during the 1790s and the 'invasion scare' years of 1803–05.[41]

Closely allied to the question of markets is that of distribution. Whereas the political and moral songs just referenced from roughly 1793–1805, such as those produced by Reeves's Association for Preserving Liberty and Property against Republicans and Levellers or Hannah More's *Cheap Repository Tracts*, self-consciously adopted the 'customary' methods of ballad distribution, 'Gathering' clearly represents something more modern: the mobilisation of specifically founded and non-commercial journals, presses, papers, and so on. Until this point, and as with 'The Good Fellowes Complaint', even the most purposefully political of songs tended to rely on established commercial networks of booksellers, stallholders, chapmen, flying stationers, and ballad-singers for their distribution. Many, if not most, were primarily concerned with profit and livelihood rather than a political cause. For moral reformers, there was something of a sheep-in-wolf's-clothing dimension to this activity – seeking to change public attitudes almost by stealth.[42] For more radical and democratic causes, there was an alignment of message and medium, with ballad-singer as *vox populi*.[43] Radical ownership of political organs of dissemination – from the United Irishmen's *Paddy's Resource* to the Chartist *Northern Star* or the socialist songbooks of the late Victorian period[44] – were the second era's reworking of this dissemination practice, removing it from a somewhat exploitative and capitalist model to a more equitable one. Revocation of previously prohibitive stamp acts, which had imposed high duties on the sale of newspapers in particular, made the truly cheap worker's periodical a feasible proposition. 'Question Time''s distribution has, of course, been far less rooted in embodied and physical practices, though its release through digital platforms such as YouTube and Apple Music signals a conceptual return to the ballad era: distribution within the established commercial model.

Contexts

Finally, we can consider these songs as operating within historically defined contexts: the literal (physical space); the socially constituted realm of networks; and the formal context of legal regulation that involves aspects of incentive, risk, and repression. To some extent, all of these have conditioned the aspects already discussed, yet they reward further elucidation.

Spatially, we witness a series of shifts, as much in the conceptualisation as in the material makeup of sites of song. 'The Good Fellowes Complaint' was sung by professionals or amateurs in informal venues – indoors in an alehouse or home gathering; outdoors in a street or marketplace. Its performances and transactional realities were anchored in ill-defined public or semi-public space. This could entail physical and sonic contestation, if the balladeer had to contend with other street-criers or noisy alehouse companies, as well as with the other demands upon their audience's attention. Few members of a ballad public (though there were exceptions) came with the express intention of being an audience: they would be passers-by, with other commitments or other demands on their attention. The street – with other vendors, noises, needs, the weather – was the ultimate space of competition and compromise. Its promiscuously public nature also exposed the singer-vendor to legal risks – related not only to the song's content but also to the mere fact of singing.

By the era of 'Gathering', the very nature of this public space, the street, was legally being contested, with repeated assaults upon rights of assembly. And from a capitalist perspective, there was a clamping-down upon obstructions of the thoroughfare in the name of improvement, progress, the circulation of legitimate capital.[45] In the case of 'Gathering', when talking of performance en masse by demonstrators, this conflict increases ten-fold: the public square is much more than the public street. Yet both 'The Good Fellowes Complaint' and 'Gathering' had secondary spatial contexts too. Once bought, a ballad could circulate in sociable and domestic spaces – public houses, taverns, coffee houses, homes. Less easily policed, more intimate, often enhanced by stimulants, and with their own social codes, these spaces could fuel further conflict when a controversial song was aired. 'Gathering', subtitled 'March and Song', was less suited to these spaces, instead invoking other typical nineteenth-century sites of mass assembly: camps on moors, fields, and hillsides, and interior spaces such as halls and, very often, churches. In both instances, outdoors and behind closed doors, these were sites likely to constitute a sense of unity and belonging, with a presumption of shared sentiment by all those present, rather than the intrinsically disputed realm of street and square.

At first glance, 'Question Time' seems to resist this focus upon physical space. We risk equating a digital mode of dissemination with an abstracted, incorporeal space of reception – between the ears, via a pair of airbuds. Yet a song must be received in space. Whereas a street ghetto blaster or club soundtrack might return us directly to the 'historic' spaces described above, songs such as 'Question Time' usher in the distinctly contemporary environment of the bedroom – and also the commute, exercise routine, and so on, but the bedroom is most exemplary of the trend towards privacy (the listening experience is not shared) and atomisation. While late-modern broadcast media such as the radio seemed to realise the promise for a shared national experience of song that Victorian Chartist periodicals had aimed towards,[46] the pathways to individuated private listening begun by the Walkman and headphones and taken further by Internet-enabled personal devices have created something very different. There is now the potential to allow as well as stifle unfettered expression and consumption, and to separate as well as connect individuals from or to a shared and politicised identity. These technologies, then, have played a clear part in the redistribution of protest. Rather than being directed at the state, the peer-to-peer model that characterises much contemporary song has writers and listeners perceiving themselves more often as individuals within a problematic society than as part of a collective subaltern identity placed in confrontation with authority.

This brings us to a consideration of networks: networks of reception, rather than of production. If 'Question Time' is less likely to prompt physical association, its online presence has catalysed many interactions and responses: more than ten thousand YouTube comments, many in nested threads, and a number of 'reaction' videos on this platform alone – to say nothing of forums and discussion groups. It does not, however, lend itself to mobilisation in affiliation with any particular cause or organisation. Its lyrics interrogate both of the UK's leading political parties and cover a broad range of issues that militate against the creation of a coherent, organised response (perhaps in contrast to the identity-based thrust of Dave's subsequent song 'Black'). This stands in sharp contrast to 'Gathering', used explicitly to mobilise, unify, and self-define networks of reform-minded workers in time, space, and political intent. 'The Good Fellowes Complaint' is more explicit still, yet constructs an audience of multiple interest groups rather than one defined by a partisan ideology (save for the overarching social ideology of resenting perceived economic injustice and the interference of the state). Its opening verse calls to 'You that of severall Trades, / have borne the [tax] burthen long', contrasting these worthy auditors with the unspecified 'Knaves' responsible for said burden, before proceeding to appeal specifically to blacksmiths, shoemakers, glovers, tailors, weavers, and more, counting them as also 'Good Fellows'. It also goes on to deplore the 'female Sex' who 'do scould and brawle', in order to appeal to male listeners that they will not 'cease to vex' until the price of liquor falls, thus extending a political-economic protest into a more familiar domestic-social realm and seeking to create a shared interest and sensibility among all its male listeners (and potential purchasers).

In practice, of course, the formation of an assembled crowd from disparate passers-by or revellers was a conditional and limited act. A ballad-singer might command attention without ensuring agreement: even to take pleasure in a song was not to stand persuaded.[47] In common with most individual ballads, we have no direct accounts of listeners' reception of the song, but analogous instances are instructive here. As explored further in chapter 6, seventeenth-century audiences might often gather to 'hear out' a singer's whole song – before proceeding variously to attack them physically or report them to authorities.

Finally, then, we might consider the songs' changing political conditions – a question addressed in much greater detail in chapter 6. While the repeated assaults upon freedoms of protest, expression, and assembly by the Conservative government of the 2010s and early 2020s guard us against propounding a Whiggish teleological narrative, the overall drift of the centuries in question has been to lower the immediate personal risks of protest song. Dave can arraign successive prime ministers in his lyrics without fear of reprisal. Indeed, such lyrics are much safer, legally, than those of non-political Black British rap and drill tracks by young urban artists, which at time of writing are being used as 'evidence' by the Metropolitan police in a succession of highly contentious investigations that have nothing to do with protest. All three songs were, of course, written and published at particularly volatile periods of English political history: 'The Good Fellowes Complaint' in a brief moment of peace between two civil wars; 'Gathering' in a context of widespread reformist turmoil; 'Question Time' in the context of disputes over the Brexit vote, the Grenfell Tower atrocity, war in Syria, and a refugee crisis. Writers and singers responded to and influenced these contexts. Yet the evidence of our wider corpus makes clear that *all* periods of English history have been politically volatile, some vital issue always at stake, protest always required – and that any 'sceptred isle' history of a stable, consensus-based civil society is a wilfully deaf piece of mythmaking. For those involved, the personal legal and political stakes have changed over the centuries. But the issues at stake have remained a constant imperative. This is the single greatest unifying conclusion that can be drawn from this 420-year narrative.

CONCLUSION

Whatever the cultural, social, and political conditions of protest song, the one great constant has been the assertion of a subaltern political voice. While early-modern ballad writers may have been educated and occasionally privileged, their songs' singers (at least the professional ones) more often were not. For both parties, as well as publishers and audiences, the insistence on projecting a plebeian voice into the realm of public political discourse was inherently wilful, subversive, and audacious. While the laws of the second era tolerated a great deal more in terms of expression – though still with changeable and strictly policed limits – the singers of 'Gathering' were manifestly unenfranchised, their collective voice an eloquent part of their argument. So too with the two females who wrote that song in a year – 1832 – when the Great Reform Bill formally and explicitly barred women from voting for the first time in English history.[48] 'Question Time' was written in an age of ostensible universal suffrage, but when much of the nominal electorate – particularly its young urban poor and its ethnic minorities – felt wholly excluded from meaningful democratic processes. Dave's lyrical conceit of holding government to account felt, for many, every bit as insubordinate as a broadside ballad doing the same. In this sense, the centuries are unified by a continued rhetorical insistence in protest song composition, publication, performance, and reception, not of its outlaw credentials, but of its political legitimacy – and its vital importance.

2

THE PROTEST SONG AS POLITICS AND POLITICAL THEORY

Protest songs are complex things, belonging to multiple categories. They are simultaneously examples of song, of the culture of particular times and places, and – we will argue – of a special kind of political expression. In analysing or interpreting a song we can make a choice about which of these aspects to focus on. That choice will affect what we see in protest songs, and so also what we understand and learn from them. For instance, we might compare them to other kinds of song or put them alongside poems, pamphlets, and physical objects from the same time period and treat them (to borrow a thought from R.G. Collingwood) as a means for reconstructing in the imagination a past way of life, helping us to better understand what is distinct about both then and now.[1]

This book does some of all these things. This chapter, however, is primarily concerned with introducing a third way of analysing protest songs. It considers them as a form of intellectual political action, ways of making and staking claims about political interests and identities, of communicating representations or mental 'pictures' of some part or aspect of society (in order to shape others' thoughts and feelings about them), and so also a way of making political arguments. The problem with this approach is that we may force songs into a box that does not fit them. We might forget to remember that they *are* songs and therefore have features and fates quite different from non-musical forms of political communication. We might treat them as species of an immutable category of political talk, ripping them from the thick cultural historical context of which they were a part, and which gave them meaning. As we shall see a little later, there is – importantly – a sense in which, very strictly speaking, protest songs are not, and cannot, be political communication. However, what is and is not recognised as a legitimately made *political* demand is itself a political question. One of the things protest songs do – which some forms of political communication cannot – is ask that question, staging and dramatizing it, and challenging some of the standard answers to it. This chapter argues that one of the things protest songs *always* do is open up the issue of who gets to speak of politics, how that may be done, and who or what decides on all this.

The goal of this chapter, then, is to make a case for seeing protest songs as a *particular* form of political thought and expression. We think one of the things these songs do is express propositions relating to politics – about how a polis (an organised civic community) should be understood, structured, or restructured, and about how we should morally evaluate the things happening in it. Other kinds of expression do this too, of course, but protest songs do it in their own way. For us, then, protest songs are expressions of a substantial kind of political thought, and much more than instrumental propaganda (although songs certainly have been this too). We admit that this is to look at songs in a narrow way and to risk neglecting some aspects of their nature as songs (something we return to in chapter 3). Here, we want to consider the songs as primarily political texts, and this entails consideration of the strategic intent behind them. That is certainly not *everything* about these songs, but it is, we aver, an important aspect of them, especially insofar as the words were created not only to be read but also to be said aloud, and to be heard, in some kind of collective (potentially) public situation. How to draw out that aspect, how to understand songs in that light – how they appear when viewed from the perspective of public political statements, as political thinking rather than musicology – are questions we hope we can go some way towards answering. Accordingly, the chapter begins with a discussion – and an argument – about how we can conceive of and analyse songs as forms of political thinking, illustrating this in the following section with two rather different examples from opposite ends of our historical time span. The chapter then steps to the side to consider how political theorists think about the formal and informal languages of politics, and to argue that the political significance of protest songs is, in part, about how they use or adapt our moral political vocabulary (the concepts we use to think about politics). This leads into an argument about the issues that arise when analysing a protest song and some of the distinctions we might make based on how they relate to particular political circumstances and general political ideas and values. In the subsequent section we step not aside but back, to think about the ways in which songs as performances may instantiate and enact an argument about who speaks of politics and how. Finally, we return to our list and consider how, over the *longue durée*, the form of protest songs has developed and adapted, waxed and waned.

EXPRESS YOURSELF

We are hardly the first to claim that songs are sometimes political.[2] The claim is clearly inarguable. But *how* songs are political and the sorts of political things they do is rather more complicated. A first thing we might think of is the use of songs as propaganda, the simple affirmation and repetition of a basic political orientation. For example, the song 'Der Fuehrer's Face', performed by Spike Jones & His City Slickers, was created to accompany a 1943 Disney cartoon of the same name, produced to promote war bonds but also, of course, adherence to and support for the US war effort. The song makes fun of Nazis' adulation of their leader, disseminating an image of an enemy around which common feeling might be formed. Other songs, with seemingly no immediately obvious political lyrical content, have helped shape and direct national moods. In 1640, players singing a courtship song called 'Blew Cap for me', about a young woman choosing a Scot as a lover, were arrested because the tune had become an anthem for songs supporting the Scottish armed rebellion against the king's religious reforms.[3] A contemporary example is 'Ding-Dong! The Witch Is Dead' from the musical *The Wizard of Oz*, which became a best-selling song in 2013 when former prime minister Margaret Thatcher died. In these cases, a song became political because of the uses to which it was put, associated with political sentiments and intentions that were fully formed apart from it.

That facility to create a shared mood, to characterise a common experience, and so to orchestrate common feeling and identity is certainly an important dimension of the politics of song, and of popular culture in general. National anthems are an obvious example, as are songs used on election campaigns or as accompaniments to demonstrations. Here the detail of the words is of secondary importance. It is the (putatively) rousing tune, easily recognised and sung, that matters. Famously, the Reagan presidential campaign in 1984 used Bruce Springsteen's anthemic 'Born in the U.S.A.' at rallies, despite the apparent gulf between the words of the song and the policies proposed in the speeches. 'Things Can Only Get Better', an upbeat love song by D:Ream, which accompanied Tony Blair's election campaign in 1997, had only the vaguest lyrical connection to new Labour. In both cases a song's sound, its feel, and a fragment of the refrain could be connected to a political mood: American pride, optimism for the future. But while these vague affinities were 'in' the song, their politics came from outside, from the relationship they had with an organised political movement. Each song could, in principle, have been used by some other movement.

These examples draw attention to the fact that the politics of a song may derive from something about their form as well as from their lyrical content. Political analyses of song that emphasise 'ideology' (or 'socialisation') often see form as the most important thing. When social theorist and music scholar Theodor Adorno defined popular music as 'standardised' and as a mass-produced product that 'keeps customers in line by doing their listening for them', he was thinking of the ways in which the musical form, and the relationship of listeners to such works, mirrors and reinforces a wider social order that demands and induces our political (and intellectual) passivity.[4] In a different but related way, some feminist scholarship has emphasised how romance and love songs, and the relationships between stars and fans they institute, may represent, reinforce, and naturalise a particular conception of gender roles and expectations (or may create space for its contestation).[5] For these kinds of analysis, the politics of song are part of the songs themselves, but only insofar as they have a relationship to and with politics at a fairly high level of general socio-cultural norms. Songs are less expressions of political ideas than symptoms of a societal order about which we are usually encouraged not to think very much.

Just as songs may reinforce traditional or dominant conceptions, they can also represent alternatives or subvert the norm. Here we might think of songs as one front in a wider struggle for cultural hegemony, and over the naturalisation and contestation of ways of thinking and acting. This conception is a counterpart to that of songs as state and party propaganda in so far as it concerns songs that express and represent social and cultural interests not fully represented by, and maybe even opposed to, the state. [6] Lyrics and style certainly can be important but often the political force of songs lies in their connection with social groups (which they may in part help to form) or simply in the fact that they happen at all, and that they are publicly shared and performed. We are thinking here of, for example, songs sung in minority or suppressed languages; songs that affirm and intensify a political-cultural identity (as soul music did for African-Americans during the struggle for civil rights in the 1960s); the performances of songs by, about, or for those with 'non-normative' sexualities; stage performances by people from minority or marginalised groups kept off a culture's 'main stage' and that, just by happening, contradict that dominant culture's representation of itself and stake a claim to public presence and citizenship.[7] This is one reason, among others, why we include in our list a song such as 'Oh Bondage! Up Yours!' (1978) by X-Ray Spex.[8] Before the song begins, singer Poly Styrene says, in mock childish voice, 'little girls should be seen and not heard', and then launches into the energetic, perhaps seemingly aggressive, song with the declaration: 'But I say, bondage, up yours'. The 'up yours' is as much in the performance as in the words, speaking for itself as an immediate refutation of a stereotypical idea of how women in 1970s England should and could act on a public stage. This sort of political move is not unique to the era of mass culture. There are numerous examples from across four hundred years. For example, Ernest Jones's 'Song of the "Lower Classes"' (1852) centres on ironising, and so refuting, the pejorative class term 'low'.[9] Declaring that the song's working-class singers are 'so very very low', each verse advances a binary couplet that is almost a mathematical proof of social injustice: 'We're not too low – the grain to grow / But too low the bread to eat'; 'We're far too low to vote the tax / But we're not too low to pay'; and so on. Earlier still, 'Vox Populi' (1642), anonymously written for protestors who marched on parliament and called for bishops to be removed, claims the position of 'loyal subject' as defined against the established church and its government supporters, who were accused of subverting the Protestant commonweal (this is discussed in more detail in chapter 4).[10] In each of these examples, people assert their presence in the polity and in so doing question the 'orders' into which it is organised.

Here, then, are three well-known and well-documented ways in which we can think of songs as political phenomena: as propaganda, as reinforcements of moods and bearers of ideology, and as a means of 'countercultural' resistance. Each of these, we think, is a good way to go about analysing protest songs. We aim to build on them and will return to them throughout the book. But we also want to do something else, which is in a way simpler and more basic, certainly more specific, but which also introduces – unavoidably and we hope productively – some complications. We want to consider protest songs as a kind of political thinking. We do that for two main reasons: one very big and one very small. The big reason is that the forms of song-politics we have just discussed tend to be conceived of as belonging only to a certain era of mass and nation-state politics. But as we have just seen, our list of songs begins before we can speak easily of such a system. As we have already argued, in the Introduction and chapter 1, considering the politics of song across a longer period might help us to see and to understand some interesting and important things about the history and development of both songs and our ways of thinking about and understanding politics.

The smaller reason is simply that songs are also words and, in the case of protest songs, words about and directed at political events and arrangements. Of course, they are not *only* words. Songs communicate through sound, style, and poetic form; how they are performed and the contexts in which they are heard can profoundly affect how they are understood. But they *are* words, and so here, for the moment, we want to concentrate on that aspect with a view to understanding something about their political nature. And after all, by its nature, politics is very much (albeit also not exclusively) a matter of words: debates in legislatures, proclamations by monarchs, orders to open fire.[11] Consequently, much of politics takes place through communicative media: oral addresses, pamphlets, books, televised events, memes, social media rows – and songs. Such communications express in words, and are most often intended to persuade others to share, a particular way of thinking about political people, situations, and arrangements.[12] When we focus on *that* aspect of songs then, it seems to us, we can see that protest songs are *also* examples of political expression that can be placed alongside, and so be compared with, those speeches, pamphlets and books, television events, memes, and twitter rows. Let us look at two examples from opposite ends of our list.

PROTEST SONGS AS POLITICAL THOUGHT: 1603 AND 1982

The earliest extant song in our list is 'Come all you Farmers out of the Countrey' from 1603.[13] It is a response to – and a rejection of – the newly crowned King James's decision to give knighthoods, for a fee, to anyone with landed income higher than £40 per annum (*c.*£120,000 in today's money). Unsurprisingly given the target, it was unprinted and circulated only privately. The song's argument turns on the proposition that the new rule entails ennobling a new class of people – the men who have made money from improving agricultural methods – wholly unsuited to becoming landed gentry or aristocrats. It is (if we can be permitted the anachronism) a defence of established privilege against what would later be called the nouveau riche, trading on commonplaces about the inferiority of rural life, or what it calls 'Gestures rusticall', while affirming the naturalness of claims to honour and nobility: 'Though thow has neither good Birth nor Breeding / If thou hast Money, thow art sure of speeding'. The song is thus drawn into an argument about the dangers of elevating the power of money (obtained through productive activity rather than inherited ownership) over culture, nature, and the traditions of leisurely nobility, and a lament for what it thinks will be the ensuing decline in natural virtues:

> Knighthood in old Time was counted an Honour
> Which the best Spiritts did not disdayne
> But now it is us'd in soe base a manner
> That it's noe Creditt, but rather a Staine.

The superficiality of this shop-bought nobility is represented metaphorically through clothing. The farmers are urged 'Bidd all your Home-sponne Russetts adue / And sute yourselves in Fashions new'; 'Cast off for ever your twoe Shillings Bonnetts / Cover your Coxcombs with three Pounds Beavers'. They are also urged – with what we might now call snobbish irony – to obtain fine clothes for their common-named wives: 'To buy your new-moulded Maddams new Gownes / Joan, Sisse, & Nell shall be all Ladified / Instead of Hay-Carts, in Coaches shall ryde'.

At the other end of our list is the song 'How Does It Feel (To Be the Mother of a Thousand Dead)?', released by the anarchist punk band Crass in 1982, as a political response to, and in the aftermath of, the war fought between the UK and Argentina over the Falkland Islands in the South Atlantic Ocean.[14] The rhetorical question of the title is directed at Prime Minister Margaret Thatcher. She is the 'mother' when they sing:

How does it feel to be the mother of a thousand dead?
Young boys rest now, cold graves in cold earth.
How does it feel to be the mother of a thousand dead?
Sunken eyes, lost now; empty sockets in futile death.

The questions assume and thus reinforce the idea that it is she who is directly responsible, not only for the policy decision to go to war with Argentina but also for all its effects, represented in the vivid imagery of horror. Indeed, the song is very insistent on this point, locating the causes of the decision to go to war in the person and personality of the prime minister rather than any wider range of social, political, or historical factors. A refrain, repeated at the end of five of the verses, insists: 'you inflicted, you determined, you created, you ordered / It was your decision to have those young boys slaughtered'. What reason does the song give for her taking that decision? It says that she employed 'blood-soaked reason', shutting down other opinions, because 'So keen to play your bloody part, so impatient that your war be fought' naming her 'Iron Lady' with a 'stone heart' and explaining:

Your arrogance has gutted these bodies of life,
Your deceit fooled them that it was worth the sacrifice.
Your lies persuaded people to accept the wasted blood,
Your filthy pride cleansed you of the doubt you should have had.
You smile in the face of the death, because you are so proud and vain,
Your inhumanity stops you from realising the pain.

In the middle, the song makes a larger point drawn from this example:

Throughout our history you and your kind
Have stolen the young bodies of the living
To be twisted and torn in filthy war
What right have you to defile those births?
What right have you to devour that flesh?
What right to spit on hope with the gory madness?

The refrain reinforces the point: '1 - 2 - 3 - 4 - We don't want your fucking war!'.[15]

Obviously, the song is a political (and in part a political philosophical) argument against the war in the Falklands, refuting claims for its justice by showing it to be the outcome of the vices of the leader who decided to wage it: her arrogance, deceit, dishonesty, pride, and vanity. Furthermore, such vice is – the song argues – typical of politicians, of people who want to be in charge of states.

Some 380 years apart, two songs: one privately circulated and, we presume, if performed at all then, sung by (or to) small groups among themselves; the other, in addition to being sung live, pressed on vinyl accompanied by text and images on a fold-out poster and listened to by individuals at home (if they could find it – HMV, the record retailers, refused to stock it). 'Farmers' was likely sung with little to no accompaniment; Crass's song was performed – raucously and aggressively – with the screamed question 'How Does It Feel?' carried by full electronic amplification. One uses verse to communicate genteel mockery from above; the other is profane and angry in expressing hostility from below. And it perhaps goes without saying that the issues each song addresses are not obviously similar and that they come from almost entirely different political universes. What possible basis for comparison could there be?

The answer, we suggest, is that both songs express a kind of political thinking. They aren't recounting folk tales, issuing dance instructions, or documenting romance. They are, instead, articulating a view about political and societal leadership and, more specifically, on the relationship of leaders to the people they rule. And both protest that the proper sort of relationship between the parts of a polity is being displaced or ignored. Furthermore, both express a view on that relationship in two ways simultaneously: as direct statements or propositions, albeit expressed in ironic or hyperbolic language, and performatively, through their very expression.

'Farmers' clearly expresses the view that there is a right and natural order of persons – one that has roots in the past and in tradition – which has been ignored by the newly arrived king. In its place, the song says, has come a breakdown of order, and so also a blurring of the line between true and false, reality and appearance. Money, it implies, has devalued the established hierarchies of society. And though it is never said in the words of the song, the implication is that the policy of the king is to be deplored. 'How Does It Feel?' is also about the relationship between leaders and led, albeit in this case, an elected prime minister rather than knights or a monarch. It explicitly (if polemically) asks about the right by which a leader can declare war and put citizens' lives in danger. It characterises the present relationship of ruler to ruled as one that is instrumental and callous: Thatcher is represented as having no care for the young soldiers she has sent to die in battle – and it is implied that she has sent them for reasons of political self-interest – to make a statement and to look tough. But notice how the song also explains and condemns the decision in terms of personal vices: Thatcher is represented as arrogant, deceitful, prideful, dishonest, and lacking in sympathy. One inference is that there are some virtues that leaders ought to possess, although the song – as we might expect from anarchist political thinkers – presents its subject as an example of a problem intrinsic to hierarchical rule as such.[16]

As well as describe such relationships, the songs, by their very nature, also stage just such a relationship. They are words meant not only to be read quietly to oneself in private but also to be sung aloud in the presence of others and perhaps in unison. We may not know how, where, and when 'Farmers' was sung, but to sing it was to participate in criticism of the policy of a monarch believed to hold power derived from God. Though the song argues for a certain natural order, it also – *by existing and by being sung out loud* – performatively enacts a different order in which subjects of the Crown hold it to account by using their words and thoughts to measure it against an ideal of good and right order. In this respect, the song draws on – and feeds back into – wider traditions and emerging cultures of political thinking that limited monarchical power by appealing to greater or more fundamental natural, ethical, and common principles. The capacity of songs to do that would become more apparent and more important later in the seventeenth century. As Angela McShane notes in her study of seventeenth-century broadside ballads, songwriters were well-versed in classical as well as Christian theories of politics, morality, and social order and 'From 1640 to 1689 ballads debated and explained the ideal constitution, the nature of tyranny, the importance of love, the outcome of political virtue and the effect of vice in the nation. Ballads followed the journey of the state, offering advice and direction to governed and governors, as governments tried to find the *via media* between excess and deficiency of love, the greatest Christian virtue, which bound together all parts of the state into a patriarchy and a commonweal'.[17]

During the Civil Wars, and much of the ensuing century, such songs sought to make plain the distinction between, on the one hand, the extreme and unbalanced drives of the envious, proud, enraged, and ambitious papists and, on the other, the excessive lusts and passions of dissenters. Indeed, McShane suggests that political songs from the period can be understood as 'largely a commentary on tyranny as defined in classical texts, in particular the analysis set out in Aristotle's *Politics*'.[18] Crass's song also draws on longer traditions of thinking, including anarchist critiques of leadership, of the intrinsic connection between state power and violence, and on a certain tendency of anarchist thought to – like 'Farmers' – imagine a natural kind of sociality and morality that has been corrupted by those whose ambitions for leadership are indicative of their lack of true virtue. Crass also expressed that position performatively. Their lifestyle and conduct – living in an anarchist commune (see chapter 5), producing records independently, keeping prices low – and the style of their music and lyrical delivery offered up a rebuke to the kind of propriety and manners that prevent us from stating the plain truth about order, class, and war.

This is the basis for a kind of comparison between these very different songs. Each is involved in expressing a theory of political order and in thinking critically about how the relationship between parts of a polity should be understood, especially that of leaders and led. They make propositions about where rulers derive their authority from, and about the moral order that limits them. Furthermore, both songs enact that theory to the extent that they are protests questioning something authority has done. They implicitly propose (and explicitly demonstrate) that part of what is proper to the relationship between subjects/citizens and rulers should and can be criticism, a relationship which people take up just by singing along with the song, or indeed by applauding it, circulating it, or jumping up and down in time with it. 'Farmers' was not published, in part because doing so would undoubtedly incur sanctions from authority, but also because the authors deliberately sought to restrict its critique. Ironically, the song prefigured a sub-genre of retailed songs protesting wasteful consumption as much by those who authored 'Farmers' as those against whom it was directed.[19] Crass did not face quite such a threat but they were indeed subject to police investigation and censorship (see chapter 6). This would not happen were it not for a recognition on the part of authority that such works were some kind of challenge to it.

This moment of public expression and performance brings form and content together in a way that helps us think about the political nature of occasions when people share a song, attend a concert, or – perhaps – simply listen to a song alone at home. These are musical but also *political* occasions and, in a particular way, moments of protest. The rhetoric scholars Gerard Hauser and Erin McClellan argue that public protest actions – such as when people surround a nuclear base, chain themselves to an oil refinery, or pull down a statue – are also performances that function as 'powerful framing devices for ideological critique whose impact is magnified when they are expressed dramaturgically'.[20] The protests do not work only directly, for example, by halting the work of the oil refinery; nor are they just a photo opportunity and a chance to hand out leaflets or press releases. They are also a kind of argument, one made through and as a form of dramatic performance that stages and simulates an idea about the relationship between situations, scenes, agents, attitudes, purposes, and so on.[21] For instance, when suffragettes chained themselves to the grille separating the Ladies Gallery from the floor of the House of Commons, shouting 'We have been behind this insulting grille too long!', and forcing parliamentary authorities to remove it, they were also putting into question how political space was divided, and access to it allocated, by re-staging that very division. In such protests, Hauser and McClellan write, 'bodily displays, modes of dress, provocative use of language' may force attention 'on previously undisputed elements of the political, economic, or social order'.[22]

The singing of songs, banging of drums, and chanting of slogans is often a part of such protest performances. Apart from such occasions, performed in a concert venue or listened to on the radio at home, protest songs are not exactly like dramaturgical performances. They are, in some measure, 'about' protest and not necessarily 'doing' it. However, we can nevertheless understand part of the protest in protest songs as 'dramatizing' in the sense that, as we saw with the earlier example of Poly Styrene, but also in the cases of 'Farmers' or 'How Does It Feel', bodily display, dress, and language-use can open up questions of who gets to speak of politics, where they can do it, and how. As we explain further in chapters 3 and 4, these may be performances of opposition or solidarity, ways of (re)staging relationships between parts of a community (between authority and citizens, for example). On such occasions, the public performance of a protest song can create an experience of relations between people (performers, audiences, and the subjects of the song), inviting them to think these through. That is one way that songs can enable us to theorise our politics. With that in mind, we turn now to political theory and the protest song.

POLITICAL THOUGHT IN THE WILD

The study of political theory has, in the past, been confined to a list of great texts – by, say, Plato, Thomas Hobbes, or John Rawls – thought to contain ideal expressions of particular ways of thinking. Conversely, 'everyday' ways of thinking about politics (how the proverbial person in the street does it) have been treated as data for pollsters to aggregate, a manifestation of false ideology to be corrected, or as an incipient consciousness to be moulded into shape by an activist vanguard. However, over the last few decades, historians of politics and political thought have come to be interested in the languages of politics at all sorts of levels, including the vernacular or everyday.[23]

To be political is, in part, to have learned a vocabulary and how to use it. To be a 'conservative' means knowing how and when to use terms such as Tradition, Markets, Order, Individual Liberty, and so forth; to be a 'socialist' requires knowing how to use other concepts in distinct ways, including Equality, Capitalism, Solidarity, Justice. Such languages of political theory, the concepts of which it is composed, do more than describe situations. In their works, political theorists and philosophers can refine the meanings of those concepts, perhaps rearranging the ways in which they are connected, changing how we understand situations. And because our understanding of it is part of a political situation, change in the former is also change in the latter. But this ability to alter the meanings of concepts is hardly confined to political theorists and philosophers (and these days, when such people are mostly confined to and disciplined by the structures and rules of the university, they are perhaps the least likely to be doing it). People of all kinds – citizens, politicians, and revolutionaries – also use these kinds of words and concepts to think and talk about political situations and, in communicating their thoughts, can change our understanding. The history of political thinking, then, is about not only the 'great works' of political theory but also all the ways these terms are used and reused, by philosophers, activists and citizens, artists, writers, and musicians, and how these shape and reshape each other's vocabularies; about the development and change of 'sub-languages: idioms, rhetorics, ways of talking about politics'.[24] Accordingly, political historians, theorists, and contemporary analysts must explore the forms of political expression found in speeches and sermons, books of etiquette, proclamations, and so on, understanding that, as political theorist Elizabeth Anker argues, our political ideas and identities, our political strategies and actions, 'are mediated by the different modalities in which they are depicted and made legible' and which themselves are the outcome of all kinds of cultural forms and expectations and of 'institutions of power that can include but are not limited to the state'.[25]

In examining political theory in this way, we are not so much interested in the pure or logical meaning of an idea or concept as with the uses to which it is put. For instance, while the 'right' to declare war is a matter of substantive legal and ethical argument and might take us into rich and interesting territory concerning the justice of war in general, we are concerned with how people – the members of Crass – use the concept of right in relation to war to do something political, such as dispute the Falklands War and criticise the state. Historian Quentin Skinner has argued that concepts can be 'tools and weapons of ideological debate' and has shown that a significant kind of political work is done by what he calls 'innovating ideologists' who find new ways to put concepts together and who express them in ways that affect how we understand and act on our political debate.[26] In our study of protest songs, we are interested in how songwriters and performers might be such 'innovating ideologists', using words and concepts in ways that contribute to the history of our political thought.

Skinner has argued that one sort of language is especially important: that of moral evaluation and appraisal, and our disputes over it. He draws attention to how our language of appraisal draws on the 'neighbourliness' of 'forms of behaviour described by contrasting evaluative terms', and to the rhetorical trope of *paradiastole* or redescription.[27] For instance, an act described positively as generous might be redescribed as an extravagance. So too, what is kindness in one description could be represented as indulgence in another, what is prudent be called cunning, and what is courageous be labelled recklessness. At issue in such descriptions is how we assign a thing or an action to a category that we consider to be a vice or virtue. That may seem a small thing, but changes to how we do that can be very significant. For example, parental actions that might once have been considered appropriate when described as disciplining or chastisement have been redescribed, and so reconceived, as violence, harm, and abuse – terms of negative appraisal.[28] More broadly, applications of the term 'violent' to institutions as well as individuals (and to non-physical as well as physical actions) are an important part of political and moral argument today.

This matters for us because songs are especially good at this sort of thing. As verse and poetry, they can paint vivid pictures describing situations. As song and music, they can communicate in ways that connect those pictures to feelings and stir them up. And as performances, they can amplify the whole, binding a community through the experience of collective listening and singing (and assenting to a description), and staging a potential relationship between people, and between people and their politics. All that can help us to characterise situations and actions such that they move from one moral category to another. For example, the lyrics to The Smiths' 'Meat Is Murder' (1985) redescribe what happens in an abattoir as murder, so that our picture of meat eating is moved from its place in one positive moral category to another, evidently negative one. This is enhanced by the feel of the song, the sampled sounds that imitate the noises of an abattoir, and by the singer's delivery, by turns wistful, mournful, and accusatory. In a different way, 'Fulfilment Centre' (2017) by Richard Dawson uses repetition and rhythm to describe working in an Amazon warehouse so that it can never again seem like a good job opportunity:

> Over and over and over and over
> Again and again and again and again and again
> Three hundred units per hour
> Hour after hour after hour.[29]

Tom Robinson's famous 'Glad to be Gay' (1976), lyrically a little complex because of the layers of irony it builds, can also be understood in this way. At the start Robinson paints a picture of police action:

> Raiding our pubs for no reason at all
> Lining the customers up by the wall
> Picking out people and knocking them down
> Resisting arrest as they're kicked on the ground
> Searching their houses and calling them queer.[30]

The image is clearly one that redescribes what some might have thought of as good policing, as abusive, authoritarian, and similar to other kinds of state violence people might know of or have experienced.

This sort of thing is not at all confined to the more recent protest songs in our list. For example, 'The Parliament Routed' (1653) paints this picture of the House of Commons:

> Full 12 years and more these Rooks they have sat
> To gull and to cozen all true-hearted people
> Our gold and our silver has made them so fat
> That they looked more big and mighty than Paul's steeple.[31]

It is a vivid characterisation that very clearly and simply displaces the members of the Long Parliament from any positive category (as, in early-modern terms, 'England's comfort', or in later ones as the 'people's representative') and identifies them as part of the category of corrupt things. It does this by identifying them metaphorically with rooks: noisy, greedy, and sneaky, always flocking together. Indeed, the 1532 Vermin Act ordered the destruction of jackdaws, crows, and rooks because they were blamed for poor harvests (predators taking food from the people). Such a description, if accepted, makes Cromwell's dissolution of parliament seem as necessary and right as the extermination of the birds.

In the wake of the French Revolution, the single most loaded word from the political vocabulary was not that of 'democracy' – still beyond the pale in mainstream English discourse – but that of 'patriotism'. The latter concept was hotly contested by radicals and loyalists, both desperate to associate their ideology with its immense and fundamentally incontestable political and emotional capital.[32] Though this contest was decisively won by reactionary loyalists, especially during the invasion-scare years of the late 1790s and 1803–05, numerous protest songs were produced by Jacobin sympathisers in the early 1790s, attempting to recruit the language of patriotism, nation, and liberty for their cause. For example, 'A Patriotic Song by a Clergyman of Belfast' (1792), written at an optimistic moment as French forces won notable victories at battles like Valmy, sought to associate 'Tyranny' with the *ancien régime* forces of Prussia and Austria whilst assembling impeccable classical examples such as Sparta on the side of France.[33] The Spartan allusion lends significance to the otherwise purple prose of 'The satraps of pride and oppression' – satraps being the regional governors of the Persian empire imposed upon subject populations, and very much 'the baddies' in the exemplary history of the Battle of Thermopylae. The 'true patriot', the song claims, is the one who unites (like the ancient Greek city states) in the cause of liberty and mankind. To advance this end, the song takes as its tune 'Poor Jack', one of Charles Dibdin the Elder's most famous sentimental sea songs, indelibly associated with martial valour and the British nation. Though Britain's entry into the war soon after the song's composition rendered its optimism not only vain but also actively seditious (see chapter 6), it is a spirited attempt to leverage the potent signifiers of both British patriotism and an exemplary classical education to redescribe subversive support for the French Revolution as the act of a true, respectable British patriot.

As with 'A Patriotic Song', such rhetorical redescription can be advanced through musical as well as lyrical strategies. 'The Death of Parker' (1797) is another such example, using the form of the tragic ballad or lament to rehabilitate a condemned man's reputation and subvert the official judicial process.[34] Richard Parker was a junior naval officer designated 'President of the Delegates of the Fleet' when, in 1797, much of the Royal Navy went on strike for better conditions and rights. The state designated the act a mutiny and Parker the ringleader; in June he was court-martialled and executed. Rather than directly contesting this verdict, the song places Parker in a completely different category by adopting the narrative voice of his widow. In the lyric, Parker is 'my lawful husband' and 'my bosom friend'. Thus, Parker is represented not as a lawless mutineer to be despised, but as a lawful husband to be mourned as a 'brave' and 'bright genius'. The politics are left unstated, but audiences could clearly infer the moral standing of those who would execute such a man and leave behind so tragic and grieving a widow.

This might all be thought of as 'mere' emotion and narrative. But recall that in each case there is also – sometimes explicitly – an alternative conception in play: a proposition about what good and virtuous rule and conduct might be. This is what political theory and political speech of all kinds does. It shapes and reshapes our understanding of how the parts of a polity are to be characterised, of how they relate to each other, of what is going well or badly, and what could be better.

Songs work with and on our political vocabulary. Putting it like that makes it sound rather general and abstract and perhaps a bit too much like political theory. It is important to remember that each song – while drawing on a general historically evolving vocabulary – is also part of a specific politics and political moment. In this respect, songs are – exactly like any political speech intervention – always making an argument both about a particular moment (an event, an issue, a political situation) and about more general ideas (of, say, right, or justice and equality).

From these observations, we can draw out not a method – that would be too grand and is not really necessary – but something that is more a way of orienting ourselves to the analysis of a protest song understood as political thinking or political theory. We need, naturally, to know something about the political situation it is characterising, be it war, selling honours, or contesting parliament. We also need to know something of the vocabulary of the time. For instance, we need to know the symbolic resonance of describing people as 'rooks' or the connotations of two-shilling bonnets and three-pound beavers. We need also to appreciate the extent to which, in 1982, gory imagery of war was considered appropriate in political discourse, and the rhetorical force and shock value at that time of using curse words. More deeply we need to have a sense of the shifting meanings of key political terms such as 'right', 'nature', and 'justice' so that we can understand the degree to which a song is relying on a dominant meaning or contesting it. From there we can ask how a song invites us to evaluate events, persons, and actions both morally and politically.

The songs used so far as examples tend to focus on a particular event or situation represented in a way intended to show it as a breach of common values. That is the essence of their protest: that something has happened, is being done or not done, which must be addressed because it is at odds with our common values. This is evidently the case with 'Farmers'. It sings of a breach of established codes of virtue, and in so doing affirms those codes and perhaps – insofar as it invites its audience to do so together – intensifies adherence to them. The pattern is the same for the first verse of 'Glad to be Gay', 'The Parliament Routed', and so on. In all these songs, the protest is primarily carried by the description and redescription and the emotional colouring attached to it. General evaluative categories are taken for granted: 'Parliament Routed' does not argue that politicians taking our gold and silver is corrupt; it assumes that everyone knows that it is corrupt and seeks only to show us that this is what they have done. Tom Robinson does not argue that police brutality is bad – we know that it is – only that the treatment of gay people by the police is an instance of brutality.

In many ways, 'How Does It Feel?' also works like this. As we have seen, that song is mostly concerned with showing us an image of a leader wanting in recognised virtues and concluding from this that the war she has embarked upon cannot be justified. But there is, as we noted earlier, something more going on here. The song moves to a more general level and suggests that what the prime minister has done is just what rulers throughout history have done. A particular situation and action is used to say something about our general concept of leadership. The song calls into question our common understanding of the concept of political leader; it is not that Thatcher has breached the codes of good leadership but that leadership as such is at fault. To this extent we are invited to reconsider things at a more fundamental level and the song opens onto a more radical sort of protest. Where many songs interrogate a particular issue when it is measured against a general category, here the general category, by being shown to be instantiated in a specific instance, is called into question. Crass are protesting not only about the Falklands War but also about leadership itself.

This sort of protest, we suggest, is most often found in songs informed by a wider political theory, philosophy, or ideology. Crass were anarchists and so came to songwriting with the view that leadership is always a source of corruption. Many of their songs can be seen as representing examples of the truth of this claim or as extended meditations on it: the intrinsic wrongness of states, patriarchy, religion, and so on. Indeed, political theorist Stuart White has interpreted some of their songs as political-philosophical arguments about the dangers of authoritarian revolution and as contributions to our grasp of concepts such as 'democratic individuality'.[35]

Robinson's song is an interesting instance of this. It builds on its redescription of policing, using a rousing chorus of pride and gladness, to become not only a specific protest about police harassment of gay patrons of the Coleherne public house in Earl's Court, London, but a general protest about the treatment of gay people and ultimately a way of changing our moral and emotional understanding of the concept of 'gay'.

Songs involved in this general sort of political protest are often more embedded than others in a political world view and tend to be more prominent at times of wider political strife. Some of these involve very direct engagement with what academics would recognise as political theory. For instance, in his counter-revolutionary tract *Reflections on the Revolution in France*, politician and ideologue Edmund Burke referred to the 'Swinish Multitude'. That epithet became the name of a pamphlet by James Parkinson in which he famously remarked 'Whilst ye are … gorging yourselves at troughs filled with the daintiest wash; we, with our numerous train of porkers, are employed, from the rising to the setting sun, to obtain the means of subsistence, by … picking up a few acorns'.[36] Robert Thomson's 1793 song 'Burke's Address to The Swinish Multitude' takes things further, using parody to attack Burke's claims.[37] Pretending to be in Burke's voice, it develops an argument for a divine right 'to flog you and feed you and treat you like swine' and paints an image of corruption of the state, church and monarchy. It closes with the verse:

> To conclude, then, no more about MAN and his RIGHTS,
> TOM PAINE, and a Rabble of Liberty Lights;
> That you are but our 'SWINE', if ye ever forget,
> We'll throw you alive to the HORRIBLE PIT.

As well as making fun of Burke – redescribing him through parody as a kind of tyrant – the song develops and defends the use of concepts such as The Rights of Man, giving them definition and force through the contrast with Burke.[38] The protest against Burke, then, creates space for a form of political advocacy and for the propagation of Paine's 'ideological innovation'. Paine also appears in a parodic version of the national anthem, Joseph Mather's 1793 'God Save Great Thomas Paine'.[39] Here redescription is in part carried by the parody, the substitution of a king for a commoner with ideas so radical he was expelled from the nation. It is also explicit in the song's ironic proposition that 'Facts are seditious things / When they touch courts and kings' and in its description of its time as one in which:

> Armies are rais'd
> Barracks and bastiles built
> Innocence charged with guilt
> Blood most unjustly spilt
> Gods stand amaz'd.

That is to say, right and virtue have been turned on their heads by 'Despots' who howl and are 'in league with hell'. The obverse is the rights of man, as enunciated by Paine, which far from being disruptive of order are what can put the parts of the polity back into a proper relationship.

This discourse of rights was also, logically, employed in protests against slavery. The author of 'An African's Appeal to the British Nation', first distributed in cheap print in 1778, remains anonymous.[40] But the song itself seeks to reduce the anonymity of the enslaved by adopting the narrative voice of one. Here the argument works primarily by humanising its subject, redescribing the dispossessed and abject as, but for the chance of birth, like the Britons to whom it is addressed:

My mind can reason, and my limbs can move
The same as yours; like yours my heart can love;
Alike my body food and sleep sustain,
And e'en, like yours, feels pleasure, want, and pain.

Echoing Shylock's famous speech in *The Merchant of Venice*, the song is an appeal to a rationalist conception of universal humanity, all under one sun and one God. Like that play, and unlike most political theory, the song can easily dramatize its basic proposition. The song's demonstration of the rational capacity of the enslaved is achieved in part by the staged address of the song, the words being said by such a person, as well as by highlighting a simple logical fallacy:

But I was born on Afric's tawney strand,
And you in fair Britannia's fairer land.
Comes freedom then from colour? blush with shame!
And let strong nature's crimson mark your blame.

Britons listening to the song are directly addressed within it, thus also implicated in the situation it dramatizes:

I speak to Britons – Britons, then behold,
A man by Britons snar'd, and seiz'd, and sold.

O sons of freedom! Equalize your laws,
Be all consistent – plead the negroe's cause;
That all the nations in your code may see
The British negroe, like the Briton, free.

A different, later example of a song doing political theory is 'The Land Song', originally inspired by the Georgist movement, followers of the economic ideas of Henry George. He thought that all taxes should be reduced to a single tax on the unimproved value of land to break the power of landowning rentiers and free up small business to create wealth.[41] American in origin, the song became an anthem for the Liberal Party and is still sung at the end of the Liberal Democrats' party conference. It is in many respects an anthem – an affirmation of a common identity and purpose already shared – especially with its chorus of: 'We'll never cease from fighting 'til victory we win / And the land is free for the people'. That claim rests on an argument according to which

God gave the land to the people!
The land, the land, 'twas God who made the land
The land, the land, the ground on which we stand
Why should we be beggars with the ballot in our hand?
God made the land for the people.

The song works with the idea that land naturally belongs to all and, therefore, aristocratic landownership is unnatural and protest against it legitimate.

Such songs do not really seek to intervene into a very particular moment. They are primarily about a general situation and general ideas. An obvious and interesting example is Leon Rosselson's much-loved 'The World Turned Upside Down' (1975), which uses the story of the seventeenth-century Diggers (who, famously, had their own song) to give shape to a protest about inequality and hierarchy in general.[42] It asserts its political case through ventriloquising past political arguments, making the Diggers – and their fate – exemplars of injustice and of the struggle against it so that the final words become not just a commemoration but also an affirmation of shared purposes and resistance:

> You poor take courage
> You rich take care
> This earth was made a common treasury
> For everyone to share
> All things in common
> All people one
> 'We come in peace'
> The orders came to cut them down.

It is a radical song insofar as it encourages its audience to be steeled for a fight against the men of property, and not simply (like the Liberal Democrats) to march with God on their side. The risk of such a protest song, however, is that it loses all political specificity, turning the political fight it describes into a kind of permanent, unchanging, moral struggle. That is why such songs easily become like national anthems or hymns – momentary orchestrations of common political feeling, with vocabulary that risks turning from innovative to clichéd.

Another example is Cornelius Cardew's 'Smash the Social Contract' (1979).[43] Cardew wrote to express a thoroughgoing political theory (as well as a radical critique of politics). He was a founding member of the Revolutionary Communist Party of Britain (Marxist-Leninist), which was particularly militant in its opposition to capitalism and at times aligned with Maoist ideas and with Enver Hoxha, the dictator of Albania. At one level the song is specifically a protest against the then-Labour government's policy of a 'social contract', an agreement with unions for wage restraint in return for the restoration of workers' rights. The song is also – by implication – addressing a much wider concept of the social contract and protesting about the very idea that the ruling class, the state, and working people can agree on common interests. Indeed, the song can be described as a piece of Marxist political analysis, almost like an op-ed in a party newspaper. It mocks the Labour government that is 'bound to fail because they "labour" under history's inescapable curse', trying to get themselves out of a crisis that is inevitable given the nature of capitalism. 'Liberal, Labour, Tory: all the same. They play the part of monopoly capitalist hacks', and their policies, their social contract, is just a way to protect ruling-class wealth. The song celebrates class-conscious action in the motor and maritime industries, urging a proletarian party 'steeled and strong' to lead and guide the working class. But it risks turning from protest into agitprop, especially with its chorus that becomes more of a chant: 'So smash, smash, smash the social contract / It's the cry of workers all over the land'.

In different ways, protest songs pick up and circulate political vocabularies and concepts. In some songs the emphasis is on describing situations and connecting them to general principles inviting a particular evaluation. At other times it is the general principles that are put into play through attention to a particular situation or event. There is not necessarily a clear dividing line between these two, and in particular instances it is a matter of the relative balance between them. In either case, though, we can say that the songs express, invite, and promote a specific sort of political thinking and that this is one way in which we can look at, interpret, and understand them. However, this is to focus on the words. But as we have seen, through the interplay of voices within them, songs may dramatize and stage the conflicts with which they are concerned.

THE BENEFICIAL LIMITS OF PERFORMING PROTEST SONGS

We return now to points we made earlier when arguing that both 'Farmers' and 'How Does It Feel?' made a kind of political claim just by existing, and that the performance of protest songs can dramatize social, economic, and political relations. A central concern of political thought in the Western tradition has always been who can best speak of politics and how they should do so. If we consider Plato to have founded that tradition, then it is a foundational concern. For Plato – to simplify a little – this was a three-sided fight. There are the philosophers, who we may think of today as the experts, be they economists, scientists, or biologists.

Then there are the rhetoricians, those good at arguing and motivating crowds, but also at explaining and illuminating. We might today think not only of politicians but also of all sorts of activists, orators, and journalists who promote ideas and interpretations. Then there are the artists, the storytellers, poets, and dramatists, who represent society to itself, retell its myths, and showcase its heroes and villains. Plato's recommendation was to let the philosophers rule, abolish the rhetoricians, and limit the artists to depicting only virtuous conduct.

The dispute between these has been unceasing. Today it is complicated by a complementary dispute about how each of these three things (philosophy, rhetoric, the arts) should be done and who, in fact, can do them. Can anyone be an expert, an orator, or an artist, or are only a few born to it? Can people be trained to do these things, and if so, should they be – and how? Must each art be conducted only in conformity with certain rules and procedures of logic, rhetoric, or literary composition? Can we allow non-citizens (foreigners, migrants) to take on these roles? Should they be open to all regardless of sex and social background? Should we insist that practitioners match up to an ideal of diversity?

Many contemporary political theorists accept that everyone and maybe anyone can be involved in political decision-making as this is what democratic politics involves. But that does not always mean that they think everyone should be encouraged to be an expert, politician, or artist. Indeed, one of the defining features of politics today is a kind of horror at what happens when, through the Internet, anyone can set up a stall in the 'public sphere' and promote their own thinking. Political theorists generally prefer to set rules of deliberation – of fair and proper argument, of taking turns, and so on. That is, of course, something embedded in the very idea of parliamentary procedure. Infamously, in the British parliament it is forbidden to call another member a liar. But this rule exists to ensure that members address themselves to the content of arguments about politics and policy and do not devolve into endless ad hominem attacks.

What has this to do with protest songs? In the first instance, when contrasted to such rules of deliberation, protest songs necessarily seem improper. 'Farmers' is rude. It makes fun of the monarchy. 'How Does

It Feel?' is aggressive, employs ghastly imagery in an excessive way and uses language many (especially in 1982) would find offensive and inappropriate in the context of reasoned political debate. More generally, songs by their nature are likely to be short and repetitive. They will probably emphasise emotion, entertainment, and collective participation, which seem to be in conflict with serious and rational consideration. But through this very impropriety, songs advance an argument about who can speak of politics and how. Like Samuel Johnson kicking the stone in response to Bishop Berkeley, they decisively refute the Platonic implication that expressions of political views should be neither artistic nor oratorical. And often they are a means by which people who do not hold official political positions can make their views known to the public, answering the question of what sort of people can speak about politics by demonstrating that the answer is 'people like me'.

An interesting and illustrative example of this is 'Question Time' by the rapper Dave.[44] Released in 2017, the song very directly considers contemporaneous political and social events: the UK's Brexit vote (to leave the European Union), the subsequent resignation of Prime Minister David Cameron and his replacement by Theresa May, the leadership of the Labour Party by the left-wing Jeremy Corbyn, war in Syria, spending on the National Health Service (NHS) and the working conditions of nurses, and in particular the 2017 fire at Grenfell Tower in London that caused the deaths of seventy-two people. The language of the song is informal, often profane, and Dave uses the first person throughout making the song a personal as much as political statement. The lyrics very clearly do the sort of thing we have been describing. They represent situations through (re)description, comparison, and contrast in ways that show leaders to be embodiments of vice not virtue – represented as cowards, dodging responsibility, incapable of empathy, and as 'addicts', 'in a big fat game', 'gambling' with lives.

Of special interest to us, in the present context, is the fact that three of the five verses of the song start with the phrase 'A question for the new Prime Minister', the fourth starts 'Look, I've got a message for our old Prime Minster', and the fifth with 'I've got a question for the leader of the Labour Party'. The language of the song intersects with that of Prime

Minister's Question Time, which in the British system is a prominent ritual of political accountability. In so doing, it prompts further political thoughts. Who gets to ask questions of leaders? How should they ask them? By what criteria should we evaluate the conduct of the holders of high office? In 'Question Time', Dave, a well-known musician but otherwise a person with no formal political standing, publicly asks questions normally asked only by other politicians and a few elite journalists. The song's vernacular and raw performance of honesty is an implicit contrast to the arcane formalities of official political expression and so also of how we are normally oriented towards our political life. Simon Frith proposes that rap music 'foregrounds the problematic relationship of sung and spoken language' and that in it 'musical (or poetic) devices such as rhythm and rhyme are material ways of organizing and shaping feeling and desire' that 'offer listeners new ways of performing (and thus changing) everyday life'.[45] Dave's lyrics offer a new way of performing political life. He performs accountability in front of us and if we follow along with the words then we 'perform' it too. The song dramatizes a political practice, such that, through both its form and content, listeners are invited to entertain – in their imagination – a particular relationship to political leaders.

That said, let us now add an important reservation. Dave's song, and most, though not all, of the songs we have discussed, are not acts of political speech. As the philosopher J.L. Austin famously showed, there are times when to say a thing and to do it are one and the same. When we say 'I name this ship' or 'I do' at a wedding, we are doing these things.[46] However, that is only so if we are the correct persons, authorised or recognised as such, doing this in a properly sanctioned location and with the requisite intentions. If you are on a ferry, you cannot throw a can of lager at it and have its name changed; no matter how serious we are, if there is no official present, we are not legally married. Things in politics are not so clear. Nevertheless, when a political leader declares war, it might be war, but not when just anyone says it. When a minister makes a proposal for policy change, something is at stake – there is a potential significance and force in play; that is not the case when we say it to our increasingly bored relatives over family dinner. When a political leader makes a statement about the economy, it has a weight not present when voiced by your cab driver. Protest songs are mostly sung by people with no official position and often not even (Cardew aside) speaking as representatives of a political party (and for much of the period we have been considering, parties were not themselves authorised political institutions). For this reason, their political speech acts are, in Austin's phrase, 'infelicitous': they do not work. However, this is also why a song can say political things in ways that are scabrous, offensive, entertaining, and so on. Indeed, the fact that the song lacks a certain official political force gives it opportunities for other kinds of political acts both felicitous and forceful.

Staged entertainment of any kind creates a complex relationship between expression and performance. What is said 'in character' may or may not be what a performer or writer would say. For example, who is 'I' in a love song? Do The Beatles want to hold our hand? Or are they, in some sense, expressing the fact that we want to hold the hand of an unknown third party? Song listeners can imaginatively move between these and other possibilities. The performance of the song simulates something so that we can, in our imagination, pose questions and entertain alternatives. A song, then, is not a political speech or a work of political theory, but it may simulate one. Because it is not a real speech or tract, it can do things those forms of communication cannot, while enabling us to respond freely, to wonder what it would be like to hear such sentiments in a 'real' speech. And also to think about what we might want from political communication that, we may come to understand, could in principle be expressed by just anyone. In this sense, then, protest songs simulate politics, dramatizing arguments, ideas, and voices. This is what Frith is getting at when he argues that 'song words are not about ideas ("content") but about their expression' and that 'political and love songs concern not political or romantic ideas, but modes of political and romantic expression'. They 'work with and on *spoken* language' with effects 'not on how people vote or organize, but on how they speak'.[47] This is a good way to think about at least part of what protest songs do. They hold political language up for scrutiny and invite a kind of play with it, potentially affecting how we think about it and how we use it (though, as we shall see in later chapters, they sometimes *do* organise, or choreograph, people).

It may be that this is why so many believe protest song to be useless or a failure. If we treat protest songs as a kind of political speech, strictly speaking, we will quickly see that they do not work very well and never in the way of an 'authorised' political speech.[48] One ought not to be surprised by this. Protest songs do not do politics in that way. They are artistic works, even the most sloganizing and agitprop of them. They certainly make serious arguments, and they can justify them. But, ultimately, they create spaces within which we can entertain and consider our politics in its most immediate manifestation as 'issues of the day', as acts that we evaluate in line with our shared moral values, as a way of contesting and reshaping those values, and as a way of organising and managing the relationships between different kinds of persons and activity. If the ideas and aspirations we entertain in this kind of speech never come to fruition, we can no more find the song a failure than we can consider Paul McCartney a bad writer because nobody is holding our hand. Political failure is a problem of politics, not of songs

CONCLUSION

Our argument is that protest songs can be read as ways in which people make political propositions and, in so doing, also 'propose' a kind of broader political theory. That theory concerns the relations of parts of a polity (ruler, ruled, contenders for rule, and so on), defining, representing, and narrating these so as to demand particular evaluations. In this respect, protest songs are primarily *moral* in their political expression, and they are one means by which a society and a culture reflects on its moral concepts, how they can and cannot be applied. In performance, protest songs bring into being another set of relationships – between the song/singer/audience and the subject/topic of the song. This can be thought of as an intrinsically democratic moment in that a 'people' is momentarily formed, authorising itself to think and talk about something political and to exercise judgement over it. This is so even when, as is the case for more than half of our timeline, there is no democracy, and the concept is regarded with more than a little suspicion.

Ultimately, however, this is a kind of simulation of a democratic moment since from it nothing must necessarily follow. When we call on a prime minister to resign, that matters, but it is not the same speech act as when the PM's backbenchers shout 'resign' during a Commons debate. Cornelius Cardew can encourage the abolition of the social contract, but he is not able to actually do it. He is a musician being a musician. This does not mean that nothing has happened when a song has been heard or performed and that 'simulation' is of no great political value. On the contrary, its value is rooted in the fact that it is a different kind of speech, contending for authority with philosophy and oratory, and dramatizing questions about the whole political scene.

In making these arguments, we have focused primarily on the words of songs, which we have treated as relatively straightforward kinds of expression. But they are – to return to our starting point – *songs* defined by rhythm and rhyme, reliant on both original imagery and hoary cliché, mostly fairly immediately intelligible, and, of course, set to music. Thus, in the next chapter, we consider protest songs not as political theory but as political rhetoric.

3

THE PROTEST SONG AS RHETORIC AND ORATORY

In chapter 2, we saw that protest songs make propositions about political situations: what they are like, how to understand their causes, the interests in conflict within them, how to morally evaluate those involved, and so on. We also saw that they stage an argument about political argument: how and where it can take place, the appropriate styles, who can take part. Accordingly, protest songs could be conceived of as a species of political theory 'in the wild'. In this chapter, we take the idea that songs are political arguments in a different, complementary direction and think about them as rhetoric and oratory.[1]

Imagine a typical political occasion. It is likely to be centred on somebody delivering a speech of some sort. If the audience is carried along by the words, it is because the speech also includes rhythm and repetition, the pitch of delivery varies, and the performer dramatizes their words through gestures, intonation, and emphasis. The audience perhaps nods along, vocalises agreement and disagreement, and, if experienced in this sort of occasion, likely anticipates some of what will be said: the end of a three-part list, the articulation of a recognised slogan. They might applaud at the end. Quite likely there will be musical accompaniment at the beginning and closing of the speech, maybe a band playing an anthem, pop, or rock song that supplements, complements, and extends the meaning and experience of the speech.

Now imagine a typical musical occasion at which a song is sung. It likely also includes many of the above elements. Elevated on a stage, somebody is the centre of attention, be they a lone singer or accompanied by a band. Their words hold attention and interest through rhythm and repetition, and – we hope – the pitch varies. The best singers add dramatic gestures and expressions to their delivery. The audience probably moves in time with the words and music, sings along, and, if experienced in this sort of occasion, anticipates lines, phrases, and musical motifs. If the song is good, they will applaud at the end. It is quite likely that the singing will be accompanied – perhaps at the beginning or end of each song – by speech that explains, contextualises, or otherwise comments on the song, enhancing and extending its meaning and the audience's experience.

These descriptions highlight some of the features shared by performances of speeches and songs. These are also shared with events such as theatrical performances or religious services (and some protest songs are also these). But a protest song shares features with the political speech that it may not share with these others: it is not fictional, and it wants to persuade its audience to take a particular view of its subject matter. To pursue this comparison further, we will think about songs as a species of oratory (a kind of public speaking) and as rhetoric (words used to persuade). In the sections that follow, we first explain what we mean by rhetoric and the questions that we might ask of protest songs when thinking of them as 'rhetorical'. We then look in more detail at how protest songs 'prove' the claims that they articulate; how – through words and music in performance – they appeal to our moral or cultural as well as political identity, to our emotions, and to our reason; and how figurative language and musical expression contribute to these. We conclude with further reflections on what makes a song like – and not like – a political speech.

RHETORIC AND SONG

To consider protest songs as examples of rhetoric is absolutely not to think of them as characterised by superficial, verbose, or misleading language. Nor is it to reduce them to ornamental language, or the tropes and schemes of poetry (though these certainly matter).[2] Rhetoric is properly understood, to use a famous statement of Aristotle, as the art of identifying the 'available means of persuasion' in situations. It is the adaptation and deployment of language to make something intelligible to certain people in a certain way, so that they come to agree and to share an understanding of it and then act on that basis.

This approach, treating songs as rhetoric, has some differences from studies in the semiotics of song. The latter concentrate on how songs express meaning in general. That entails identifying the elements of song out of which meanings are made, and how these work not because of their inherent or essential features but because of social and historical practices of music-making and listening, and from the ways in which songs draw from and refer to each other. Analyses of the semiotics of song can be important contributions to the political, ideological analysis and critique of songs and song forms. In particular, they can show how the signifying systems of music can lead to some songs, or elements of them, acquiring the 'second-order' level of meaning that Barthes famously called 'myth', functioning politically by naturalising social phenomena.[3] Contesting such myths, or subverting them, is clearly a part of the politics of song. For example, 'God Save Great Thomas Paine', discussed in chapter 2, conveys political meaning and gives political pleasure today insofar as listeners recognise it as re-signifying the UK national anthem, and thus as criticising by exposing the mythological accretions of the 'original'. In such a case, however, the meanings are in part intentional and inseparable from the political context into which the songwriter (and subsequent performers) are seeking to intervene. While remaining alert to the broader semiotics of music, and particularly the ways in which 'genre' can come to signify a cultural-political orientation, we want to focus on the intentions behind, and the political contexts of, songs and on specific and direct moments of political thought, action, and expression.

Rather than attend to politics in the expanded sense of all social relations and any use of power to create meaning, we are concerned with moments when actors in a specific political situation sought to express a position that they wanted others to understand and share. Thus, we prefer to speak of rhetoric, not of meaning in general but of language used to persuade. As literary critic Terry Eagleton has explained, rhetorical analysis approaches 'speaking and writing not merely as textual objects, to be aesthetically contemplated or endlessly deconstructed, but as forms of *activity* inseparable from the wider social relations between writers and readers, orators and audiences, and as largely unintelligible outside the social purposes and conditions in which they were embedded'.[4] If semiotics is concerned with the politics of meaning in general then we are concerned with the meanings of particular political songs. Consequently, in our analyses we focus on the arguments the songs are trying to make and which can only be understood with some reference to their political situations. In that respect we are interested in them as examples of politics rather than as examples of song. However, in analysing their rhetoric we do not confine ourselves to the meaning and force of the words. The music is also part of the argument, part of the potential rhetorical force. In this respect we are also interested in these as examples of songs rather than of politics alone.

In studying protest songs as rhetoric, then, we treat them not as words or as music alone but as combinations of these used in particular instances of political action; protest songs are 'done' by people for themselves and for each other in the hope of attaining some specific outcome. It follows that we need to know something about what that was and about the singers and audiences brought together through a song. Rhetorical theorists and analysts call this the 'rhetorical situation', which takes shape in relation to an 'exigence', the issue or thing that it is thought rhetoric might be able to affect, and the 'complex of persons, events, objects, and relations' at which persuasive speech is directed.[5] Rhetoric, as political theorist James Martin explains, is 'strategic' action involving the communication and circulation of ideas in ways aimed at attaining goals. It is more than just stating or explaining something. It is one thing to explain the directions to the pub we might meet at; quite another to do so as part of showing that, because of the convenience or the pleasantness of its location, it is definitely the best pub to choose. In the latter case, we are not just describing an aspect of reality but also hoping to affect it by bringing about the situation in which we find ourselves in that pub. To study such speech, as Martin says, is to study a force 'assembled in the content of arguments' and to see how 'plausible stories' organise affects.[6]

Understanding rhetorical situations is not always straightforward, not least because one of the things rhetoric may seek to do is define and redefine the situations in which we find ourselves, and the issues within them.[7] Consider, for example, Clause 28 of the UK government's 1988 Local Government Act, which sought to prohibit the 'promotion of homosexuality' by local authorities, especially in the schools for which they were at that time responsible. A speech by an MP in the House of Commons urging fellow MPs to vote against that clause, a rhetorical analyst might say, is shaped by that exigence: it is a response to this proposed law; the intention is to prevent the passing of Clause 28 by affecting the way MPs think about it, showing them that it is wrong in some manner that they are likely to understand and agree with, and by motivating them to walk through the No Lobby in the House. But what about a speech at a public protest or rally against the clause? This takes place at some remove from the scene of national law-making. The audience members are not MPs and their refusal to support the legislation cannot directly and immediately affect the voting outcome. Here, rhetoric is formed in relation to a different exigence. It is still rooted in opposition to the proposed law, but the orator is likely seeking to promote or consolidate that opposition in ways that could put pressure on MPs and thereby affect their actions. That is why they might urge their audience to lobby their MPs and seek media coverage for the rally to indicate the force of their numbers. Alternatively, they might connect Clause 28 to other issues – to gay rights in general, to criticism of the government, to the cause of freedom – as part of organising and mobilising yet wider societal opposition, with the goal of building a movement of such size and voice that it can take power at some later point.

What, then, is the rhetorical situation of a protest song, such as 'Smash Clause 28' (1988) by the anarchist collective Chumbawamba or 'No Clause 28' (1989) by the pop star Boy George?[8] If performed at a rally, these songs could be understood as rather like the rousing political speech, consolidating opposition. But in 1988–89 they were most likely to be heard as TV performances, radio broadcasts, or records at home. In these circumstances, the exigence is rather ambiguous. Part of it might be commercial: a song is situated in a marketplace where it competes for the attention and interest of DJs, television producers, and paying customers. In some cases, this might be the most important rhetorical situation for a protest song. But often artists have wider goals, though the looseness of the rhetorical situation can make those hard to pin down. Songs 'happen' somewhere several times removed from the scene of political decision-making or rabble rousing, often in contexts where people are not expecting politics to take place at all. This is one reason why protest songs tend towards making very general arguments and communicate attitudes as much as ideas. Chumbawamba's song combines its denunciation of homophobic repression with a wider attack on past and present religious, political, and cultural repression. This can be understood as part of their wider goal of using music and live performances to promote political education about oppression, domination, and the value of solidarity. Boy George's song also brings into its argument about Clause 28 a range of political and policy issues (AIDS, NHS funding, the clamping of cars) and articulates opposition to a moralising political culture that, it argues, fails to address the real causes of our problems.

That argument, however, is not only contained in the words. The sound – as musical semiotics has shown – also carries meaning, and so here, it also contributes to the intended persuasiveness of the song. The video to Boy George's song is based around a DJ spinning decks, reinforcing its club style: verses, backing-singer hooks, a guest rap, all anchored by a tight disco groove that is at once aligned with its target audience – countercultural clubbers – and evocative *of* that expressive, liberated culture. Chumbawamba's punk thrash, by contrast, is much looser, almost a collage of shouted rhetoric, musical samples, measured spoken word, bass-led breakdowns, and intense rhythmic clatter – a succession of literary references high and low and reinterpreted that enjoins mental concentration whilst allowing a degree of bodily entrainment. You can sort of bop along whilst thinking and paying attention, but that attention is more integral than in Boy George's more generous dance track. There is, however, a payoff for the engaged listener, who is given cathartic moments of release for their accumulated anger in the final crescendo passages. In short, the musical approaches differ in attempting to serve the same purpose: in the former, music and message are aligned; in the latter, music is subordinated to message – but in both, the intentionality of musical rhetoric is clear.

Both songs take part in an 'exigence' that involves a very wide 'complex of persons, events, objects, and relations' – one with 'fuzzy' edges – into which they introduce a vocabulary, imagery, emotional experiences, and the kind of broad moral evaluation we saw at work in 'Come all you Farmers' and 'How Does It Feel (To Be the Mother of a Thousand Dead)?'

Central to the rhetorical analysis of protest songs is an understanding of the political context against which they were written and of how writers and performers found a place within it (including audiences to communicate with) and, in so doing, came to constitute situations as rhetorical (and as we shall see in chapter 5, how that interacted with their institutional, political, and commercial situation). To make things yet more complicated, analysis might also require consideration of how, if a song survives the depredations of time, it comes to enter into and out of new contexts and new rhetorical situations. For example, songs about Clause 28 have been superseded by political change: the clause did become part of an Act, but it was repealed in Scotland in 2000 and in England and Wales in 2002. In contrast, Tom Robinson's 'Glad to be Gay' has not been superseded, though the meaning of its argument for rights, resistance, and pride has changed as rhetorical situations have changed (and as Robinson has adapted the lyrics and added verses to take in new issues).[9] Sometimes, protest songs become part of the background of new rhetorical situations, resources that can be drawn on in saying new things, part of the 'available means of persuasion'. Rewriting a song, quoting from it, or reusing its tune can be a way of making and performing an argument.

Given that rhetoric is about the means of persuasion in particular situations, in addition to the situations, we need to look at those means. There are lots of ways in which people can be induced to act. They can be threatened or bribed, for example. Psychologists specialising in marketing – in the sorts of books often piled high in airport shops – claim to show us how our emotional and rational weaknesses can be exploited. But the concern of rhetoric is forms of persuasion achieved in and through speech – with how, as Cicero famously put it, our words may 'prove, please and persuade'. Understanding that requires looking at how arguments and evidence are arranged and at how language is used to communicate vivid, delightful, or emotionally powerful images so that we are 'moved' to change where we 'stand' on an issue or in relation to an idea, maybe even to 'cross the floor' from one side to the other. In looking at songs, we are asking how they prove and how they please, and how these things combine within specific styles of music, to make songs that – performed in a certain time and place for a certain audience – can affect the way people think and feel about something.

Classically, rhetoric identifies three general classes of proof. The first is rooted in ethos or character – that of the speaker but also of those being addressed. The second is pathos – the appeal to our emotions (which is vital if we are to not only agree with a proposition but also feel motivated to act on it). The third is logos – the appeal to reason, which involves logical or quasi-logical claims about the world. We consider each of these in turn and look at some examples of protest songs making use of them.

FORGING IDENTITY AND IDENTIFICATION: ETHOS AND THE PROTEST SONG

One of the ways in which we might persuade people to agree with us is by highlighting something about ourselves. That might be our expertise in a certain subject ('I'm a scientist'; 'I've done this before'), our moral character ('You know you can trust me'), or something that shows we share the same interests and concerns ('I work here too'). This is the appeal to ethos. It is an essential part of any public argument since the first step in persuading people is to give them reasons to listen to us and to take us seriously. People are not wrong, when judging politicians or entertainers, to want to know why they are saying what they are saying, to ask why they should be listened to, or to worry about underlying motivations. At a deeper level, ethos is about establishing what rhetorical thinker Kenneth Burke called 'identification' between speaker and audience, an understanding that we share something with each other, are on the same side.[10] In political theory something similar is understood through the concept of 'the representative claim'.[11] Beneath the assertions of representatives – our union negotiator, an MP, the spokesperson for a campaign group – is a claim to be representative of an interest group and therefore someone who needs to be taken seriously as 'standing for' lots of people. And beneath that is a claim made to those people to be that representative. The validity of the claim is not just a matter of somebody's statistical averageness or, conversely, how exemplary they are. It rests on their 'performance' of that role, their capacity to convince us that they are 'one of us', which is also an argument about who is 'us', what 'we' are like, and what 'we' need. Ultimately, then, the rhetorical appeal to ethos isn't only a claim about an individual orator. It is an argument about social and political identities as such, and an invitation to identify with or as something: a steelworker, a Protestant, a soldier.

It has been argued that protest rhetoric is primarily concerned with this – that it is 'self-persuasion', fulfilling an 'ego-function', and that protestors are the primary audience of their own rhetoric, 'constituting self-hood through expression'.[12] This perspective rather unfairly contrasts protest rhetoric to speech that adapts particular demands into rational propositions made to an imagined 'disinterested' audience exercising its critical judgement in deciding what is best for the polity as a whole. But protest rhetoric, by definition, is making a demand not already accounted for by the 'disinterested' consensus. It articulates claims for and by people who are not part of an established order of 'legitimate' bodies, voices, and demands: women without civil rights; workers excluded from economic decision-making; religious minorities unrecognised by the constitution. Protest rhetoric – more explicitly than other kinds of political rhetoric – appeals to constituencies that have to be brought into being. The burden of argument it carries is not simply to show that enacting some policy will advance the interests of the polity as a whole. It has to persuade some people to see that they share an identity and therefore have common interests and persuade other people that that identity has a place in the polity.[13] This is why ethos is so central to the rhetoric of protest (and, indeed, to protest songs).

The rhetoric of social movements is greatly shaped by this 'functional' need to bring the movement into being, to provide it with a history, a belief in its role in the present (because 'the times they are a-changing'), consciousness of what is to be done (and of the possibility of doing it). Some of this rhetoric may take the form of great oratory and passionate writing, but movements are also shaped by 'vernacular' rhetorics, which create and circulate ideas and identifications 'as part of everyday processes in and through which collective reasoning happens, and common understandings [are] shaped and reshaped'.[14] Protest songs can be an important part of such vernacular rhetorics.

This rhetorical situation – the need to bring people to an awareness of an identity – gives rise to what may seem to be the relatively restricted argumentative repertoire of protest songs. As David Carter finds, in a study of songs created by the Industrial Workers of the World (IWW): 'A song tells the story simply. Heroes and villains are identified, struggles and crises are amplified, and the hopes for salvation and nirvana are shouted. Songs become means of uniting against and coping with a common enemy'.[15] Similarly, Ralph Knupp, through a content analysis of eighty-seven songs from the labour and anti-war movements of 1960s America, found those songs to be reactive, simplistic, and expressive, responding to an exigence in the form of a 'need for in-group solidarity and morals'.[16] It was a finding replicated by Charles J. Stewart who, having analysed 705 American protest and social movement songs from 1800 to 1985, reported that: 'Terms that denote innocent victim and wicked victimizer dominate the selected songs, and the vision of reality is negative, dangerous, threatening, unfair, and unfulfilling' with victims 'duped, deceived, framed, and embezzled'.[17]

In the universe of English protest songs, we also find the oppressed (the marginalised, excluded, disenfranchised, and suffering) up against an oppressor (the wicked ruler, boss, or dominant group; exploitative, parasitic, and, as in 'The Man Who Waters the Workers' Beer' from 1938, fat at the expense of others). There is often an ideal condition, lost in the past or over the horizon, and in the gap between now and then is the movement of resistance: united, strong in 'Solidarity Forever'(to reference an IWW song), more powerful, and more certain to prevail than the flinching cowards and sneering traitors. Consider 'The Agricultural Labourers' Union Song' (1872), which begins:

To the labourers, the pride of the nation
And the true hearted sons of the soil
By tyrants and cruel oppression
Have been robb'd of the sweets of their toil

Having named the group defined by its subordination, the song immediately affirms that group's capacity to seize the moment:

But the chain of oppression is broken
And a freedom for serfs stand in view
And now is the time lads, or never
To stand to the Union so true.[18]

If this is the mere exercise of 'an ego function', then it's one that is inseparable from a proposition about effective collective action.

Similarly, in Samuel Bamford's 1818 call for civil rights, 'The Lancashire Hymn', we again find that the naming and description of an oppressed group is one part of an argument that concludes with a call to resolute action:

When fell oppression o'er the land,
Hung like a darksome day;
And crush'd beneath a tyrant's hand
A groaning people lay;
The patriot band, impell'd by thee,
Nobly strove for Liberty.
And, shall we tamely now forego
The rights for which they bled!
And crouch beneath a minion's blow,
And basely bow the head?
Ah! no—it cannot, cannot be;
Death for us, or Liberty.[19]

In some of the most enduring songs, melody and vocal performance also contribute to the orchestration of common feeling, amplifying the rhetoric to give people an experience of empowered unity. Most obviously, multiple vocal lines arranged in harmony – such a key characteristic of working-class protest in the nineteenth and early twentieth centuries – could foster exactly this sense, not only of communal identity but also of empowerment: of the sum of the collective being greater than its parts. For both public listeners and, just as importantly, participating singers, the vision of an ideal society could be not only taught but also actually *felt* in choral arrangement: voices male and female, high and low, weak and strong, bent to the same ends and together creating something magnificent. In a sense, before universal suffrage, this made *all* choral singing on some level political, or at least imbued it with political potential. It is perhaps no coincidence that the Anglican Church forbade the singing of hymns until the 1820s, just as the Royal Navy forbade its sailors to sing worksongs whilst on duty: the shanty was wholly a product of the merchant marine, not the military.[20] 'Citizen Shanty' (2017), by Commoners Choir, adopts the call-and-response form of just such a seafaring worksong in order to contrast the lone voice of a (sampled) Theresa May with the many voices of the self-proclaimed 'citizens of the world'.[21]

Harmonic arrangement could also allow for the sonic construction of alternative, idealised communities – not simply as an argument for but also a manifestation of a particular ethos. David Kennerley's analysis of Chartist song arrangements posits a deliberate strategy to challenge social hierarchy by dividing the lead melody line among the different voices of certain songs.[22] Published arrangements of the suffragette anthem 'Shoulder to Shoulder' (*c.*1910), written to the tune of the regimental march 'Men of Harlech', replaced the lower and specifically male registers of tenor and bass with additional soprano and alto lines, so that all four parts could be exclusively female.[23] These examples show how the combination of words and music, in particular political settings, can work rhetorically and make a particular political argument at the level of both meaning and form that is instantiated or 'dramatised' in the act of performance.

To the extent that these songs are focused on identity, it is as part of the rhetorical appeal to identify with a group, and to act on that basis, confident of victory. It is too easy to dismiss all this as nothing other than unsophisticated political melodrama, crude sloganizing, or dangerous populism. These rhetorical features are characteristic and essential parts of *any* political rhetoric. As political theorists such as Ernesto Laclau have demonstrated, part of the fundamental 'logic' of politics is the positing of an 'antagonism', a divide that also constitutes a potentially common identity between 'us', who feel that we are unable to attain or achieve something because of 'them', against whom we must organise ourselves.[24] Tony Blair, while not generally considered a leader of a social movement and certainly no populist, led his 'new' Labour Party to power by distinguishing it and its putative supporters from 'the forces of conservatism' of both Left and Right, said to be holding back a new generation – 'a young country' – whom he urged to seize their moment, to embrace and implement 'modernisation', social, cultural, and economic change.[25] Protest songs do not do much that Tony Blair or any politician would not do.

Some of the songs on our list are long. 'Sit Down Neighbours All. Bow Wow Wow' (*c*.1786) takes a little over eight minutes to sing; others from the seventeenth and even the twentieth centuries are still longer. But none has as many words as the average book, political pamphlet, or hour-long speech. And, as we argued above, they are at some remove from immediate political power and decisions. Their rhetorical situation and the constraints on their form demand that, even though they are concerned with contemporaneous political issues and problems, they must be more general than most political speeches, which have the luxury of developing an argument at length and of addressing it to an already-empowered audience. One consequence of this is that protest songs are often like parts extracted from a political speech, especially the beginning call to self-recognition and the rousing peroration. Consider, for example, Edith Nesbit's short Fabian socialist song 'Come Gather, O People' (1888). It begins by proposing a political division, calling a people into being and setting them up against their enemies because the time is ripe:

Come gather, O People, for soon is the hour
When princes must fall with their pomp and their power
For the power of the Future, we know it shall be
A People united and sworn to be free.

Compare this with the opening of Tony Blair's speech to the Labour Party conference in October 1996 (the year before they were elected to office). Blair said:

> Next year, the British people willing, an end to 18 years of the Tories and we will meet as the new Labour government of Britain. It is exciting! But it is also a great responsibility. A chance to serve – that is all we ask … at the time of the next election there will be just one thousand days until the new millennium, a thousand days to prepare for a thousand years.

Like Nesbit's song, the speech begins by situating the audience in a moment in time – a decisive moment of significant change – and at an opening onto a new and better future. The rhetorical identification of the people in Nesbit's song is affirmed by the chorus:

> Firm and fast we will stand,
> Heart to heart, hand in hand!
> In fair or foul weather,
> Brothers together—
> A People united and sworn to be free.

And here is Blair, not speaking in verse but extolling the historic provenance, virtue, and commitment of his party and supporters:

> We are part of the broad movement of human progress, the marriage of ambition with justice, the constant striving of the human spirit to do better, to be better … it was there long ago, there even when the ancient prophets of the Old Testament first pleaded the cause of the marginal, the powerless, the disenfranchised … And it is here now, in this room, as we build around the Labour Party the new force for progress in British politics to bring in the new age of achievement for all our people.

Nesbit's song ends with the declaration that:

Our war-cry is 'Freedom' and those who withstand
That cry have no place in our conquering band
We strive for her sake from the cradle to grave
'Tis Freedom we fight for and Freedom we'll have.[26]

And in his peroration Blair declared:

> Think of the possibility of change. No more squandering the nation's assets. No more sleaze. No more cash for questions. No more lies. No more broken promises. I say to the Tories: enough is enough! Be done, be gone! The glory days of Britain are not over, but the Tory days of government are.

This all builds to the closing lines: 'Let us call our nation now to its destiny. Let us lead it to our new age of achievement and build for us, for our children, their children, a Britain – a Britain united to win in the 21st century'.[27]

The rhetorics are not the same but they are thematically similar insofar as they invite people to share in the identity of a movement, defined by its timely purpose and historic virtue, and by the corrupt – but soon to be spent – forces against which all are united. Blair gets to say a lot more about how his vision will be made real than Nesbit could say in a song. But it is surely unjust to dismiss hers for simplicity while not recognising the place of such in all winning political rhetoric.

Furthermore, one reason for resonance between Blair's words and Nesbit's is that one is a direct descendent of the other. Nesbit's song featured in *The Socialist Sunday School Song Book*, editions of which were printed into the 1950s.[28] It was not in *The Labour Party Song Book* but similar songs were, such as Edward Carpenter's 'England, Arise!' (1886). Songs of a united virtuous people, committed to seizing the future, were part of Blair's rhetorical inheritance. Their sentiments lodged deep in the sensibility of his audience, they were part of the rhetorical situation in which he acted and a resource on which he could draw in seeking to show his own ethos – fidelity to his party's tradition – and also in motivating the Labour Party. In other words, songs such as Nesbit's drew on, recreated, and circulated a 'vernacular' rhetoric informing the everyday identity of the British Left, British socialists, and the British Labour Party. We might even say that Blair was singing Nesbit's song.

Of course, a speech and a song are not the same. We have been able to treat them as if they were by specifically attending to ethos as a property of the words. But when it comes to ethos, the music also counts, in particular because of the rhetorical significance of musical genres or styles. As a number of music scholars have argued, and as Matula summarises, 'listeners approach music from positions that are framed by their existence in social and cultural settings' and bring to the experience of listening 'a host of musical and non-musical experiences and values', not the least of which is 'preconceived notions of what makes good music, what kind of music is most highly valued, and what kind of music appeals to others within or without their social circle'.[29] That is, we come to music with some idea of what is entailed by a song being, say, a ballad, ready to judge it by criteria that have been summarised, in this context, as appropriateness or 'fitness'.[30] The labels put on music – sometimes only obliquely related to their actual styles – are freighted with meaning and part of 'the symbolic veil of culture and value through which listeners frame their response to music'.[31]

Terms such as 'punk', 'pop', or 'world music' are tools of the commercial market for music but also have social (perhaps political-rhetorical) utility in explicating something about a song before we even hear it. They name (and give rise to) conventions, shared between musicians and audiences, that set expectations. They may also be associated with judgements of taste, aesthetic value, and cultural capital.[32] Such valuations may be very different in different communities and subcultures, and this is one of the ways in which musical genre and style can be said to function as a rhetorical means of establishing ethos and signalling communal membership. This is obvious in the case of, say, reggae and related genres created and shared within England's Afro-Caribbean community. In a less obvious way, it is also the case for punk music, which both stated and created a division – marked also by subcultural style – between generations, and between professional musicians and insurgent artists, which had connotations linked to both class and racial identifications.[33]

Musical genre or style, while they may depend in part on technical conventions for musical performance, are also semiotic phenomena, available for rhetorical use.[34] Indeed, genre might be one of the most effective ways in which a song can give definition to a rhetorical situation. It is a way of connoting seriousness or significance, positioning music – through the 'character' of sound – as 'on the same side' as some things and against others. The obvious, and much studied, example is the way in which the construction of 'traditional' and 'folk' music after 1945 came to connote an ethos of 'sincerity' and 'authority'. Experienced as objects 'recovered' from a lost past, folk-song style signified something natural in contrast to the artificiality of modern life, spontaneity rather than calculating commercialism, and the comforting weight of tradition in place of the superficiality of endless modern reinvention.[35]

Such meanings were not stable and were sites of contestation. Folk music could signify the lost innocence of the rural working class or the spirited consciousness of the urban proletariat – the universal class to come. In either case, political and rhetorical claims were embedded in and expressed through aesthetic choices: the unadorned and therefore authentically expressive voice; the refusal to use technology; the adoption of collective singing. This sort of rhetoric is replicated in claims that rock music is authentic, in contrast to pop. Writing in the 1980s, Simon Frith argued that 'the rock claim was that if a record or performance had, in itself, the necessary signs of authenticity then it could be interpreted, in turn, as the sign of a real community – the musical judgement guaranteed the sociological judgement rather than vice-versa'.[36]

One chief means of exploiting ethos in political song of all stripes was, for centuries, the use of familiar tunes as settings for new words, tunes that were assumed to carry and lend signification for the songs' target audiences. This contrafactual practice was the default method of composing new songs at the level of the street, but it was especially prized by top-down activists as a means of adding authenticity to a fundamentally inauthentic (because politically purposed and top-down) lyric. This practice was as common among reactionaries or moral reformers as it was among subversives – the bluestocking Christian moralist Hannah More had a particular preference for the tune 'Derry Down'/'King John and the Abbot'/'A Cobbler There Was' that we analyse in more detail below. Edith Nesbit set her 'Come Gather, O People' to the tune of 'Hearts of

Oak', thereby seeking not only to harness its inherent musical qualities but also its markers of patriotism, tradition, and respectability as a long-standing military anthem. Such tune re-purposings did not seek to draw attention to the songwriters' musical choices, but to use these valued, unremarkable melodies as a form of rhetorical ethos, allowing their songs to 'pass' as authentic properties of the cultural communities into which they were introduced.[37]

Means of connoting sincerity can also involve rhetorical subversion of ethos and authenticity. The lyrics of Neil Innes's comic 'Protest Song' (with which we began chapter 1) mock the empty portentousness of a certain kind of acoustic folk protest:

> Rain on a tin roof sounds like a drum
> We're marchin' for freedom today … hey!
> Turn on your headlights and sound your horn
> If people get in the way[38]

But the power of the parody lies in its use of the aural signifiers of genre: nasal voice, intrusive harmonica, very basic guitar playing. These are used to show a genre as merely that: a set of clichéd gestures signifying the very opposite of authenticity. Innes's song is a rhetorical assault on the rhetorical ethos of that kind of protest song.[39] A different example is Mike Read's 'UKIP Calypso' (2014), a conservative political critique of government policies on tax, immigration, and foreign policy that proposes, as a solution, making UKIP's (United Kingdom Independence Party) leader Nigel Farage prime minister.[40] The song is a weak imitation of calypso, including a crude impersonation of a Caribbean accent by the white DJ singing it. That, and the misuse of the musical style, has rhetorical effects. The pretended embrace of UK Afro-Caribbean culture is really a mocking appropriation marking the distance between social groups and cultural forms, an old-fashioned sort of comedy and perhaps experienced by its intended audience as in harmony with the rhetorical ethos of UKIP.[41]

'Genre' in a more general sense is a potential problem for protest songs, however. Political speech and oratory also has its generic aspects, often associating it with certain kinds of formality, the use of tone and language conveying seriousness of purpose and decorum. In English culture, music is likely felt to exist somewhere else on the spectrum of speech genres, perhaps signifying leisure, fun, and sex. Thus, there is a risk of music seeming at odds with any sort of political message. For example, listeners might experience some dissonance from the contradiction between Boy George's pop sounds and the serious themes of 'No Clause 28', which it may be felt to trivialise. A related problem is that musical form induces misappropriations of political songs (as with the example of 'Born in the USA' discussed in the previous chapter).

One way, in theory, that protest songs might evade these problems is by developing distinct generic markers: stylistic tics to indicate that something serious and political is happening. That is one approach to understanding the 'folk' style. And yet, surveying those songs in our list from the era of recorded music, it is remarkable how few of them stress sonic or musical qualities that might mark them as protest song. Instead, the vast majority, from Noël Coward's 'Don't Let's be Beastly to the Germans' (1943) to Sault's 'Wildfires' (2020), retain the generic musical signifiers of their creators' non-protest repertoire. Reggae protest songs sound like reggae, new wave protest songs sound like new wave, hymns that protest sound like ones that do not, and so on. Perhaps part of the reason why punk music as a whole has been over-associated with explicit political protest is that its generic markers – fast tempo; fuzzy power chords played with choppy, regular downstrokes of the plectrum; and shouted or screamed vocals – have been more widely interpreted as intrinsically political. By the same token, the packaging of 'authentic folk' music in the same era has led to the simplistic parallels between one nasal voice and a strummed acoustic guitar, and idealistic protest.

On the contrary, there appears to be no correlation between a song's subject matter, in terms of protest, and its musical style or features – a notable and memorable exception being The Smiths' 'Meat Is Murder' (1985): as we saw in chapter 2, Morrissey's vocal takes on a more than usually dolorous tone. Here, the melody assumes some of the characteristics of monotonous chant, intensified by the sampled sounds of distressed cattle and industrial machinery. But compare this with the same album's 'The Headmaster Ritual' and 'Barbarism Begins at Home', both of which might be interpreted as heartfelt protests against the physical abuse of children, but which are musically among the band's most upbeat, toe-tapping, and mellifluous tunes. One clear conclusion is that, rhetorically, signifying protest via musical gesture is less important than – or even antithetical to – the appeal to ethos. For an artist or band to step outside their customary generic parameters might be to endanger that very sense of authenticity that we have previously discussed as problematic. Furthermore, to appeal to their established followings or even casual listeners, it seems important to couch political lyrical content in consensual, established musical modes, trading on the connections and affinity this affords with those listeners and their predisposition to attend to the sort of music they already enjoy. Musical pleasure and entertainment need not be viewed in opposition to political engagement: in fact, they might more often be its preconditions.

Protest singers and bands have also evolved a number of solutions to misunderstandings or failures of rhetorical ethos. One is to provide supplementary material. That includes explaining to people what a song is about when performing it, as well as notes and information on album covers, record sleeves, and inserts. Another means is to cultivate their own ethos – a personal style and a celebrity character – that transcends any single song, and the meaning of which can be lent to them, clarifying their political meaning and perhaps even authorising singers to address such matters. John Makay and Alberto Gonzalez, for instance, identify Bob Dylan's cultivation of an image as a kind of outlaw figure embodying a mythic ideal of integrity and simplicity and of opposition to corrupt authority.[42] Just as one expects Billy Bragg to bring politics into an evening's entertainment, so would nobody have found it incongruous for Chumbawamba to be singing about Clause 28 (and Boy George doing so might have given his arguments – paradoxically – more force). Conversely, the attachment of a certain ethos to protest song – a certain kind of man singing about certain kinds of things in a certain way – can be constraining for others who find that they are not taken seriously as musical political orators. Grace Petrie illustrates this in her song 'I Wish the Guardian Believed that I Exist'

(2016), an objection to that paper's attachment to a static conception of the ethos of protest singer.[43] She asserts her presence and identity against settled conventions of who counts, and against an invented tradition of 'proper' protest music, singing of 'the good old days of picket lines and flags', of a time when The Specials and The Jam 'ruled the charts'. Having marked this distance between herself, the main newspaper of liberal sentiment, and an older generation, Petrie then cleverly uses the ethos this creates to align herself with her own generation, and names a distinct political moment, marked by unemployment, wage freezes, a collapsed housing market, and student debt. She ends by closing the gap between persons, aesthetic forms, and politics, denying the existence of the category of protest singer ('it's a made-up thing') not because of declining interest in politics but, rather, because 'there's politics in everything we sing'.

COME TOGETHER: EMOTIONS AND PATHOS IN MUSIC AND WORDS

In stage musicals, the audience is aware that songs are sung in character. But most of the songs we consider here are not like that. In many cases we perceive them as being sung by the real individual to us, the listener or audience member. Mark Booth correctly observes that this may foster particular sorts of identification, especially if we sing along (aloud or in our minds). 'When this happens', writes Booth, 'the singer's words are sung for us in that they say something that is also said somehow in extension *by* us, and we are drawn into the state, the pose, the attitude, the self, offered by the song'. There is a ritual aspect here, he adds, as audience members 'enter into a common pattern of thought, attitude, emotion, and achieves by it concert with his society'.[44] This is intensified in the case of those songs – and there are many of them, especially from the nineteenth century – written to be sung together, often while marching. As Dana Cloud and Kathleen Feyh write of 'The Internationale', 'alongside the motion of the music, the agentive lyrics of the American and British versions feature "action" verbs like "arise," "revolt," "change," "rally," "fight," "unite," "condemn," and "free." Singing these words as part of a collective experience creates a sense of potential action in the bodies of those participating in the ritual'.[45] This brings us to the entwining of formations of ethos with rhetorical appeals to pathos, or emotion, which seek to stir our feelings in order to win our assent and, for that reason, are often considered to be an inferior sort of political argument. But the absence of emotion – an attempt to calm things down or to get us to see things in a passionless way – is also itself a way of organising an argumentative appeal to the emotions.

This might be a very important part of the rhetoric of protest songs, especially if we agree with Deryck Cooke's influential, if not consensus, view that music is 'the supreme expression of universal emotions'.[46] There is a long and rich history of interest in how music and rhetoric might share common features and powers when it comes to stirring and moving the emotions.[47] The great Roman rhetorician Quintilian wrote that 'eloquence does vary both tone and rhythm … and in every expression of its art is in sympathy with the emotions of which it is the mouth-piece', likening the effect of variations of voice with varied musical instruments.[48] Such emotion is a fundamental part not only of the words and sounds of a song but also of its performance. As Frith observes, 'song words work as speech and speech acts, bearing meaning not just semantically, but also as structures of sound that are direct signs of emotion and marks of character'. All pop singers, he continues, 'have to express emotion'. The words are 'the sign of a voice' and 'an apparently transparent reflection of feeling'. Indeed, he suggests that it is non-verbal devices that may most forcefully make a point: 'emphasis, sighs, hesitations, changes of tone; lyrics involve pleas, sneers and commands as well as statements and messages and stories'.[49]

Songs, like other art forms, are a means by which we not only can express but also come to experience and understand our feelings. They do not fabricate emotions out of nothing. Rather, they give names to affects and direct them to issues and phenomena, inciting our bodies to march, dance, and parade. Our concern here is not with the emotional power of music as such. It is with the ways in which, in particular rhetorical situations, it can be part of an argument and a means of making protest songs persuasive. Here the emotional nature of music and its performance can be a problem for political rhetoric: rather than underpin and add emphasis to an argument, it can overflow and drown it out. Often, in political campaign contexts, songs are used as nothing other than emotional triggers – the lyrics don't matter. It was the emotional mood of Springsteen's 'Born in the U.S.A.' and Fleetwood Mac's 'Don't Stop' that the Reagan and Clinton campaigns respectively wanted. The recordings helped shape a background sensibility.[50] Unsurprisingly, the songs that most effectively fulfil that function for politics are unlikely to be protest songs.

This has the benefit of reminding us that the rhetorical force of the emotion in music may come most from its part in a social situation, in which it affects mood and receptivity. Songs are ways of reporting and forming experience, and of intensifying solidarity through singing, drinking, and moving together. In specific times and places, songs might function to 'unite, to defy, and to reach out', but also to divide and intensify prejudice. In the nineteenth century, Oskar Cox Jensen shows, songs could be catalysts for the formation of unruly crowds cultivating an authority, 'exerted at an intimate affective level through appeals to sentiment, emotion, and self-identification, and conducted in the vernacular language and rhetorical gestures of the everyday'.[51] The great forms of mass collective singing – such as the hymns and anthems that accompanied reformist and Chartist gatherings (Eliza Flower and Harriet Martineau's 'Gathering of the Unions', 1832) – orchestrate individual experiences of, and feelings about, the forces of social and economic change. They rearticulate them as songs of hostility to the ruling class (Allen Davenport's 'The Corn Laws', *c.*1837), solidarity (Ernest Jones and John Lowry's 'Song of the "Lower Classes"', 1852), hope for the future (John Leatherland's 'Base Oppressors, Leave Your Slumbers', *c.*1840), and conviction of the inevitability of victory (Thomas Cooper's 'The Time Shall Come', 1852).

Emotion in rhetoric – and as we shall see, in the rhetoric of protest songs – is closely connected with the emphatic representation of aspects or elements of the world. Rhetorically this can be understood as *enargia*, making things vivid through description and 'setting the scene before our eyes' as Aristotle says in Book II of *Rhetoric*. Contemporary rhetoricians use the term 'presence' to name the ways in which a speaker seeks to emphasise elements of a situation and to elevate them above others (though this is not exclusively achieved through emotional appeals). Presence, say Chaim Perelman and Lucie Olbrechts-Tyteca, 'acts directly on our sensibility' such that we feel as well as know about a thing: 'one of the preoccupations of a speaker is to make present, by verbal magic alone, what is actually absent but what he considers important to his argument or, by making them more present, to enhance the value of some of the elements of which one has actually been made conscious'.[52] In songs this can be achieved by some simple devices such as repetition, a chorus that repeats the theme, and by the use of music and performance to intensify and focus attention on particular expressions.

Musically, one outstanding example is the melody that has come to be, by virtue of its ubiquity for upwards of a century, almost our project's theme tune: the air known variously as 'King and the Abbot', 'King John and the Abbot of Canterbury', 'Derry Down', and 'A Cobbler There Was'. In this case, as in that of other melodies from the long eighteenth century, the music serves to shape and enhance the delivery of text to rhetorical ends. It is structured as four measured lines – the notes ideally spaced for the conveying of a clear and comprehensible message – followed by a one-line refrain. Lines one and two serve as an opening proposition, a neat couplet, with line one ending on the (low) dominant, or fifth note in the key, and line two resolving on the tonic or keynote – a familiar device well suited to a declarative statement or question. Line three climbs a whole octave to end, again, on the dominant – but this time high up, poised, at the apex of the melody, perfectly designed to highlight a key word, create suspense, set up a crisis. Line four takes a precipitous rush down the scale and on into the emphatic refrain, by which time we discover we have modulated to the relative minor key from that in which we opened, the effect being intensely satisfying to sing as well as to hear: practically a growl of resolution. As with 'Bow Wow Wow', the short refrain resembles a peroration, a punched fist, a series of cheers, practically enjoining agreement and enthusiasm from the listener(s). Skilled lyricists such as Robert Thomson, author of 'Burke's Address to the "Swinish Multitude!"' (1793), could take full advantage of this melodic skeleton, loading the first two lines with questions, creating powerful and meaningful rhymes for lines three and four, playing with the 'down, down' words of the refrain – words very much in sympathy with the melodic trajectory – in order to make their subversive point.[53]

Stirring the emotions requires a rhetoric that steps away from generalities to specifics – just as journalists know that a great tragedy is most powerfully conveyed through the example of individuals caught up in it. A good example of this is Thomas Hood's 'Song of the Shirt' (1843), a poem immediately set to music, the inspiration for which was a real-life case of a widow making a living from sewing at home. Required to pay a deposit for materials, she found herself trapped in debt and fated for the workhouse.[54] Poem and song intensified awareness of such conditions. Their sentimentality allied to a stark narrative set a benchmark for such criticism of working conditions. The subject of the song is represented so as to inspire empathy in the audience, making present the nature of the woman's toil and despair. Its rhetoric is not like Nesbit's, which sought to inspire common political cause and the energy to commit to it. It is not a song for an audience of other seamstresses who might share its subject's plight. It is for an audience outside of the situation, an audience that is to be persuaded to feel pity and to become indignant. The song begins by describing her situation in simple vivid language, making her the object of the listeners' thoughts:

> With fingers weary and worn,
> With eyelids heavy and red,
> A woman sat, in unwomanly rags,
> Plying her needle and thread—
> Stitch! stitch! stitch!
> In poverty, hunger, and dirt,
> And still with a voice of dolorous pitch
> She sang the 'Song of the Shirt'.

The rhythm of the poem and the music that came to accompany it emphasise that dolorous voice, the repetitions creating presence, making the scene an object of potential feeling but also, as one critic notes, echoing the labour of the seamstress and 'its homogenizing influence … flattening life into a vast monotony of one endlessly repeated action: "Stitch! Stitch! Stitch!" … her life, actions, and even emotions are collapsed into the incessant repetition of the stitch'.[55] In J.H. Tully's first setting, a central motif based around a ceaseless return to the keynote, the lower D of a D minor scale, reinforces – in the musical sensibility prevalent at the time – this sense of weariness and despair. Though the need to provide a listenable parlour tune prevents Tully literally representing the 'Stitch! Stitch! Stitch!' as monotony, the overall effect is to achieve the 'dolorous pitch' described in the lyric.

Later, the song ventriloquises the woman's plea, appealing to ideals of a rustic rather than urban England:

Oh! but to breathe the breath
Of the cowslip and primrose sweet –
With the sky above my head,
And the grass beneath my feet
For only one short hour
To feel as I used to feel,
Before I knew the woes of want
And the walk that costs a meal![56]

The appeal is made to the listeners – 'Oh, Men, with Sisters dear! / Oh, Men, with Mothers and Wives!' – and a striking image implicates them in the plight of the seamstress: 'It is not linen you're wearing out / But human creatures' lives!' In both these 'plea' sections, offering first the appeal to listeners and then the possibility of temporary mental escape, the music modulates to a major key (G major and E-flat major respectively), accompanied by a shift in the piano part from simple arpeggios echoing the melody to jaunty oom-pah-pah chords and then rippling semi-quaver arpeggios. The intention clearly is to achieve a striking affective accord with the listener. An ensuing return to that remorseless D minor opening melody and original tempo underscores the desperation of the situation with which the listener is being asked to empathise.

Here, then, the stirring of emotions is part of an argument for taking the plight of such women seriously, while gently introducing the idea that there is a connection between their situation and the (in)actions of the song's audience. It does not spell out a conclusion or demand action but implies it. Publication of the poem in *Punch* transformed sales of the issue in which it appeared. It was widely quoted and reprinted, including on handkerchiefs, until it 'echoed from the ranks of every social class … an enduring symbol for the Victorian populace generally and for reformers, painters, and illustrators specifically'[57] – which is to say it created an image available for subsequent deployment in rhetorical situations in songs such as 'The Distressed Sempstress' (1849).

These images of work remain available and are still used in songs, intensified by repetition to make present the feeling of the constraining monotony that is the effect of the division of labour. As we saw in chapter 2, Richard Dawson's 'Fulfilment Centre' (2019) makes use of lyrical repetition, sung in a world-weary voice, to rhetorically redescribe working in an Amazon warehouse, foregrounding the drudgery and tedium. That argument is enhanced by the restricted musical palette and simple mid-tempo rhythm that reinforce the lyrical mood:

> An endless array of tat for us to pick,
> Stretching and reaching and crouching and bending over
> Three hundred units per hour
> Hour after hour after hour[58]

In contrast to 'The Song of the Shirt', the voice of the song is that of the worker articulating their own plight: spent, shuffling home after a night shift only to repeat it all the next day. Lyrical and musical repetition adds to a critique of the weight and containment of consumer culture, the excitement associated with it turned to boredom through listing: 'PlayStations, Xboxes, Nintendo Wiis / Microwaves, toasters, espresso machines': 'trainers and tarot cards, dash-cams and wall-art, Lego and shaving foam, onesies and retractable extension leads'.

Dawson also deploys the same device as 'The Song of the Shirt' for his final verse, a gesture towards the possibility of a better future characterised musically by ramped-up dynamics, a soaring major-key melodic departure over suddenly much richer guitar chords, and a final stomp of propulsive drums. However negative the overall portrait, it remains important to leave the listener with at least a moment that, musically, might allow for hope and emotional uplift.

In chapter 2, we argued that the staging and performance of a song simulates political expression in ways that open up, for reconsideration, who can speak politically and with what voice. We can say something similar about the performance of emotion in protest song. In one sense, the anger is not 'real'. It is being imitated as part of a performance. Anger in the mind of the listener is an internal representation affording an experience of the emotion. But this is not a limitation on protest songs. On the contrary, it means that they can stage and explore emotion and its expression, and introduce questions about what kinds of people get to express their anger, in what ways, and with what social meanings. Such performances can be very significant for people seeking to come to terms with their experiences. They can be a route into identification, adopting an ethos, as well as a means of apprehending personal situations as parts of political causes. Jayna Brown writes of her experience watching Annabella Lwin from Bow Wow Wow as she 'leapt and screamed under the stage lights', relating that 'when she sang, I heard my own anger and defiance, my own strife as I tried to negotiate the landscape of sexual exploitation as a young brown woman'.[59] The voice of Poly Styrene, Brown continues, 'carries with it an explicit critique of patriarchy and capitalism'. Such performance is also an argument. It proposes that there is something we should feel angry about, but also that this is what anger looks and feels like, and that its expression is legitimate. This can also be an argument against a gendered emotional economy: 'Both Poly Styrene's and Annabella's screams … interrupt a masculinist claim to dissidence as they disrupt the very ground of dissonance'.[60]

A related example is Petrol Girls' 'Touch Me Again' (2016).[61] This song asserts women's rights to bodily autonomy and freedom from sexual harassment and assault, beginning with first principles: 'My desire, my right to choose or refuse this encounter … my body and my choice'. That argument ends with the repeated and unambiguous assertion: 'Touch me again, And I'll fucking kill you', which continues after the music has stopped, leaving only the singer Ren Aldridge's shout. In performance, she passes the microphone to others so that they can join in with the statement. The emotions of the song – anger and defiance – are explicitly identified as shared affects feeding back into a common ethos as part of a jolting empowerment of the audience and as the conclusion to an argument about not only why something is wrong but also how it can and must be resisted. Anger is an energy.

GIVE ME A REASON: THE RHETORIC OF REASON IN PROTEST SONGS

For a number of writers, the rhetoric of song is largely confined to ethos and pathos. Elizabeth Kizer is blunt and to the point: 'Ethos and pathos are the main types of artistic proof in protest songs. Extensive use of logos is lacking'. Logos is the appeal to reason, which rhetoricians understand to encompass all kinds of 'quasi-logical' claims. Kizer argues that the words of protest songs are 'designed to elicit an emotional response rather than being polemics for cognitive examination' and that they do not 'call for intellectual processing from the auditors to whom they are directed; the treatment of topics, and the topics themselves, appeal to the emotions'.[62] In a similar vein, writing of songs during wartime, G.P. Mohrmann and Eugene Scott conclude that 'a song is, after all, a song, and it is an unsuitable medium for complex persuasive appeals. A lyricist may write a soulful plea or make a compelling assertion, but the effective range of communication seems inherently limited, confined to the reinforcement of existing predispositions'.[63] We do not entirely agree.

On the whole, one might think, you cannot develop a highly complex discourse in a short song: you can sing the elements of the periodic table, but an explanation of the origins and epistemological grounding of modern chemistry is not an ideal topic for a musical number. But songs do and always have made arguments: some of the best examples of song's argumentative capabilities come from our earliest songs They had the advantage of a strophic verse form and – importantly – length (typically between ten to fourteen verses), while at the same time being composed and sung by people educated in rhetorical devices and techniques in grammar schools, universities, and inns of court, and experienced in hearing rhetorically inflected exhortation in weekly sermons delivered to the vast majority of the population. These arguments often incorporated words, tune, and image: take, for example, a song discussed in chapter 1, 'The Good Fellowes Complaint' (1647).[64]

Published between the two Civil Wars, the song protests the 'temporary' imposition of excise on ale and beer to raise money to pay for parliament's army. The new excise led to riots in various parts of the country. Set to a well-known tune, relating to beggars, the balladeer – who aligns himself with all those worst affected – begins emotively, by observing that if people thought times were bad before, this tax is worse than anything. The song's argument is that while wine tax is just because it falls upon the rich who drink it, the beer tax is un-English (it was a Dutch idea) and creates a burden for the working and indigent poor. Suppliers and providers have doubled their prices while making the beer weaker. Tradesmen such as blacksmiths, who work in extreme heat, cannot afford to slake their thirst, while increased costs have led to a breakdown in sociability and charity, as landladies will not give drinkers credit. Most importantly, old women who live on tiny poor-law pensions cannot afford it and will starve. Ultimately, the writer proposes a solution: that the government must promise the tax will be rescinded as soon as the Civil War is over (it still has not happened). At the same time, ballad illustrations literally created a 'picture' (in Ludwig Wittgenstein's sense) that – influenced by the context of the song – induced the listener/viewer to make a judgement and to draw a conclusion in a quasi-logical fashion. In this case, the song is illustrated with carefully chosen contrasting scenes – a richly dressed classical figure attended by a servant serving wine from a giant barrel, and a poor, disabled old woman. Together they highlight the key points of the argument.[65]

The political ferment from the Civil Wars to the Glorious Revolution were crucial to the development of argumentative song forms, only some of which survived into the later period. The forms that disappeared were those that, like 'The Good Fellowes Complaint' and 'The Anarchy' (1648), laid out a detailed argument based on fulsome critique over many verses. Several innovative forms survived to influence the shorter songs of modern periods. These included songs that anticipated debate and voiced the protestors' part in it, such as 'Vox Populi' (1642) (discussed in chapter 4) and 'The Sea Martyrs' (1691), which could involve specific complaints of badly paid groups, linking them to wider questions of constitutional change; satirical approaches that evoked a spirit of protest by recounting a dialogue or telling a tale, such as 'A New IRISH Song; OF Lil-li bur Lero' (c.1688); or themes that heroized and called for justice for an individual suffering for championing the oppressed, such as 'The Subject's Hope' (1681) and 'Free Nelson Mandela' (1984). And especially more subtle approaches that *implied* arguments even as they relied heavily on raising the emotion of listeners to deliver protest and rebuke, such as 'The Lamenting Ladies Last Farewell' (1650) and 'Hollow Point' (2009).

Alongside nineteenth-century innovations of marching hymns for large group singing, these developments set the model for the IWW songbook, which, as Carter noted, was 'intended to persuade the workers that the IWW was the answer to labour's problems', to arouse discontent and promote efforts to change conditions. Descriptions of the miserable condition of the workers, alienated from their labour, dominated by despots and parasites and emphasising their powerlessness and separation, were not just about creating common identity and inspiring emotions of indignation and anger. They were elements of a larger argument, the conclusion of which is meant to be that capitalists should be opposed by a workers' movement, and that the IWW is that movement. The suggestion by scholars that 'soulful pleas' and emotional responses are the antithesis of political argument cannot be sustained.

This brings us to the central form of rhetorical argument, which Aristotle called 'the body' of persuasion: the enthymeme. The best way to think of this is as a kind of everyday informal reasoning. If philosophers like to spell things out laboriously – telling us first that all bachelors are unmarried men, then that Steve is a bachelor and therefore that Steve is an unmarried man – most of us in everyday discussion would just say that Steve is a bachelor. Now suppose that, in talking about Steve to our friend who is thinking about going on a date with him, we then add: 'but he's been married four times'. You do not need to be a philosopher to see that we are making an informal argument against going on a date with Steve, using the fact of his multiple marriages as a sign that he might not be the best at relationships. That argument relies not on the pure logic of the formal syllogism but on our friend inferring from that sign what we intend them to. It's not a claim we can make with the same certainty as we might make claims about mathematical formulae (Steve might just be really unlucky), but it is also not a ludicrous point to make. Enthymemes, then, use argumentative premises that are probable rather than fixed, making arguments relying on an audience's inferences. We point to signs, define situations, and show that things are 'like this' or 'like that', and our audience provides the conclusion: if 'meat is murder' then a moral person ought not to eat it.

In short, protest songs absolutely do make arguments rooted in logos, and like political rhetoric of all kinds, they do so by invoking an audience's stock of commonplaces: idioms, phrases, proverbs, quotations, allusions, and what Aristotle called 'notions possessed by everybody'. In rhetorical enthymemes, Lloyd Bitzer argues, 'the speaker does not *lay down* his premises but lets his audience supply them out of its stock of opinion and knowledge', such that *'the audience itself helps construct the proofs by which it is persuaded'*.[66]

This sort of logical operation is central to most if not all protest songs, though it is hardly unique to them. Songs give names to things, and sometimes they rename and redefine them (as we saw in chapter 2 in our discussion of *paradiastole*). They paint for us mental pictures of situations, put things into dramatic relationships with each other in order to suggest cause and effect, specify who is villain and victim, and invite an emotional response. But they often stop there, relying on audiences to supply the missing piece: that the treatment of seamstresses is shameful and unjust and ought to be stopped; that work in an Amazon warehouse is analogous to nineteenth-century exploitation of labour and that workers need rights; that Clause 28 is an authoritarian act and ought to be opposed.

In this context, the poetic language of songs has epistemological as well as aesthetic significance. Metaphors are important for rhetorical presence because, as Max Black put it, they 'organise' our conceptions, acting as a filter or a screen through which we see something anew.[67] Rhetorical figures can, for example, locate singular actions or phenomena in some larger class, such as when – in Joseph Mather's 'Watkinson and his Thirteens' (1787) – one bad boss is represented as pharoah (and his workforce, it is argued, should all be set free 'like bond-slaves of old in the year jubilee'). In the same song, oppression is metaphorized as a kind of living beast – 'That monster oppression, behold how he stalks / Keeps picking the bones of the poor as he walks'. In 'A Patriotic Song by a Clergyman of Belfast', from 1792, evil is an army: 'While Tyranny marshals its minions around, / And bids its fierce legions advance'. And in 'Song of Choice' (Peggy Seeger and Ewan MacColl, 1973), fascist tyranny grows when seeds and weeds are left unchecked.[68]

Synecdoche (a part of something standing for the whole) and metonymy (an attribute turned into the name of something) help cognitively to organise experience, showing that something belongs in one place or category rather than another. Such figures, in giving 'presence', make us, as it were, turn our head to look at something, lean forward to see it more closely, and change what it is we think we are seeing. There are many examples of this to choose from: almost all protest songs do this in some way, with more or less knowingness and more or less art. One fine example is Maggie Holland's 'Perfumes of Arabia' (1991), written in opposition to the first Gulf War. Taking its title and core image from Lady Macbeth, haunted by the image of Duncan's blood – 'All the perfumes of Arabia will not sweeten this little hand' – it begins, as narratives often do, as a journey.[69] The singer is driving and listening to the radio. Recounting the story told by the news reports ('voices telling me a foreign war'), Holland's imagery gives presence not to the glory of war but to its horror:

> I heard the voice of the airman as his plane fell from the sky
> I heard the man in the foxhole as he watched his brother die
> I heard the last sad song of the dolphin as he drowned in a filthy sea
> I heard the mother weep aloud for her dead child on her knee.

Turning into a garage to fill up her car, the scent of petrol becomes, for Holland, the smell of blood upon her hand, a synecdoche of the oil industry as a whole and so also of the war fought over access to it. In a petrol station in a small Hampshire village, Holland finds herself implicated in and connected with, and so also in some way responsible for, the events she has just heard about on the radio, and concludes that, although 'I've tried sandalwood and roses, I've tried Eau de Cologne as well / Calvin Klein, Chanel Number 5, it cannot erase the smell'. In common with so many other protest songs, 'Perfumes of Arabia' invites a 'way of knowing'. Holland's voice is part of this: the song as an unaccompanied vocal repeating four-line verses removes all possible obstacles between the affect of the singer's words and the listener. Arranged and produced so minimally as to evoke the ballads of a pre-recorded age, there is a dissonance with the topical (for 1992) references that serves to bring them into still sharper relief. In choosing to listen to 'Perfumes of Arabia', and entering into that relationship, we have no choice but to become thoughtful, to reflect: the music places us in a necessarily receptive mood. Such songs 'bring things to mind', providing names, labels, pictures, and slogans. They proffer definitions, map relations, and urge evaluations. Through the power of repetition, and enhanced by the performance – the sound and the emotional support it gives – they point at something, give it presence in our minds, and ask us to agree that 'yes, it is like that' and then to do what necessarily follows.

To the enthymemes in the text, we must add the enthymemes in performance. As we have consistently emphasised, a protest song is not just an idea, a text, some poetic language. It is a social action that can bring these together with an audience; in performance it creates a fact, an event that took place not in the imagination but in the world: these people, at this time, singing about these things, constituting an identity and expressing emotional force. And from that fact one can infer things: about collective experience and interests, the reality of solidarity, the emotional resonance of an issue or situation, the likelihood of opposition succeeding. Christophe Traïni calls this aspect of protest songs a 'syllogism of festive and participative democracy'. That is to say, the gathering together of people in the context of political and protest music is part of a perfectly logical demonstration of a truth about democratic politics, and who is (and who is not) doing it. Traïni explains this in terms of a 'primordial proposition' in which 'musicians emphasise their ability to conduct enthusiastic festivities which allow the participation of all their fellow citizens in the form of dances, choruses, acclamations etc.', accompanied by a secondary proposition, 'the fact that political competition obeys a professional logic that now only interests the minority of specialists who work in it'. The conclusion of this logic presents musicians 'as the heralds of a participative democracy rising up against the professional politicians, who now only represent themselves'.[70] That is too specific and contemporary a problem to encompass the long history of protest songs in England. But something like this syllogism is always potentially in play when a musical performance takes place: a people is gathered and collectively expresses a view on matters of state. That is to say, protest songs – no matter how many people sing along – are never only *about* politics. They are also one of the ways in which politics happens.

CONCLUSION

To conceive of protest songs as rhetoric is to see them as a means of conveying social meaning to particular audiences in particular situations and about particular things, and in ways that affect how we apprehend, experience, and evaluate them. Such songs are not monological but part of a conversation. Audiences bring their own conceptions with them. If the work is successful, there will be some kind of alignment between a speaker, an audience, and an issue; between identify, affect, and reason (if only for a short while).

Political speeches are likely to blend and combine rhetorical appeals – to identities, to feeling, and to reason. How these are blended – the differing amounts in the mix and where the emphasis is placed – is one of the things that differentiates ideologies and forms of politics from each other. Protest songs are also such a blend, but as we have seen, ethos, or identification, has an especially prominent place, in part because these songs *are* protests and necessarily involve political identities in (re)formation. The emotional force of music and lyrics adds to this mix, and there is always some kind of rational proposition in play. Protest songs constitute cultures and traditions by forging links to a political situation and context. Through the combination of poetic language, musical form, and performance, they create a 'picture' in which things are seen in relation to each other in a certain way, and from all this, audiences may draw the obvious conclusions for themselves.

Ultimately, the rationality or rightness of such claims cannot be judged by looking at the songs alone, nor by applying a standard created independently of the situation. In some respects, the judgement of a protest song is a political one and we will make it on the basis of our prior political orientations. That said, and as we have seen, protest songs are trying to make an argument and to be persuasive. Any judgement we make of a song will also be a product of its success in creating harmony between its claims and political experiences, ideas, or values we already held. Songs may have more or less 'fidelity' with the social, economic, and political experiences of their audience. Cloud and Feyh propose a more nuanced term – 'affective fidelity' – which they define as 'a condition under which the emotional constructs of a constitutive discourse align with the class standpoint of its addressees', suggesting that 'the fit between text and experience (i.e., the text's fidelity), is a criterion for discerning … an accurate from a mistaken "binding job" of constitutive rhetoric' or a socially and historically grounded political interest from an 'ersatz' identification.[71]

This returns us to the rhetorical situation in relation to which arguments – and songs – are formed. In the case of protest songs, this is first and foremost a political situation. For all the reasons that political arguments and movements of all kinds fail, a single song may have no effect. Up against everything else that happens, a song is a small thing. But the pictures songs paint, the names they give to things, and the evaluations we make on the basis of them may remain available as ways of thinking and speaking and as part of the circulation of ideas and phrases across a political culture. This is a foundational political activity.

4

PERFORMING PROTEST AND CLAIMING REPRESENTATION

The politics of a protest song do not reside only in the words and the music. They are also part of a song's performance and the ways in which those performing claim to represent a particular group or cause. To some, this might seem intuitive. The Fall emerged amid punk's mid-1970s tumult, abrasive in sound and acerbic in word. Mark E. Smith was the singer and lyricist, fronting the band until his death in 2018. In that time, Smith's distinctive voice (Mancunian, smoke-inflected, and prone to end each statement with an 'ah') spoke lyrics of a phantasmagorical England, where speed-freaks lurked and spectres haunted landscapes real and imagined. He stalked the stage, turned his back on the audience with apparent disdain, chided his band for 'showing off', and presented The Fall as uncompromising in both their sound and performance.[1]

In interviews, Smith perfected the persona of a gnarled pub intellectual, spouting 'common-sense' opinion on all and sundry, a lottery of insight and nonsense depending on how many lagers were sunk and what mood he was in. The politics, though, were harder to define. Quite how does a hymn to a northern uprising, 'The N.W.R.A.' (The North Will Rise Again), situate itself politically when a key character lives underground in an ostrich headdress with orange-red lines on their chest and tentacles swinging from their body? In their references to revenging the Battle of Culloden and rampaging in Manchester Arndale shopping centre, the lyrics invite a political interpretation, as does the 'common sense' of the interviews.[2] But arguably the heart of the protest lies in the performance.[3]

First performing in 1977, The Fall had links to communist and feminist organisations; they worked with the Mental Patients Union and appeared in support of Rock Against Racism (RAR). Their song 'Hey Fascist!' was a *cause célèbre* in certain leftist circles, meaning Smith was sometimes questioned as to why he soon tired of such a direct approach.[4] His reply was telling, complaining about RAR asking him to hold up posters. 'I would say – we're a political *band*, that's what we sing about. But they want you to make announcements between songs; they see you as an entertainment – you might as well be singing Country & Western ... SWP [Socialist Workers Party] workers walking around with leather fists – that's the *alternative*?'[5]

Smith's comment is worth unpicking for what it shows us about how the performative aspects of protest songs, as argued in chapter 3, unfold in the actual (live, communal, unpredictable) situations of performance. The politics of The Fall, and any associated protest, were communicated through who the band were: working class, comprised of male and female members, resolutely Mancunian/northern, refusing to kowtow to either the media or the music industry (let alone political directives from outside the group). Equally, the politics of The Fall were registered in the *way they played*, without recognised pop/rock affectation, and *what they played*, raw and repetitiously riffed songs with lyrical subjects localised but creatively reimagined.[6] In other words, the legitimisation and resonance of The Fall's protest – registered in their *refusals* and Smith's barbed socio-political observations – resided in their performance of a rhetorical ethos that subverted what it was to be a singer, or a musician, northern, or working class, but their performance also laid claim to represent what it was to be distinct and different.

How successful The Fall were in doing this may be open to debate. Nevertheless, their approach raises questions as to how the public performance of a protest song links with claims to represent (to speak to, for, or about) a particular cause or social constituency. This chapter therefore begins by insisting that representation involves more than just the 'I/we/you' of a lyric. To consider just how the performance of protest songs gives force to claims of representation and rebellion, we utilise three case studies: 'A New IRISH Song; OF Lil-li bur Lero' (1687, 1688, 1689) – Protesting Disguise; National Songs – Performing England and Englishness; and Bob Vylan's 'We Live Here' (2020) – Contesting Identity.

THE ART AND POLITICS OF PERFORMANCE

The communication and performance of protest in song goes beyond the lyrics. Integral to the process of transmission are factors such as who is singing, where they are singing, how they are singing, to what music, and to what audience they are singing. Likewise, the media that present and frame the protest song become essential to its simultaneous existence as a product to be sold, consumed, and used. Arguably, therefore, the resonance of the Sex Pistols' 'God Save the Queen' was initially located in the fact that the song was being written and performed by a disaffected working-class member of the Irish-Catholic diaspora, whose torn clothing détourned symbols of establishment power and whose lyrical promise of 'No Future' came wrapped in a record sleeve that defaced and muted Elizabeth II as she celebrated her Silver Jubilee (1977). Form and substance aligned, underpinned by a pugnacious rock riff and the ongoing furore as to punk's embodying Britain's supposed decline through the 1970s. In that moment, and for all the contrary narcissism that followed, we can believe that Johnny Rotten meant it.[7]

Defining what makes a protest song credible or resonant is partly subjective and partly related to our understanding politics as a form of music and music as a form of politics.[8] By 'subjective', we may mean the point-and-purpose of the writer and performer, or the reception of the song by its audience and/or individuals within that audience.[9] To perform a protest song is necessarily to represent either a particular constituency or a particular cause. It is, in other words, a simulation that embodies a protest and proposes that the audience embodies it too. There are five elements to this: the staging, the space, the visual and the material, the sound and the voice, and the reputation.

The Staging

The staging refers to what the performers – who might include the audience singing along and responding to the song – look like and how they present their protest. The politics are embedded in their physical representation, as with the rapper Slowthai's appearance at the 2019 Mercury Prize ceremony waving a replica severed head of Boris Johnson or Stormzy's Union Flag stab-vest performance at Glastonbury in the same year. Chosen to headline the main stage, Stormzy became the first Black male solo artist to do so. His wearing of the Banksy-designed vest alluded both to the nation and to the knife-crime epidemic afflicting the working-class London community he came from. This item of stage wear was used to claim representation of a people and a problem, a claim endorsed by the audience's enthusiastic response to Stormzy's chant of 'Fuck Boris [Johnson]'.

Of course, such spectacularly mediated performances are neither the norm nor historically conventional. Songs of protest were obviously registered and reported in the pre-TV and social media age, their words shared, printed, and later relayed. But they were not visually transmitted through virtual time and space in the same way. In the seventeenth-century beginning of our timespan, when performer and song were not always so closely linked, woodcuts of hungry poor men remonstrating against greedy farmers raising food prices provided clear identifiers of the cause and class being represented, regardless of who actually wrote or performed a song. More generally, songs performed at a political gathering, on a march, outside a mill, or before a symbol of power

4.1 • Stormzy in his Union Jack stab-vest performing at the Glastonbury Festival in 2019.

necessarily signalled – and signal – a display of opposition or resistance. Banners and flags inform the panorama of protest. The assembly of a crowd frames both the song and the singer(s), be it in the twenty-first or seventeenth century. The British Union of Fascists marching and giving voice to E.D. Randall's hymn to their leader 'Mosley' (1934), striking lemonade workers bemoaning the sacking of Annie Lowin in 1911 ('Idris Strike Song'), the forest community in Charnwood Forest performing an 'opera' in opposition to the appropriation of common land in eighteenth-century Leicestershire, crowds supporting those in parliament demanding political and religious reforms in 1641–42 singing 'Vox Populi' and leaving printed copies of the lyric strewn across the street: the songs and the protest found focus in, came together to speak of and for, a political protest of remonstration.[10]

The Space

The space in which a song is performed also constitutes the protest it expresses.

Listening alone to a protest song is a different experience to sharing in a live performance of it, which is different again from hearing it at a demonstration. Each may inspire political responses – Tracey Thorn, for example, describes a political education acquired from her bedroom listening habits.[11] But the response and its politics may be different in each case, and may be influenced by the marketing strategies of the industry that produces it, or by the political organisations associated with it.

In earlier centuries, it was the publisher who would coordinate the author(s), printers, and distributors of the published song. The politics of capitalist production was crucial to a song's existence and dissemination. For the 'Vox Populi' singers, the very performance of the song took politics 'out of doors' in ways that broke all ascribed rules, yet they simultaneously claimed the identity of the king's loyal subjects and rejected the label of 'disloyal rebel' imposed upon them by those antagonistic to parliament's reform agenda.[12] Live performance might also enable a communion between the performer and the listener.[13] Proximity to the audience, be it close-to in a collective space or at a site of demonstration (a rally for example), allows for a symbiotic relationship between the song, the performer, and the protest. As Billy Bragg made clear when he lent support to the 1984–85 miners' strike, songs such as 'Between the Wars' had to 'speak to people who were deeply involved in politics with a capital P in a manner that reassured them I wasn't just a pop star from London who was exploiting this to further my career'.[14]

Put simply: context matters. The meaning and impact of a protest song is partly dependent on where – and/or the place in which – the song is performed and heard. We might posit that Stormzy's protest would be received and interpreted differently if performed in a small East London club rather than on a corporate festival stage. Equally, a song sung to co-workers in a local tavern no doubt resonated in ways the same song might fail to if performed to a crowd of strangers in another part of the country. We expect certain songs to be sung in a folk club. The venue helps give sense to a politics or protest: it positions the song and its intent. Though we might take protest songs with us (in our heads, to our homes, on a march), communication and reception refract through the space in which the protest is heard and seen.

The Visual and the Material

The protest song is accompanied by visual and material elements that further seek to communicate the meaning and the message. This might entail clandestine lyric sheets proffering words of rebellion to be sung at conspiratorial meetings or at the gathering of a crowd. Early socialists – not to mention feminists and, in the twentieth century, communists and fascists – produced songbooks that depicted both their future vision and their critiques of existing wrongs or injustice. Akin to seditious pamphlets, they communicated and documented a protest, ensuring the words and the songs were bound (literally in some cases) to the ideas and ideologies espoused by the parties and movements who performed them.

These elements are also the result of a market, serving to help brand and advertise a product. Charges of marketing the revolution and turning rebellion into money have long been made against rock's rebels as they decry war and vent frustrations at the ills of society whilst oiling the wheels of capitalist production. One response from those who wanted to make their political message clear was to try to take control of the product and its image. For this reason, whether it be the Marxist rock group Henry Cow, the left libertarians at Rough Trade, or the punk-anarchists of Crass, attempts were made to circumnavigate – or provide alternatives to – the existing means of production. Though printing your own sleeves and cutting your own records rarely meant *literally* doing so, the establishment of independent labels run co-operatively or collectively at least endeavoured to limit any inherent contradiction in attacking a system whilst engaging with its processes. By doing-it-yourself – and demonstrating *how* to do-it-yourself – the notion persisted of a music emergent from below rather than above, a consequence of creative agency immune from commercial interest and attuned to the interest (and often the associated protest) of a particular culture or political position/

milieu. Here again, moreover, the politics were bound up as much in the practice as the lyrics or subject matter of a particular song. Nevertheless, the Desperate Bicycles' 'The Medium Was Tedium' (1977), released independently with a lyric bemoaning the 'commercial ventures' of pop music and wrapped in a sleeve explaining the process of production, at least came close to fusing form and substance: 'It was easy, it was cheap, go and do it'.[15]

There is, then, a longer prehistory to consider. Changes in the technologies of print culture allowed for political meaning to be enhanced or inflected by material paratexts: from font choices and illustrations to the actual stuff the lyrics were printed upon. From the outbreak of the Civil Wars in the mid-seventeenth century, political campaigners avoided the retail market (which customarily published popular songs in 'old English' fonts, known as 'blackletter', but today called Gothic) and commissioned printers to print their song lyrics in a roman font (similar to the serif fonts we use today). On the one hand, this meant they avoided interference as regards quality and saleability by the ballad trade, and the social denigration of their carefully honed words being sold from ballad stalls or on the streets to a socially and geographically broad audience. On the other hand, they missed out on the trade's highly developed distribution systems. This was deliberate. Campaigners paid accomplices to distribute their sheets for free to strategically useful groups (such as urban apprentices) to whip up support for street protest or similar. In the later century, as political tensions grew, this squeamishness dissipated somewhat as Whig and Tory campaigners sought to influence the whole political nation and published in both formats.

Throughout our timeline, long before the rise of recorded music, the decision to publish at all was fraught. There was not only risk of persecution but also risk as to interpretation. Single-sheet ballads – both the large, landscape-format broadsides of our first 150 years and the smaller, portrait-format slips of later years – came with down-market associations but also a certain status. They had an implicit association with the *vox populi* and its moral authority that political actors of all stamps sought to exploit in order to win over, and claim representation of, 'the masses'.[16] Publishing a song within a different medium – such as a newspaper or journal – reframed its context entirely, removing it from the realm of the ballad-stall or street ballad-singer and placing it in the domain of the 'rational' reading public, whilst still allowing for the possibility of oral performance and mass distribution. Chartist newspapers such as the *Northern Star* included songs in advance of major public demonstrations, so that their readers might be able to rehearse songs beforehand and come ready-equipped with a lyric sheet in a manner that was both efficient and semi-respectable. 'Respectability' was key to claims of representation in that it granted authority to the claim.

Still greater respectability was to be conferred by a bound book, a collection of songs: the oeuvre of a single writer or the repertoire of a movement. Compared to the single-sheet ballad, a songbook conveyed a sense of solidity and permanence that might bolster a protest song's credentials as more than ephemeral. This process began very early. One hugely popular collection, *The Garland of Delight*, was produced by Thomas Deloney (our first protest singer), as were collections for other professional songwriters and protest-song authors in our list.[17] It is no coincidence that the protest songwriters who sought to establish themselves as the new celebrities of the working-class movement often self-published their own collections in the manner of John Freeth (see chapter 5). The archetypal figure here is Samuel Bamford, whose collections evolved from 'The Weaver Boy', a short pamphlet produced in his early days as a radical youth. Later, as he began to present himself as a more moderate elder statesman of the reform movement, his songs came in voluminous collections in which protest mingled with poetry and pastorals.[18]

The element most often absent from the printed record of songs was, of course, its music. There are exceptions, such as music-printer Nathaniel Thompson's single-sheet ballads and song collections (see chapter 5). Engraved music was much rarer; though Charles Corbet, Thomas Moore, and Thomas Cross did produce engraved single-sheet political songs from the late 1680s. More usually, a tune might be stated, implied, or left open to interpretation. Images, however, were common, be it a woodcut or engraving.

Again, changes in social praxis and technologies over time were closely entangled with the visual choices made by publishers. From the

1620s, as the market for ballads grew exponentially, publishers pushed further by enlivening their songs with illustrations. These became political tools by the 1640s – adding their own meanings to a song's text. For example, 'The Parliament Routed', published in 1653 in response to a republican crisis, incorporated an illustration of the monarch turned upside down, which made visually explicit the royalist argument that to right the government, the monarch should be turned heads up again, a point that was only implicit in the lyric. In 1820, the hugely influential Newcastle printer William Marshall contributed a three-song broadside in response to the Queen Caroline Affair, at a time when radicals everywhere, to advance their cause, were protesting the new King George IV's treatment of his wife.[19] This sheet, *Excellent New and Popular Songs on Queen Caroline of England Adapted to the Most Popular Tunes*, specified its three tunes as Burns's 'Scots Wha Hae', a radical staple, along with 'God Save the King' and 'Rule, Britannia!' in a proud appropriation of loyalist rhetoric: 'we are the queen's staunch defenders, the real patriots; it is the wicked king who has disgraced the name of monarch, which we hereby uphold'.

Visually, this audacious tactic was endorsed by a woodcut of the royal coat of arms (replete with motto) positioned above the song. Contributed by Samuel Bamford, the woodcut signalled an unlicensed, brave, and thoroughly impressive use of establishment credentials to reinforce the song's sense of righteousness. Not dissimilarly, an unattributed edition of 'What's Old England Come To?' – a fairly generic protest at the woes of economic depression – was greatly bolstered by the image at its head: a John Bull figure dressed in the clothes of a respectable countryman, bent double under the weight of an enormous sack labelled 'taxes'. Rhetorically, the image is ambiguous if you unpick it: logically, the man must be the tax collector, not the oppressed masses. But the visual message is immediately striking: once-prosperous England is being crippled by the impositions of a money-grabbing state. The image leans into the iconography and values of middle England in a way that the more working class–directed lyrics do not, perhaps expanding the demographic appeal of the song.

Bound books understandably offered still greater scope for visual rhetoric. This could be simple, as with Robert Thomson's 1793 Jacobin collection *A Tribute To Liberty*. The title is augmented with an ornate sunburst, while the preface comes with a classical image of Britannia's shield and a helm crossed by wreaths, a sword, a Phrygian cap of liberty, and the caduceus of Hermes/Mercury. Here, the symbolic meaning of the individual objects becomes secondary to the overall impression of classical vigour and virtue. As a result, a collection of modern and often scurrilous songs corresponds to the high-minded heroics of the Greek and Roman republics. In other words, the songs are elevated by association with appropriated iconography.

Fast-forward a few centuries and the imagery of radical pop/rock/punk records could be more explicit. Photos of battle-torn bodies, for example, were common on punk records decrying the horrors of war. Both Discharge (for example, *Why* from 1981) and Crass (for example, *The Feeding of the Five Thousand* (1978) and 'Nagasaki Nightmare' (1980)) utilised gruesome war photography to augment their message. But to register a continuum, we might look to Hone's aforementioned 'Political Christmas Carol' of 1820, which included caricatures by leading artist George Cruikshank to make clear in the familiar – and legally acceptable – lexicon of visual political satire the song's targets and context. It is not a million miles from the cover of Iron Maiden's single 'Sanctuary' (1980), which envisages the murder of then Prime Minister Margaret Thatcher in a similarly of-the-minute cartoon idiom.

Generations after Cruikshank, socialist songwriter-publishers William Morris and Edward Carpenter each augmented their collections of protest songs with familiar motifs from their movement. Morris's *Chants for Socialists* (1885) is headed with an engraving of the Socialist League featuring the slogan 'Agitate, Educate, Organize'. The words are emitted from the flaming torches of classically robed and muscular men; or shown haloing the head of a benevolent angel, with acorns and oak leaves symbolising both the national strength of the movement and indicating the vast potential of small beginnings. The high-blown style of the image exactly complements the perhaps misplaced lyricism of the songs but is nonetheless impressive. Carpenter's *Chants of Labour*, meanwhile, features two specially commissioned designs by Walter Crane. Their arts and crafts resplendence adds grandiosity and glamour to the

4.2 • Walter Crane's designs for Edward Carpenter's *Chants of Labour*, 1922.

contents, from the frontispiece of the noble labourer and rising sun – again with a Phrygian cap held aloft – to the group composition of an idealised community replete with babes-in-arms. At left, we see a family reading – or singing – from a book, presumably the same book we ourselves are reading. Once again, the claim to represent a people and to legitimate or authenticate a protest is conveyed in the visual and material form of the song.

The Sound and the Voice

A song's protest is not just conveyed in the spaces it occupies or forms it takes, but in the sound it makes. The sound and voice of a protest can be defined in various ways. Genre convention, for instance. Or vocal grain. Or with regard to particular tunes, rhythms, timbres, instrumentation, arrangement, and production.[20] To quote Morrissey: 'I thought that if you had an acoustic guitar, it meant that you were a protest singer'.[21] As this suggests, certain musical forms may be recognised to signify protest (even where a protest or a politics is not necessarily apparent). Folk, for example, alongside punk, reggae, and hip hop, often comes with the expectation of a political message. In other words, music that is historically aligned to a subaltern milieu, or is played aggressively, or accommodates a chant or slogan, or has a tradition of communicating dissent can indicate at least the potential for protest. Yet, our list of songs reveals that protest transcends genre and may be found across the array of musical styles and forms. For example, Autechre's *Anti* EP from 1994 protested against the Criminal Justice and Public Order Act, legislation designed to prevent 'illegal' raves by defining music as a 'series of repetitive beats'.[22] The record was instrumental, with the longest track, 'Flutter', programmed to have non-repetitive beats and to be playable at variable speeds.

Another recent example may be found in Extinction Rebellion's 2019 claim that 'the samba saved Parliament Square'.[23] This referred to a time when, during an occupation outside of parliament, police attempts to arrest demonstrators were thwarted by the arrival of the XR drummers. Kimwei, who was one of those drummers, remembered it rather differently, though he made the point that drums tend often to be seen as 'magical and spontaneous', when in fact they are 'much more planned than that'.[24] The planning is, in part, a consequence of the multiple roles that drums can play. They can be used for 'site-holding', 'outreach', 'de-escalation', 'morale boosting', or 'distraction'. Whatever the role, the idea is that drums helped to organise the people in particular ways and to represent their interests, whether in protecting the space they occupy or boosting their morale. To this extent, we can talk of rhythm as a constituent component of the performative claim to political representation in the midst of the protest.

Michael Denning makes the case for the political significance of music-as-sound in his account of the impact of recorded music on colonial societies. He writes: 'Even when these musics carried no apparent political meaning, their disruptive noise challenged not only the musical codes of empires and racial supremacy, but also the improving and uplifting ideologies of many colonial elites'.[25] He explains that the 'anticolonial meaning of a record often lay in neither the politics of the musician nor of its lyrics, but in the way its very sound disrupted the hierarchical orders and patterns of deference that structured colonial and settler societies'.[26] Denning's argument, and the evidence on which it is based, does not speak directly of protest, but it does suggest that music has the capacity *as a sound* to convey political ideas and to ally those to particular communities of interest. To this extent, it alerts us to the possibility that music as sound can constitute a political claim on behalf of a cause or constituency. In the same way, the songs of the disenfranchised labourer or suffragette can be understood to carry an implicit political meaning, giving a voice to the protest.

Giving 'voice' is not just a matter of reciting words. As sociologist and music scholar Simon Frith has argued, the voice exists as 'a *musical instrument*, as a *body*, as a *person*, and as a *character*'.[27] In these guises, the voice can express protest and claim representation. This might well be the case in relation to recorded music of post-1945, but it may have less salience for the performance practice before then. Written songs, most often incarnate in the lyric sheet, were blueprints for renditions by any number of different voices, especially those of the songs' purchasers and readers. In domestic contexts, singers were very often singing to themselves and/or their own families; their individual voices would be associated with all the songs they consumed (political or otherwise), so lacking that dedication and exclusive connection to the song in question. In many cases, the melodies they envoiced could be associated with multiple sets of unrelated lyrics. There is, therefore, a case to be made that for the majority of our period, the lyric sheet (in broadside, slip song, pamphlet, or book form) was the aspect most closely bound to the unique qualities of the song.

Nevertheless, and despite the lengthy lyrics offered from early modern ballads to anarcho-punk tirades and hip hop testifying in more recent times, Frith insists that protest songs 'don't furnish us with arguments or even messages but with slogans' (which can sometimes be misinterpreted).[28] Ergo, the language used and the grain of voice become integral to how the song is received – whether it is believed or taken seriously; whether the listener relates to the singer and the song. Can the singer be *trusted*?

Questions of this kind used to be raised in the 1960s in debates about musical authenticity. They were concerned about not just white performers of the blues but also the 'showbiz' style of Motown artists. They were to reappear in punk's apparent disdain for the glam rock of David Bowie, T. Rex, Elton John, and others in the 1970s. More recently, something similar can be witnessed in arguments about cultural appropriation in music.[29] What all this has in common is a concern with what counts as 'authentic' musical expression, itself tied to notions of credibility. Put another way, they are about the claim to represent, to speak for a community or an experience, and about how a performance can (or cannot) establish that claim. It is about how the performance *appears* to those who witness it. Bruce Springsteen's stage clothes – often jeans and a T-shirt – help to establish his claim to speak for the experience of blue-collar workers.[30] Bob Dylan's look performed a similar task, but so did his music. As Greil Marcus notes of 'Blowin' in the Wind', it takes its melody from Odetta's 'No More Auction Block' and 'borrowed authority from that melody'.[31] Much of this – the link between sounds, styles, and authority or credibility – depends upon the reputation of the performer.

The Reputation

Finally, then, the reputation of the person(s) delivering the song becomes important with regard to the legitimacy of the protest and the message conveyed. In the aforementioned genres of folk, punk, reggae, and hip hop, performers often spend time authenticating their right to speak for a particular constituency, documenting and detailing where they come from and what they've seen. Do they talk it as they walk it? Hence, the controversy around Joe Strummer of the Clash's claim to sing for 'the guttersnipe' when he was born of middle-class parents and educated privately.[32]

In the early-modern period, the complexity of the ballad-singer's place and voice in society is embodied in the figure of Autolycus, immortalised by William Shakespeare in *The Winter's Tale* (1610/1623). Shakespeare's character lays claim to the gifts and talents of both his namesake, Autolycus, son of Mercury and inheritor of his father Mercury's crafty tricks and thefts, and his twin, Philammon, famous for the beauty of his song and his handling of the lyre, as described in Ovid's *Metamorphosis*. Moreover, in Shakespeare's play, Autolycus is socially complicated: though he plays the part of a rogue as he sells ballads at Bartholomew Fair, he is both a courtier and an actor. The real ballad-writers and singers, for all their faults, were nonetheless regarded as 'tom-tell-troth' figures, able to sing truth to power.

A century later, the status of those impoverished guttersnipes who typically mediated street-songs was no longer regarded as a political asset by the writers of progressive protest songs. Instead, the 'authenticity' of the disreputable street-singer, as an embodiment of the *vox populi*, was seized upon by reactionary and conservative songwriters. Frequently citing the maxim of the Scottish theorist Andrew Fletcher of Saltoun – that 'if a man were permitted to make all the ballads, he need not care who should make the laws of a nation' – moral reformers such as Hannah More and the Cheap Repository Tracts organisers of the 1790s–1800s produced moralizing and counter-revolutionary songs to be promulgated by lowly street-singers in order to influence mass opinion. On rare occasions, this resulted in what we might call protest songs, such as 'The Plow-Boy's Dream' (1795), which protested widespread cruelty towards farm animals.[33]

4.3 • 'The ENRAGED POLITICIANS or Political Ballad Singers', cartoon by Charles Williams, 1805.

Charles Williams's 1805 caricature 'Political Ballad-Singers' is a brilliant evocation of how the tropes of rags, coarse features, and poverty associated with street ballads gave many songs a subversive quality that troubled authorities (regardless of their origin) without necessarily advancing the causes advocated for by the lyrics.[34] The cartoon is a knowing parody of William Hogarth's famous *The Enraged Musician*, with the Tory politicians Henry Dundas and William Pitt the Younger taking the places of that original titular figure. In the street below, five balladeers holler five songs, two of which are on our 250: 'Bow Wow Wow' (*c.*1786) and 'Tyburn Tree' (1728). With their muscular forms and savage countenances, the singers are explicitly reminiscent of caricatures of French revolutionaries, lending their otherwise politically acceptable songs an association with violence, the mob, and democracy (a dirty word at the time).

As the nineteenth century progressed, protest songwriters deliberately sought to move away from any such associations.[35] Seeking above all to extend the electoral franchise to working-class men, their aim was the reverse of Strummer's: to represent the mass of the urban poor as clean, educated, respectable, and deserving of a place in the establishment. In practice, this meant sober, well-ordered communities singing en masse, often on a congregational basis, demonstrating their piety and respectability as God-fearing churchgoers and also their intellectual and social capabilities by singing arrangements in four-part harmony.[36] So, for example, the radical working-class activist Francis Place, who appeared before parliament to argue at length that the masses (who now deserved the vote) no longer sang the bawdy, profane songs of a generation before. Instead, they preferred to sing rational and improving music.[37]

Of course, reputation can be both projected onto a performance and given expression by the performance. An expectation, a presumption, may be applied to the reprobate balladeer singing from the ale house in seventeenth-century England or the DJ chatting in a 1980s dancehall, with notions of class, race, gender, age, education, and context being assumed to give substance to the meaning and intent of the song. When Rock Against Racism (RAR) formed in the UK in 1976, it was important that their gigs and carnivals comprised both Black and white musicians appearing together. For Wayne Minter, a RAR central committee member, racism was 'a white problem', so 'it wasn't important to have black people in the audience, but it was important to have black and white people on the stage playing together'.[38] The protest, in this case anti-racism, resonated as much in the performance as the lyrical content of a particular song. As The Fall's Mark E. Smith recognised, the politics were bound up in *the who* and *the where* and *the how* as much as – not more than – the songs sung and the slogans bandied around. For this reason, perhaps, the multiracial dynamic of 2 Tone, which fused punk with ska and comprised bands with both Black and white members, embodied anti-racism far better than RAR. It was not just punk or rock bands playing alongside reggae or soul bands – for example, the punk of Sham 69 and Misty in Roots' reggae played in the same building and on the same stage. Rather, the protest of The

Specials and The Selecter was embodied in the mesh of peoples and musics that *performed* the anti-racism 2 Tone espoused.

So far, we have talked in wide-ranging terms about how the performance of songs contributes to the protest that they express. The three case studies that follow explore the details of the relationship between performance and protest. We have chosen to draw from examples expressing or contesting national identity. This helps us to consider an ostensibly diverse range of songs – across a notable expanse of time – to find common connections with regard to how performance and presentation imbue such protests with meaning. Though our songs sound nothing alike, and comprise varied modes of performance, their similar focus enables us to explore how extra-lyrical and extra-compositional factors might coalesce to varying effect. Be it parodying the Irish in the seventeenth century ('Lilliburlero') or asserting a claim to belonging in the twenty-first century ('We Live Here'), the space, place, and material trace of a song frames or underpins how the message is presented and received.

Case Study

'A New IRISH Song; OF Lil-li bur Lero' – Protesting in Disguise

'A New IRISH Song; OF Lil-li bur Lero' perfectly illustrates how the politics of protest can reside in the power and reach of its performances and the authenticity of its claim to represent the concerns of its target audiences. At first glance, 'A New IRISH Song', better known today by its chorus 'Lilliburlero' and arguably the most effective protest song in English history, does not seem to set out any clear political agenda (contrary to our definition of protest songs). The Catholic-Irish voices it ventriloquises are deliberately *in*authentic and, it would seem, *un*representative. The song was originally a trifling entertainment written and sung by and for a small, politically frustrated group of three Whig English social elites enduring the reign of James II. Yet, two years later, the song had taken over the country. It was said to have driven James II from his three kingdoms, helping to bring about a revolution in government, and to this day, it acts as a divisive vehicle for protest and identity politics in Northern Ireland.[39]

Who did 'A New IRISH Song' purport to represent if not people similar to the characters that voiced its words, or its socially elite writers? The song was co-composed in February 1687 by at least three Englishmen in angry response to James II's appointment of Richard Talbot, Earl of Tyrconnell, a Catholic, to be lord deputy of Ireland.[40] One of the writers was Robert Ware (1639–1697), a well-to-do government lawyer based in Ireland, described by Kenneth Fergusson as 'able, mischievous, and highly political … an ultra-protestant, disdainful of Catholicism and the Irishry'.[41] Ware was immediately dismissed as a result of Tyrconnell's appointment and returned to London, where he sought out London's Whig clubs, notably the 'Treason Club', held in the Rose Tavern on Drury Lane. Here he met with his two fellow-writers.[42] One, Thomas Wharton, a known wit, had long campaigned to exclude James II from the throne. The other, Wharton's younger brother Henry, was an officer in the Coldstream Guards and had a good singing voice. Like Ware, the Wharton family had personal as well as political reasons to be aggravated by Talbot's appointment, believing that their Irish estates might be at risk of confiscation. More importantly, all three men were deeply suspicious of the growing presence of Catholics – many of whom were Irish – in James II's (illegal) standing army. Indeed, MPS from all sides increasingly feared that the king might use his army to impose Catholicism on his Protestant subjects. These suspicions sparked tensions within the army: for example, Henry Wharton had recently killed a Catholic army officer in a duel.

The song's 'inauthentic' (though, as it turned out, prophetic) lyric voices an imagined dialogue between two pseudo-Irish protagonists, who lay bare their devilish plans. Using a mock-Irish dialect, 'Teague' (a stereotypical English name for an Irishman) and his 'brother' welcome Talbot's appointment as the new 'debutie'. They anticipate that Talbot will provide 'commissions galore' for Irishmen in the king's army, augment their forces with French soldiers, who were all sworn to eradicate Protestantism, and 'cut the English mens throat[s]'.[43] Teague also expects a papal dispensation, which will allow the Irish to 'hang up magna carto [i.e., ignore English laws]' along with the English. Augmenting these threats, the song's chorus incorporated memories of the bloody Irish Rebellion, which had helped to spark the Civil Wars. In 1641, Irish rebels seized the government of Ireland and drove out English and Scottish families. Many thousands died, while stories of brutal massacres filled the English newsbooks.[44] Parliamentarians suspected that Charles I (James II's father) secretly supported the rebellion and had hoped to use Irish rebel forces to enforce tyrannical government in England. At the end of the British Civil Wars, Irish royalists, led by Richard Talbot, were brutally defeated by parliament's forces. As the Irish scholar, Breandain Ó Buachalla argues, the chorus of 'A New IRISH Song' mimicked an Irish-Catholic slogan from the uprising, which claimed that the astrologer, William Lilly, had forecast Irish success. In Irish: 'Léir ó, Léir ó,/ léir ó, léir ó,/ bu linn an lá'; in English (as translated by Niall Mackenzie): 'It is shown by Lilly, the day will be ours'; and in the printed song: 'Lero Lero Lil-li bur Lero, Lero Lero bullen a la'.

Thus, Wharton's and Ware's adoption of the clownish 'inauthentic' voices of Teague and his brother not only expressed their own sentiments and memories but also claimed representation of the prejudices, memories, and fears of most English people. As Deana Rankin has argued, the derogatory 'versions of Irishness crystallised in the English popular imagination' in the jestbooks, songs, and satirical writings published throughout the religious turmoil of the 1680s 'were rooted firmly in the fears generated by the Irish Rebellion in the mid-seventeenth century'.[45]

Between spring 1687 and summer 1688, the manner and spaces in which 'A New IRISH Song' was performed, the material forms in which the song was distributed, the audiences it consequently reached, and

A
NEW SONG:
To an Excellent IRISH Tune, much in Request.

HO, Brother Teague, dost hear de Decree,
Lilli burlero Bullen a-la;
Dat we shall have a new Debittie,
Lilli burlero Bullen a-la:
Lero, lero, lero, lero, Lilli burlero bullen a-la;
Lero, lero, lero, lero, Lilli burlero bullen a-la.

Ho, by my Shoul, it is a T——t,
lilli burlero &c.
And he will Cut all de English T——t,
lilli, &c.
lero, lero, &c.
lero, lero, &c.

Though, by my Shoul, de English do Prat,
lilli, &c.
De Law's on dare side, and Chreist knows what,
lilli, &c.
lero, lero, &c.
lero, lero, &c.

But if Dispence do come from de Pope,
lilli, &c.
Wee'l hang Magna Carta & demselves in a Rope,
lilli, &c.
lero, lero, &c.
lero, lero, &c.

And the good T——t is made a Lord,
lilli, &c.
And he with brave Lads is coming aboard,
lilli, &c.
lero, lero, &c.
lero, lero, &c.

Who all in France have taken a Swear,
lilli, &c.
Dat dey will have no Protestant H——r,
lilli, &c.
lero, lero, &c.
lero, lero, &c.

Oh! but why does he stay behind?
lilli, &c.
Ho, by my Shoul, 'tis a Protestant Wind,
lilli, &c.
lero, lero, &c.
lero, lero, &c.

Now T——l is come ashore,
lilli, &c.
And we shall have Commissions gillore;
lilli, &c.
lero, lero, &c.
lero, lero, &c.

And he dat will not go to M——ss,
lilli, &c.
Shall turn out and look like an Ass.
lilli, &c.
lero, lero, &c.
lero, lero, &c.

Now, now de Hereticks all go down,
lilli, &c.
By Chreist and St. Patrick the Nation's our own,
lilli burlero bullen a-la;
Lero, lero, lero, lero, lilli burlero bullen a-la,
lero, lero, lero, lero, lilli burlero bullen a-la.

FINIS.

Printed for A. B.

4.4 • 'A New Song to an Excellent Irish Tune' (n.p., *c.*1688–89). This edition of the song was produced in the typical retail ballad format: verses in blackletter type and illustrated with generic woodcuts. Authorship attributed to R. Ware, T. and H. Wharton, 1688. Published by permission of the Master and Fellows of Magdalene College, Cambridge.

the power of protest it was able to wield, all changed markedly. The first performances were given in 1687 within socially and politically constrained spaces (such as the Treason Club) for the amusement of the writers and their Whig friends and allies. Perhaps too, manuscript copies circulated allowing others to perform the song at private gatherings.

By spring 1688, however, growing frustration and fear at the huge increase in Irish soldiers and officers recruited into the army prompted Henry Wharton to give a much bolder public performance, disguised 'in the habit of a player', before James II and his court at the playhouse.[46] On 10 June, the urgency of the political situation changed with the birth of James II's son, the Prince of Wales. In August, James II assembled his army at Hounslow Heath, just outside London. Though ostensibly an opportunity for military exercises and training, many suspected that the king's real motivation was to intimidate his political opponents. At the same time, James's agents were canvassing and coercing the county gentry with a view to persuading them to increase the king's powers over the army and to legislate to free Catholics and Dissenters from all penal restrictions if a new parliament was called. In any case, the king pre-empted legislation by issuing a 'Declaration of Indulgence' granting freedom of worship to all non-Anglicans. When seven Anglican bishops wrote to the king to protest and refused to order the declaration to be read from the pulpit, they were imprisoned and tried for sedition.

It was now clear to Whigs and Tories alike that, unless direct action was taken, a Catholic succession and the end of the Church of England seemed assured. The 'immortal seven' wrote to William of Orange, begging him for help. Meanwhile, Thomas and Henry Wharton assembled with their supporters at the Treason Club with a view to encouraging an army conspiracy. As part of a wider campaign, they decided to distribute printed editions of 'A New IRISH Song' with musical notation among the Protestant officer corps of the army. Moreover, it was perhaps at this point that a retail publisher re-tuned the song from 'Stingo', a melody requiring some skill, to the easily singable marching tune, 'Lilliburlero'. Years later, Thomas D'Urfey highlighted its simple but engaging singability when he disparaged the 'pitiful Crowdero' (ballad-singer) 'That could but tune or sing Burlero'.

The song took off. It not only voiced the concerns of officers like Henry Wharton but also became endemic throughout the ranks and across the country, thanks to a retail blackletter version (fig. 4.4). Designed to attract or to depict a military man, the retail ballad was illustrated with images of three Civil-War soldiers: a royalist artillery-man, an armed officer, and a parliamentarian halberdier – deliberately highlighting the memories embedded within the song. The confidence inspired by this loud and united community of singers encouraged and enabled soldiers and officers alike to abandon James II in the face of William of Orange's invasion – following Henry Wharton himself, who joined William at Exeter. He was to die in 1690, fighting James II's forces in Ireland.

Though by no means an unbiased observer, nor a popular music fan, in his *History of His Own Time*, Bishop Gilbert Burnet could not help but express his wonder at how 'The New IRISH Song' had impacted the momentous events of the revolution:

> the King [was put] in an unexpressable confusion. He saw himself now forsaken, not only by those whom he had trusted and favoured most, but even by his own children. And the army was in such distraction, that there was not anyone body that seemed entirely united and firm to him. A foolish ballad was made at this time, treating the Papists, and chiefly the Irish, in a very ridiculous manner, which had a burden, said to be Irish words, lero lero lilibulero, that made an impression on the Army that cannot be well imagined by those who saw it not. The whole Army, and at last, all people both in city and country, were singing it perpetually. And perhaps never had so slight a thing so great an effect.[47]

'A New IRISH Song' mattered because of who was singing, where they were singing, how they were singing, to what music and to what audience they were singing. All were integral to the transmission and impact of this protest song. Authentic performances in dangerous spaces, using clownish voices set to singable music, for socially diverse audiences that shared antipathy and fear were key to the political power of 'A New IRISH Song'. Although the true identity of the authors was unknown to the vast majority of those who sang the song in 1688 and 1689, its multiple material incarnations expanded the spaces in which and the audiences to which it was performed, bringing together socially diverse but religiously united people, and bringing about a political revolution.

Case Study

National Songs – Performing England and Englishness

The tactics of Othering were characteristic of political song in the early-modern period. This is especially apparent in those protest songs that construct a specifically English identity in contradistinction to an Other. Interloping Scottish politicians, perhaps, from 'Well Met Jockie Whether Away' (*c.*1604) to the songs of John Wilkes (1770s). Or, by contrast, nineteenth-century working-class protest songs that sought common cause with Scotland and Ireland as fellow victims of an oppressive elite defined by class rather than nationality (see, for example, 'England & Ireland Sing Erin go Bragh' (1837)). Across all periods, in fact, the issue of England and Englishness was never far from the surface of protest songs, sometimes constituting its dominant theme. In this case study, we focus on three instances when a song's performance and representation were pivotal in that construction, contestation, and reappropriation of what it meant to identify as English.

Decades of scholarship have drawn attention to the 1790s as a period of bitter struggle over which political ideologies could exploit the cultural capital of Englishness and/or Britishness. This, ultimately, was a struggle the reactionary, loyalist right conclusively won.[48] The decades after 1815 saw renewed attempts by radicals to reclaim the language of patriotism, for example, in response to Peterloo ('National Songs – No.1' (1819)) and the Queen Caroline Affair ('Britons Claim Her As Your Queen' (1820)). Rather than problematise patriotism, or even its precise definition (the slippage between England and Britain), they sought simply to represent their songs and arguments as patriotic in order to find favour and legitimacy. This tactic proved most effective in the late Victorian and Edwardian era. Charles Osborne's 'He Was One of the Light Brigade' (1890) offered a critique of the treatment of impoverished veterans predicated entirely on the assumption that fighting for one's country is noble, honourable, and deserving of reward. Representationally, it was crucial to Osborne's song that it was performed on music hall stages – the engine rooms of imperialism and jingoism – and couched in the musical style and costumes of orthodox patriotism rather than striking audiences as in any way countercultural. [49]

The same tactic was truer still of the women's suffrage movement. Highly conscious of the radicalism of their demands and their subaltern positions, suffragette songwriting made full use of the trappings of contemporary Englishness: an identity that was explicitly imperial, Christian, and militaristic. Theodora Mills's 'Shoulder to Shoulder' (*c.*1910) employed an army marching tune and opened with the couplet: 'From the daughters of the nation / Bursts a cry of indignation'.[50] This at once positioned the protestors as having a natural right to be considered part of the political nation, signalling their credentials as good, strong, righteous Englishwomen, ready to march in step and in every way resemble the idealised soldiers whose burden of service they 'share'. More explicit still was the 'Daughters of England' (*c.*1908), composed by (Irishwoman) Alicia Needham with lyrics by either J. Russell or Margaret Martin:

> Daughters of England! awake and bestir you,
> High be your hearts and with fervour aglow,
> Ye too are Britons – and England's the loser
> While half of her children their service forego.
> Rouse ye, arouse ye, claim boldly your Freedom,
> Wives, sisters, mothers of men who are free,
> Yours the same blood, the same heritage, history;
> Yours the same breeding – the same rights have ye.
> Men taunting cry, 'Ye are naught to the Empire,
> 'Taking no part in her battles and strife,
> 'We die for our Land', Yet each mother among you
> Bravely faced death to give England a life[51]

The lyrics' nuanced and rational argument equates the risks of childbirth as both equal to and the necessary precondition for the dangers of military service. It is also exceptionally complex as a proposition to make in a short song, which is where the performative dimensions served to heighten, endorse, and even simplify its message. The militarism of the lyric ('rise', 'fight', 'battle') was reinforced by the sound of martial choral music in the same idiom as Edward Elgar; by the motion of disciplined, marching bodies; by the sight of banners and regalia, flags, and uniforms. A nation where women are enfranchised, the message goes, is a nation made not effeminate but doubly martial. Again, the lyrics elide 'Britons' and 'England' as interchangeable facets of an identity that is imperial and bellicose. Ideological stress is placed upon the vigour and health of the marching singers – since 'breeding' is key to this identity – resulting in a vision of England and Englishness that is not only very much of its time (pre–World War I) but of its prevailing orthodoxies: white, pro-empire, nationalist, in many ways conservative and patrician. None of which is to diminish the achievement and audacity of women's suffrage, but rather to emphasise the fact that the cause was represented as compatible with the established national interest.

There is a coherence here of message, medium, and representational strategy that other protest causes have lacked. In the early 1930s, as later in the 1980s, British fascists sought to reconcile their Nazi-derived iconography with a more local nationalism. The lyrics of 'Britain, Awake!' (1934), penned by E.D. Randall to wholly uncontroversial and unexceptional music by J.F. Welsh, would have been heard as much less suspect at the time than they are today, trading as they do in tropes of 'ancient honour', martial valour, the strength of the 'folk', and a nation embattled against the world. In fact, its imagery, save in its gendering, is almost indistinguishable from that of the suffragettes. Yet the British Union of Fascists' logo, a white lightning bolt against blue within a red field, so clearly denoted 'fascism' that its adherents' performance could be judged definitively as inauthentic and, in the context of the 1930s, decidedly un-English. The same might be said of neo-Nazi punk band Skrewdriver in the 1980s: with a cod-medieval logo clearly rooted in Nazi iconography, and a lead singer photographed draped in a Nazi flag, their claims to English patriotism were never likely to convince any but a deluded minority.

Of course, protest songs could also critique, contest, or reject conceptions of Englishness.[52] Emblematic here is Sister Audrey's 'English Girl' (1982), a roots reggae hit both then and during the Windrush scandal of 2018.[53] Prompted by an altercation with a Jamaican national in which she took offence to being labelled as the titular 'English Girl', Sister Audrey's song flat-out rejects identification with her legal status (as a second-generation British citizen), assembling markers of Jamaican culture in contrast to a perceived Englishness rather than seeking to assert a composite English-Caribbean identity. This rejection is rooted in the hostility and hypocrisy of Home Office policy and its poor treatment of the migrants who arrived from the Caribbean in the years since 1948 (verse one) and the ongoing racism encountered by Black Britons (verse two). The song's musical style and numerous remixes, as well as Sister Audrey's own self-fashioning in Jamaican prints, textiles, and headgear, are malleable, easily claimed as part of a multicultural British identity. Yet the differences between the original 1982 12-inch record pressing's presentation and the 2018 re-release are telling.

The original, put out on the Jah Shaka Music label, foregrounds pan-Africanist signifiers: the disc is illustrated with a silhouette of the African continent and a stylised depiction of a Zulu warrior captioned 'King of the Zulu Tribe'. The B-side is a reggae instrumental called 'African Queen'. Finally, the song's title is given a question mark, ('English Girl?') so that even shorn of the context of its challenging lyric, those words may be seen as a provocation and a rejection, or at the very least a complicating, of identity. By contrast, the 2018 vinyl boasts a new sleeve illustration that insists upon a celebration of the Windrush migrations as an intrinsic part of contemporary British identity, employing the same register of visual rhetoric as the 2012 Olympic opening ceremony or *Paddington* films (2014, 2017). Sister Audrey herself, now a smiling, tea-drinking figure, is depicted between the *Empire Windrush* docking at Tilbury and London's Big Ben clock tower, a consensual image of integration rather at odds with the song's

4.5 • Record sleeve for Sister Audrey's 'English Girl', 2018.

original message, but wholly fitting the context of the 2018 campaign against the 'hostile environment', detentions, and deportations carried out by the British Home Office. Put simply, the updated sleeve reframes the song from a rejection to a reinterpretation of Englishness, a tactic of protest more prone to ambiguity and misadventure than either staunch endorsement or critique.

Perhaps the most problematic attempt to relocate or renew English identity is Show of Hands's song 'Roots' (2004), a song superficially similar in its lyrical preoccupations to Maggie Holland's 'A Place Called England' (1999).[54] Its writer, Steve Knightley, with his band colleague Phil Beer, is a prominent founder-member of Folk Against Fascism, which campaigned to block the British National Party from using the song. Show of Hands's sets also often include covers of artists such as Bob Marley.[55] As such, the extent to which the lyrics of 'Roots' sometimes seem to lean towards the same ethnic nationalism propounded by the likes of Cecil Sharp a century earlier may be regarded as unfortunate rather than intentional. Yet taken in combination with the song's video, it is easy to see the appeal to contemporary nationalists: the re-rooted England for which the song advocates appears to be largely male, exclusively white, and almost entirely rural. Reference to 'Indians, Asians, Afro Celts' with music 'in their blood' and 'Overpaid soccer stars, prancing teens … American rap, Estuary English' contain troubling implications for markers of class, race, and gender. But even taken on its own terms, the song's representational strategies are often at odds with its lyrics: images of Cornwall's Eden Project and the druidical poses of its long-haired stars on hilltops are signifiers of ancient British, thus Brythonic and Celtic, culture rather than the 'English' that drove much of this out. A musical section that evokes nineteenth-century sea shanties risks the observation that the shanty, an explicitly cosmopolitan, polyglot, and transnational musical form created by the global commercial exchanges that the song deplores, is therefore archetypal of everything Show of Hands is criticising. The instruments played in the song are, likewise, the result of international commerce and external influence.

These contradictions may matter only to the extent that they damage the song's perceived coherence and its performers' authenticity when the listener is aware of them. More important, however, is the extent to which the song *in performance* has created a certain kind of audience and identity at odds with the celebratory and ultimately benign form of protest the band are on record as seeking to create – a protest initially directed solely at a disparaging remark about folk music made by a UK government minister.[56] The YouTube discussion thread below the song's video makes clear the highly disparate interpretations the song has created, this itself fostering a far from inclusive online space for the song's consumption.[57] Even more telling is the experience recalled by one audience member during the song's performance at the 2010 Cambridge Folk Festival:

> Not as depressing, however (or as disturbing), as finding myself in the midst of a thousand white people singing Knightley's song Roots, which closed the set … I understand that Knightley's intent was to express his love of English culture and traditions, but the song does not do that, nor did it do that on the night. The chief emotions it expresses seem to be envy (of 'Indians, Asians, Afro-Celts' – as if being a Celt (whatever the hell that means) implies I am not at the same time English!) and contempt (for 'Australian soaps, American rap, Estuary English' – why yes, for what is worse than black music and common people?). Envy and contempt: prime sources of exclusion and hatred. It does not surprise me to learn that the BNP has co-opted this song. Listening to a crowd of white people (for the festival-going crowd was not the most diverse, and the tickets are not cheap) who had already been primed to scorn the Other yelling about an Englishness which had specifically excluded me on the grounds of that part of me that is Irish was vile. I walked out. If Steve Knightley doesn't want his songs to be co-opted by the BNP, he shouldn't write a hateful song, or create a space soaked in sourness, grievance, and distaste.[58]

This was the experience of a white audience member, to whom the song's performed aspects were of far greater significance than its lyrical intent. Her sense of alienation and intimidation, her feeling of unbelonging in the face of this manifestation of a certain kind of Englishness, is profound.

Case Study

Bob Vylan's 'We Live Here' – Contesting Identity

Bob Vylan's 'We Live Here' was released in 2020.[59] It begins with a spoken intro: a generic racist trope – 'was a lovely area before you come here, lovely' – relayed to set up a stinging riposte. Vylan recounts his time growing up as a Black boy in England, racially abused at school and by neighbours, told to 'go back to' the country he was born in.[60] As the title suggests, that country was in fact England, and England 'is my [Vylan's] fucking country'. 'We didn't appear out of thin air', Vylan clarifies, transferring the 'I' to a 'we' and thereby sharing his experience, 'We Live Here'.

The song then turns on those who spout the racism or deny its pernicious influence, dismissing generic excuses ('I'm just proud [of my country]') and the perennial bleats of bullies being challenged. By the third verse, we find that Vylan was born to a white mother and a Black father, the former explaining the 'bad word[s]' spat at her son as he tried to reconcile being made to feel an outsider in the place he lived. Vylan is now speaking for 'us', or at least those of us opposed to racism and who comfortably live in and accept a multicultural society; or, like the singer, come from families of various creeds and ethnic origin. Once again, his reply is blunt and to the point: 'We Live Here, you cunt'.

'We Live Here' protests at the attitudes and idiocies of the complacent and conceited. Its lyric is personal and abusive; outraged and unapologetic. It fights fire with fire and claims a space. It reveals hypocrisies and denies familiar homilies, drawing from lived experience to shout down racial prejudice. Its statement is definitive; its wrath is righteous. But 'We Live Here' is also performed, most obviously in a video that circulated on YouTube and contributed to the song's pertinence.

Vylan performs his wrath, affirming the Black identity his racist opponents seek to denounce and deny. As he sings, Vylan acts out the anger of his words in gestures, transmitting the pain and the

4.6 • Image from Bob Vylan's 'We Live Here' video, 2020.

vehemence of his lyric. He walks *at* the camera: threatening and confronting, demanding a response (are you with me or against me?). Notably, too, Vylan's leopard-patterned coat startles, the Crass symbol on his T-shirt linking him and his protest to anarcho-punk and a broader lineage of protest. Rasta, reggae, and punk reassemble into the battle armour of resistance. On his feet, oxblood boots signify the beat of the street … walking where skinheads once asserted their own working-class identity. This is about class as well race. 'Here' is the inner city and the back streets as well as England.

Indeed, the location of the song and the video is important. As Vylan eats chips, plays pool in the pub, and visits the local corner shop, he positions himself in recognisably working-class spaces, even going so far as to perform outside a garage or tyre fitters. The back streets and alleyways show Vylan as 'a local', cutting through, stocking up, winding down. He evidently does live here. By so doing, Vylan signals that he is very much 'one of us', a claim made through references to school, neighbours, bath time, and bus stops, but an 'us' and an everyday scarred by racism.

As a video, the song passes into spectacle. Nevertheless, when viewed on YouTube, 'We Live Here' plays next to – and flows into – more of Vylan's songs and music of a similar nature. One click and you are into grime; click again and hip young indie things appear. The point is that the protest projects into social media's sea of possibilities, albeit surrounded by (and previewed by) irrelevant adverts and pop-ups. The impact is contained as the message delivers. Arguably, the sentiment remains: the protest is still made.

As a material product – as a download single and an album track on vinyl and CD – 'We Live Here' was independently released, connecting to the Crass symbol on Vylan's shirt and to Crass's own strategy for circumnavigating the music industry so far as was possible, unconcerned by airplay and costed as cheaply as possible. 'We Live Here' came out on Venn Records, a label run by members of the punk band Gallows. The CD and cassette were issued on Vylan's own Ghost Theatre imprint. On the back of the album, also called 'We Live Here', a defaced image of Queen Elizabeth evokes the Sex Pistols' sleeve for 'God Save the Queen', Jamie Reid's blackmail lettering replaced by a gothic script muting and blinding the queen with the words 'racist, murderer, thief'. The lyrics are repositioned in an accompanying essay, expanding on the experience detailed in the song and thereby transferring the message into prose – a testament. A reading list then directs the listener to Paul Gilroy, Noam Chomsky, and others, establishing the song as a way into politics and extending protest (Chumbawamba and Crass also adopted this practice). Crass, of course, filled their sleeves with the addresses of radical bookshops and contacts for the Campaign for Nuclear Disarmament (CND) and other movements.

The material traces left – or generated – by 'We Live Here' document the protest. They also locate it within a continuum of radical politics (hence the reading list) and cultural form. Most obviously, punk is signified in the video via Vylan's T-shirt and on the sleeve via the artwork. With regard to the *musical* performance of the song, punk too is signalled by the riffing guitar and aggressive vocals. Though Vylan's delivery draws also from hip hop, his voice is anglicised and angry. He's neither reflecting nor complaining. Quite the opposite: he's challenging and confronting. The result might be heard as a hybrid of punk and grime. But the former prevails, channelling the reverberations of British punk through the generations for Vylan to harness and reapply.

Despite the contestations and complications of punk as a cultural form, the implication, of course, is that Vylan means it. Punk was typically presented as a grassroots culture, a medium for protest, a venting of spleen. Yet Vylan further affirms his protest through his reputation. The lyric of 'We Live Here' is presented as his story and his experience: he has walked it as he talks it. In interviews, he tells of growing up in London's working-class and multicultural community, and of dropping out of school, before later making it to university (a transition no longer so unusual) and then turning to music as an expression of outsiderdom.[61] As described in the song, he was born of a Black father and white mother. His reference to wider real-life events – the murder of Stephen Lawrence – imbues his own experience. To deny 'We Live Here' its pertinence is to deny Vylan his existence. The two are one – a factor that becomes interesting once we consider how 'We Live Here' would sound/communicate if sung by someone else.

Historically, many protest songs were written to be sung by others, to be passed on and reapplied in a way that made the 'we' open to appropriation. But we can overemphasise this historic mutability. Many songs across the centuries have made the 'we' or 'I' very clear either implicitly or explicitly: 'we', the Chartists whom you see marching before you; or 'we', the weavers who have come together to petition the monarch; or the 'I' of the song's narrator, the titular powte (a type of fish) of 'The Powte's Complainte' (1619); or the suffering and disillusioned 'I' of the sailor who proclaims 'I'll No More To Greenland Sail' as a way of warning others not to make the same mistake he did. In the first two of these examples, the 'we' is literally embodied by the singers; in the latter, the 'I' is figurative, but made explicit by the lyrics. And just as the distinct sonority and persona of Bruce Springsteen have not protected 'Born in the USA' from reappropriation by generations of jingoistic Republicans, so, conversely, have historic protest singers managed to tie songs to the specificity of their own individual performances. Archetypal here is the Sheffield file-hewer Joseph

Mather, author of dozens of outrageous protest songs in the late eighteenth century. The power and impact of these songs was closely coupled both to his own identity – as demonstrably one of those labourers whose working conditions he excoriated – and to the manner of his embodied performances. As his local biographer noted:

> [It] was not unusual for the grinders … to persuade Mather to leave his employment and go to the public-houses frequented by employers of labour, or other persons deemed obnoxious, and in their presence to sing his satirical productions … our author used to 'raise the wind' by vending his songs in the streets, seated on a grinder's donkey, or on the back of Ben Sharp's bull … He used to be seated (as Robin Hood seated the bishop), with his face to the animal's tail … It is said that he sung 'Bad Luck to the Crow and the Owl', on the market day, in front of the Cutlers' Hall, when the Magistrates were leaving it after discharging their public duties. The poet had been bound over to keep the peace [but] his satirical pieces often forced masters (reluctantly) to comply with poor industrious workmen's just demands.[62]

Similarly, returning to the 2020s, we find that Vylan's protest – and his performance of the protest – are bound to his own experience. The political is personal. Nor does the song protest against the state and/or the ruling class, but against attitudes within civil society. It is a protest beyond either party or ideology, wherein the racism Vylan opposes stems from divergent individual attitudes and perspectives. Though class is evoked, the song hones in on those who articulate racism rather than the processes and socio-economic conditions that engender racism within society. A tension between the shared experience of a protest and the subjective experience of the performer is thereby revealed: a fault line that continues to extend across the twenty-first century's identity politics.

CONCLUSION

Our three case studies illustrate the central argument of this chapter: protest songs are neither written nor exist in a vacuum. How and where – by who and to whom – they are performed matters in terms of instigating effect and affect. Protest songs need to resonate: their relevance to a people and a place or time determines how they are received and understood. For the performer, the need to embody or convincingly Other the subject of the song might signal such pertinence. The construction of an 'us and them' becomes manifest in performance and relies on an array of signifiers to bolster and augment a song's conviction. Where signals and signifiers clash, however, connections give way to contradictions. How a song is mediated, from its moment of conception through to performance and on to production and dissemination, might reframe and reposition its form and function.

As this suggests, the performance of protest songs is inextricably linked to their capacity to register their political message. There are, as we have noted, several elements to a performance, each of which provides a different means of communication. Together these elements help to sustain a key feature of the protest song across time: the claim to speak for, and about, a people and a cause. There is no one way in which the protest song and its author or performer establish the right and ability to make this claim convincing, but it is, we would argue, an intention of all protest songs.

5

PRODUCING THE PROTEST SONG

Much of our concern so far has been with what protest songs communicate, how they do so, and where their anger is directed. There is, though, an important further question to ask about the history of the protest songs: how do they come into existence? For much of the period we cover, in cases where we are able to make these judgements, the majority of the *known* authors of protest songs were straight, white, Christian, educated men. One explanation for this, as we note on our website, is this: 'Much like a murder, a protest song has traditionally required means and opportunity, not merely motive, to bring it into being – or at least the sort of being that gets acknowledged and remembered'.[1] Capital of all kinds – financial, cultural, social, political – is implicated in the production of protest songs. In the late 1960s, a sampler was advertised with the slogan 'The Revolution is on CBS'.

We have, of course, already referred to publishers and record labels, and in doing so provided some kind of answer to the question of where protest songs come from. But in this chapter, we provide a more detailed account – using case studies – of the process by which protest songs are created, distributed, and heard.

Our simple question tends to elicit two simple responses. The first is that protest songs originate with their authors; or more precisely, they originate with their authors' political values and attitudes. To ask why a particular song exists is to ask who wrote it and what they believed. It is a view that is most obviously represented in interviews with musicians and songwriters, and seems to draw a straight line between the views expressed and the songs written. This assumption is shared by the musicians themselves. Here is John Lennon being interviewed by Tariq Ali and Robin Blackburn, editors of the far-left paper *Red Mole*, in January 1971:

> BLACKBURN: Well, in any case, politics and culture are linked, aren't they? I mean, workers are repressed by culture not guns at the moment …
> LENNON: … they're doped.
> BLACKBURN: And the culture that's doping them is one the artist can make or break.
> LENNON: That's what I'm trying to do on my albums and in these interviews. What I'm trying to do is to influence all the people I can influence. All those who are still under the dream and just put a big question mark in their mind. The acid dream is over, that is what I'm trying to tell them.[2]

And here, some fifty years later, is Lily Allen being interviewed by *Glamour* magazine:

> *GLAMOUR*: Last summer you made a surprise appearance at Glastonbury with Olivia Rodrigo and performed "Fuck You" as a message to the US Supreme Court. How does it feel that you live in the US now in the wake of the overturning of Roe versus Wade?
> ALLEN: I guess, I'm concerned and scared for my children. So, yes. I live in the USA and things are quite complicated at the moment in terms of,

I guess, legislation where women's rights are concerned. I have spent a long time using my platform to talk about issues that I feel are important to myself and lots of other people.[3]

Interviews of this kind treat performers as political activists and their songs as a direct product of their political conscience or experience.

The second possible answer to the question of where protest songs come from is to view them as the product of their moment in history, as parts of what we describe in chapter 2 as a 'rhetorical situation' in which, it seems, things can be changed by words, their performance, and everything that goes along with them. In times of political crisis or upheaval, the argument runs, there will be many more protest songs than there are in times of consensus and complacency. This is an idea that features in media coverage of protest songs. When the world is beset with crisis or conflict, journalists are known to ask: 'Where have all the protest songs gone?' This headline appeared in the *Philadelphia Weekly* in 2021 and on BBC News Online 2003.[4] With a minor variation on the same theme, a *Guardian* headline in February 2016 was: 'Not talkin' bout a revolution: where are all the protest songs?'

There is, of course, an element of truth in both responses, and they are not, in themselves, mutually exclusive. Political conscience and political crisis can indeed coincide. Throughout the history of the protest song, there are instances of people with strongly held and widely expressed political views turning to song to alert or inspire their audience. In 1619, the author of 'The Powte's Compaint' warned of the threat to livelihoods posed by land reclamation; in 1793, Robert Thomson reacted furiously (and satirically) to Edmund Burke's description of the British people as a 'swinish multitude'; and in 2017, Lowkey's song 'Ghosts of Grenfell' demanded justice for 'the corporate manslaughter' of those who died in the Grenfell Tower fire. Interviewed in 2015, Pete Townshend of The Who reflected: 'I suppose the Who were rebellious, and I suppose for a while we were – or seemed to be – anti-establishment. But that wasn't us really. I think we were just reflecting what was going on around us'.[5] Johnny Marr of The Smiths tells a similar story: 'If you were an alternative musician, you were political, because of the times [Thatcherism and the Falklands War]. It was taken for granted that the bands you shared a stage with had the same politics. I'm not sure you could say that now'.[6]

However, these two crudely demarcated narratives beg as many questions as they answer. After all, there are an infinite number of political events happening at any one time. Few of these ever attract the attention of songwriters. Why not? What explains the ones that get selected and the ones that are ignored? Similarly, is it the case that songwriters with strong political views always write political songs? Or that those with only vague political awareness never write them? Brian Eno, who has made no secret of his fiercely held political views, claimed that 'I have never used my music as a mechanism of protest'.[7] The nineteenth-century radical reformer Samuel Bamford devoted most of his songs to the landscape, fairies, and love. And emancipated Black composer, writer, abolitionist, and grocer Ignatius Sancho (*c.*1729–1780) published extensive works in prose in the abolitionist cause; he also published multiple volumes of songs. None of his songs was political. The conscience argument presumes that we know the politics of singers, or that political songs express directly and straightforwardly the views of those who write and perform them. Neither may be the case.

As shown in earlier chapters, there is a real danger that, in focusing on the politics of the singer or songwriter, we lose sight of how songs themselves convey or acquire meaning, and come to have rhetorical force. Greil Marcus is wary of the relevance of biography: 'For a song, a biography of its writer or performer is at worst not a key but a prison, a way of limiting what a song can say and where it can go by returning it always to its author, cutting the listener, the person to whom the song is actually addressed, out of the picture'.[8] Marcus is not denying all significance to biography but, rather, suggesting that it is one factor among others that help us understand why songs exist and what they do. In writing about protest songs in particular, Marcus inclines towards the second of the two explanations for where they originate. He says of Bob Dylan's 'Blowin' in the Wind', 'it seemed to have been written less by a particular person than by the times in which, for which, it was made'.[9] In less subtle form, this link between context and creativity underpins the narratives of many of the books written about the history of rock music, in which events like Woodstock and the songs of the late 1960s are directly attributed to the politics of the time.[10]

This argument, that political songs derive from their political context, underpins Peter Manuel's more sophisticated obituary for the protest song. Manuel takes it as given that the protest song is in decline. For him, the pressing question is 'why?' The answer, he says, is to be found in the 'broader change in global culture'. He contends that the rise of the protest song in the 1960s and 1970s was a product of the political dissent witnessed in Latin America, Asia, the US, the Caribbean, and Europe.[11]

For Manuel, this dissent shared a commitment to enlightenment and democratic politics, and as such inspired protest music. The subsequent decline of the protest song is to be explained by changes in global politics and, in particular, in the rise of the New Social Movements (NSMS). 'Most NSMS, from gender rights to environmental causes, however worthy they may be', writes Manuel, 'have not lent themselves to expression in song, except in the most marginal, oblique, ephemeral, or contradictory forms. Protest music is even less likely to emerge from developed-world sophisticates steeped in the ironic detachment of postmodern aesthetics'.[12] Manuel's argument, which draws on an extensive knowledge of both the musics of the world and of world politics, insists on a strong association between political trends and musical creativity.

As with the link between personal biography and political songwriting, there is a plausibility to this connection. But there are also grounds for scepticism. Critics of Manuel question both his account of the decline of the protest song and his account of global political change.[13] Certainly, any account of 'decline' in the protest song confronts the problem of how such songs are to be defined and then how their decline or rise might be counted.[14] And in contradiction to Manuel's assertion, Noriko Manabe suggests that 'protest music is still going strong, but in ways different from the 1960s and 70s [*sic*]. The explanatory causes, in my view, are economic and technological. Changes in the music industry, in terms of demographics, monetization, and distribution, have affected what music gets made and heard'.[15]

Manabe's approach, in which multiple factors are called upon to account for the rise (or fall) of the protest song, provides a less constricting framework of analysis. We are not committed to seeing the protest song only in terms of context or creator, but rather as the consequence of a variety of agents and agencies, processes and practices. In this chapter, we set out the general theoretical assumptions of such an approach and the implications for their practical application. We then offer a series of case studies, distributed across the long history of the protest song, that build a richer picture of the processes by which protest songs come into existence.

THE PROTEST SONG PROCESS

Our approach to explaining the protest song owes much to developments in cultural sociology. Writers such as Stanley Lieberson and Richard Peterson have undermined the idea that cultural change is driven by events in the 'outside world', what Lieberson calls 'reflection theory'.[16] Taking the example of naming children, Lieberson argues that, while it might be tempting to believe that trends in children's names can be directly linked to, say, the names of currently famous actors or other celebrities, the evidence suggests otherwise. Lieberson concludes that internal, rather than external, factors are the drivers of change in naming. He proposes that this insight can be extended to cultural change more generally. 'Internal mechanisms are operating', Lieberson writes, 'that can affect the outcome even in the absence of new social developments; at the very least, they interact [with] and modify these social changes'.[17]

Lieberson's argument has a family resemblance to that advanced by Peterson, writing some ten years earlier. Taking as his topic the question of why rock 'n' roll took off in 1955, Peterson does not find the answer in wider sociological or demographic factors, such as the emergence of the 'teenager' or of affluence. Rather, he suggests, the explanation is to be found in changes in the music industry, as opposed to exogenous, social changes. Rock 'n' roll was not a consequence of, for example, a 'demand' created by an audience of baby boomers. Indeed, says Peterson, the music industry failed to recognize any such demand, and instead 'it was the structure of the arrangements, habits, and assumptions of the commercial culture industry that caused the blindness. Likewise ... it was the systematic change in these factors that created the opportunity for rock to emerge'.[18]

Elements of this approach to cultural change are present in sociologist Nick Crossley's network analysis of the rise of punk in the late 1970s in the UK. Crossley connects the many agencies and actors who together created the spaces and aesthetics for punk to flourish. His approach differs from Peterson in that he looks beyond industrial and economic drivers to the circumstances in which musical scenes change. He draws on Emile Durkheim to argue that '*music worlds emerge as an effect of collective effervescence within a networked critical mass of actors who are defined by shared interests of some sort*'.[19] But while Crossley sets himself against some aspects of Peterson's perspective, he shares the general view that an explanation of cultural change needs to reference the mechanisms by which music is made and distributed, rather than dwelling only on wider social changes.

We adopt Crossley's general perspective and the tradition of cultural sociology upon which he builds. For us, the presence of protest music has to be understood as the consequence of the complex interactions of actors and organisations. In our case, the emphasis falls upon political actors and organisations, as well as those traditionally associated with making music (publishers, venues, record labels, and so on). The history of the protest song is closely allied with the roles played by political intermediaries, from political parties to trade unions, from social movements to religious bodies, from theatre companies to journalists.

In emphasising the political dimensions of the protest song process, we also draw inspiration from those social movement scholars who have highlighted the role of music in political mobilisation.[20] Taking their cue from the 'cultural turn' in social theory, when culture was taken to be constitutive of identities and interests, these scholars saw music as integral to the formation and success of campaigns for civil rights, equality, and the protection of the environment, among other causes. Ron Eyerman and Andrew Jamison argue that songs provided examples of the movement's aims and ideals, and performers acted as witnesses to the cause.[21] Music is seen as vital to the ideas and ideals that inspired the movements' followers. They also suggest, as do other such scholars, that the movements provided a political environment hospitable to political song. However, in their focus on the genesis and maintenance of social movements, these scholars have less to say about the music itself – where it comes from, and how it serves the movement *as music*. They tend to overlook the processes by which the songs are created and distributed, or about how the music is drawn into the movement.

There is an exception to this general rule in studies devoted to specific movements. Often written by historians, they map in detail the networks that link political actors and the music industry, most notably in the US in relation to the civil rights movement.[22] In the UK, this gap has been filled by those who have traced the story of Rock Against Racism (RAR) in the late 1970s/early '80s, when musicians helped to lead the campaign against the racist National Front party.[23] These writers all acknowledge the importance of political and music intermediaries in the forging of the alliance that created RAR. They all recognise the role played by the Socialist Workers Party (SWP), journalists on papers like the *New Musical Express* (NME), and music managers such as Peter Jenner.[24] They do not agree as to the relative importance of these various links, but they acknowledge the need to include them in understanding music's role in political action.

Similar attention to the organisational interplay of music and politics is to be found in Trish Winter and Simon Keegan-Phipps's account of English folk and its cultural politics. They write of 'the web of the folk industry' to capture the networks that connect music to politics. Caught up in this 'web' are a range of agencies and organisations. These include venues, distributors, festivals, and media outlets (such as the magazine *Sing* in the 1960s).[25] Also involved are bodies like the Arts Council of Great Britain (now separate arts councils for England, Scotland, and Wales), the English Folk Dance and Song Society, and academic researchers. They all contribute to Winter and Keegan-Phipps's account of how folk music flourished in a particular period and of the politics to which it gave expression – as do a range of other agents and agencies, often with no formal links to the music industry.

Organised labour is one such intermediary. Unlike the small magazines, fringe parties, or churches that helped in producing the protest song, the trade unions could command considerable resources of both people and finance. In the 1930s, writes Stewart Duncan, 'labour movements increasingly used choral singing as a method of concrete political action'. Singing was not simply a way of imagining the future, argues Duncan, but of achieving it by way of forming communities, educating participants, and organising political action.[26] Labour leaders were instrumental in creating the National Labour Choral Union in 1924. This national initiative failed to flourish, but the London Labour Choral Union, which was also formed in 1924, did succeed. The choral union published song sheets for what it entitled 'socialist choral music', which included songs written or arranged by Alan Bush ('Song to Labour' or 'The Red Flag') and others by Hanns Eisler and Bertolt Brecht.[27] Another product of this process was *The Left Songbook* (1938), which, says Duncan, was intended 'to provide the labour movement with an accessible and effective musical repertoire'.[28]

In the late twentieth century, another important intermediary was Women's Revolutions Per Minute (WRPM). Founded in 1977, WRPM organised venues, recordings, and distribution networks – among other things – for music made by, and for, women. WRPM began by importing records from the US, before expanding into an organisation that aimed 'to fuse politics, music and business'.[29] In its early publicity, WRPM announced: 'Our purpose is to make non-oppressive women's music as widely available as possible … and to stimulate interest and confidence in producing more women's music'. By 1986, its catalogue contained more than one hundred titles, and its mission was now to eliminate sexism in the music industry, to employ women throughout WRPM, to train women to become recording engineers (among other skills), to raise the visibility of women artists, and to encourage songs with lyrics that are 'positive about women'. WRPM provided a platform and resources that enabled feminist protest songs to be performed, recorded, and heard. As such, it is illustrative of how intermediaries contribute to the existence of protest songs.

Other important contributions to the life of the protest song include the work of folk song collectors like Francis Child, who was important to the careers of musicians many years later. 'Without Francis Child', writes

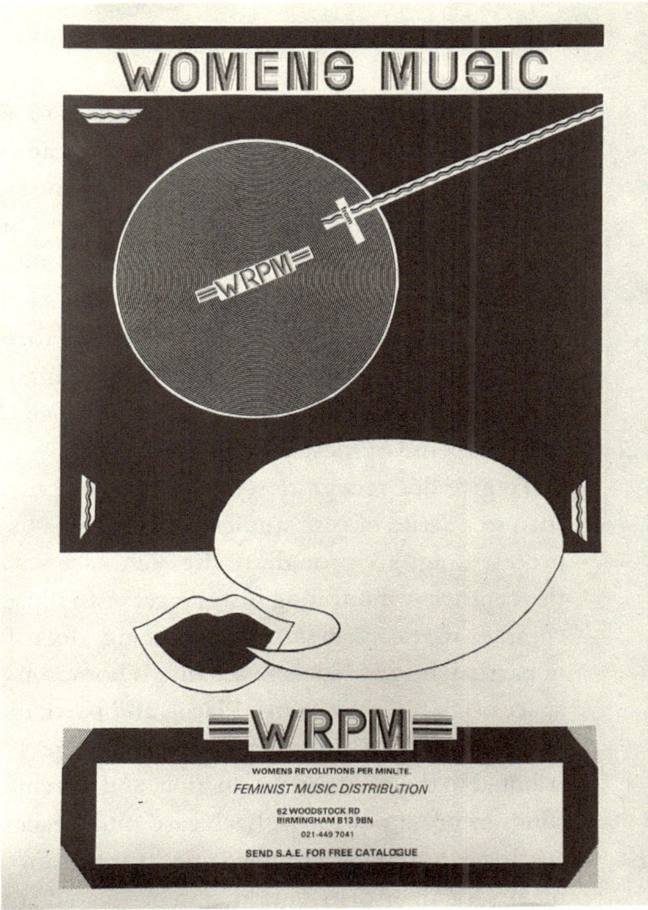

5.1 • Women's Revolutions Per Minute newsletter, n.d.

Dave Laing, 'no Bob Dylan or Steeleye Span'.[30] The availability of the protest song in the twentieth and twenty-first centuries also owed much to specialist record companies such as Topic Records and No Masters, just as it depended on publishers such as Nathaniel Thompson in the seventeenth century. Also of note is the role played by those who commission protest songs. Tom Robinson's song 'The Mighty Sword of Justice' (2015) was written in response to a request from the Justice Alliance and its campaign to protect legal aid. The song subsequently appeared on an album, funded by crowdsourcing on PledgeMusic. Latin Quarter's environmental protest song 'Dominion' (1989) was the result of a commission by documentary filmmakers. In documenting these many and various routes to the protest song, we need always to be aware that money too plays its part. From the beginning of the trade in song to the music industry of today, making a living was a key motivation. Protest and profit may not always make the happiest of partners, but there have been times when their relationship has flourished (as with 'The Revolution is on CBS') and times when financial stability was sacrificed for political belief. In short, the protest song owes its existence to any number of processes, intermediaries, incentives, and actors. Of course, the political awareness of songwriters and the political climate of their times matter too, but not at the expense of these other contributors.

To give due recognition to these other contributions, we once again turn to a series of case studies. These enable us to look in detail at how protest songs are brought to life. Five case studies, drawn from across the centuries of our long history, serve to illustrate the contingent and complex narratives behind protest songs, focusing on the life and times of particular individuals (Nathaniel Thompson; John Freeth), particular spaces (Dial House; South Place), and particular organisations (South Place again; the Critics Group and the Singers' Club), all of which contributed to the creation, production, and dissemination of specific protest songs or groups of songs. Each case study traces the networks that gave rise to protest songs, provided opportunities for them to be played, found means for their distribution, and generated an audience for them. But while each case study identifies a process by which the protest song assumes a place in the world, the processes vary. Our case studies not only mark changes over time in the creation and distribution of the protest song but also reveal the differences in the agents and agencies involved, and in the kinds of music being made and heard. We begin in the seventeenth century, when the commercial production of protest songs was in its infancy, and when the business was not just financially, but politically and personally, risky. We end with Dial House, where Crass and others worked collectively to forge links between punk and political protest, and in determined independence from the established music industry.

Case Study

Nathaniel Thompson – Campaigner and Publisher of Protest Songs

Music printer and publisher Nathaniel Thompson (*c.*1645–1687) coordinated the publication of more than a hundred political songs as part of a personal campaign of protest against Catholic discrimination. His career illustrates how both the systems and values inherent in production processes and the politics of producers could be central to the creation, distribution, and reach of protest songs.[31]

Thompson trained as a printer in 1660s Dublin. By 1668, he was in London, working (illegally) for a master music printer and learning how to print accurate musical notation (a rare skill in Restoration London). He was discovered during a search of printing houses in 1669 but could show he had lived in London for a year, giving him a right to stay. He formalized his right to work as a printer by paying a large fee for membership of the Stationers' Company, which controlled the trade. Questioned about his religion as part of the membership process, Thompson claimed he was a Protestant. But this was not true. Not only was Thompson Irish, an identity that continually exposed him to derogatory colonial stereotyping, but also a Catholic. Universally distrusted, Catholics in Restoration England, Ireland, and Scotland were viewed as potential terrorists.[32] They were legally subjected to social, political, and economic discrimination and were excluded from attending universities, from joining the professions, from serving as government officials, and from joining trade guilds and corporations, such as the Stationers' Company.[33]

Most Catholics compromised their beliefs in order to live, and Thompson was no exception. His lie to the Stationers' Company was not altogether believed; some saw him as a potential danger, but he was not expelled. Though constantly harried by searches of his premises and a victim of false accusations of illegal printing, Thompson managed to find a partner and build a successful business as a jobbing printer of musical, theatrical, and religious works.

Before 1678, Thompson eschewed political printing on his own account – his outsider status gave him trouble enough. But that changed when news broke of a shocking 'Popish Plot', supposedly hatched by agents of the pope in Rome. The plotters aimed to kill Charles II and replace him with a puppet ruler in the person of the king's Catholic brother and heir, James, Duke of York. He would then drive the country back to the Roman Church, take back all the monastic lands, and massacre all those who refused to convert. Panic spread across the country. The merest hint of 'popish' sympathy led to people's homes being searched and violent assaults in the streets. Scores of people were arrested, and many were executed for treason on little evidence.[34]

Like other Catholics, Thompson was terrified for his family, his business, and himself. Nevertheless, despite these risks, he was determined to defend the loyal Catholic interest against what he regarded as a 'Protestant plot' by using all the communication tools at his disposal. His aim was to cast doubt on the Popish Plot and to win hearts and minds to supporting the Duke of York's claims, and thus to restore Catholic reputations and guarantee better treatment for his fellow Catholics in the future. By 1679, Thompson had entered the increasingly noisy and dangerous world of political discourse with two new and, strictly speaking, illegal ventures: first, he began a weekly loyalist newspaper; and second, he began to print, sell, and distribute scores of pro-York and anti-plot songs.[35]

Thompson wrote his own copy for his newspapers but is not known as a poet or songwriter. He was, however, one of the leading music printers in the city and was likely capable of editing lyrics. He had access to all the major and light musical works of the period, was musically knowledgeable, and had an ear for a good song. Knowing from experience that his endeavours were likely to lead to trials and imprisonments, he gathered about him a few like-minded, if somewhat disreputable, authors and publishers (including his wife), to help him produce, print, and distribute pro-Tory songs, even if he was in prison.[36] In addition to commissioning or facilitating the production of songs from lesser-known authors (such as the bookseller and Tory songwriter James Dean), Thompson also sought out good songs by well-known writers that could be adapted to his own pro-Catholic stance. The best of these had been written for the theatre or for court entertainments by professional poets and songwriters, such as Thomas D'Urfey or Matthew Taubman, though whether they were willingly appropriated is unclear.[37]

At first, Thompson faced an uphill struggle. The Whig party, which sought to exclude York, was in the ascendancy (especially in London). As a known (or suspected) papist, Thompson did not dare to openly defy the narrative of the Popish Plot to which the party subscribed (men were executed for less). Nevertheless, he dispensed a stream of song and newsprint that linked Whigs to the history of regicide and claimed that their populist political scheming would soon lead to a new civil war. In late 1681, the tide turned against the exclusionists. Whig leader Anthony Ashley, Earl of Shaftesbury was imprisoned and awaiting trial for treason. Another leader (and putative Protestant heir), the Duke of Monmouth, was banished. A Whig protest singer, Stephen Colledge, was executed for treason (see chapter 6). From this point onwards, Thompson openly launched a campaign against the Plot and all those who had made the allegations. He issued dozens of protest songs under his own imprint, complete with accurately printed music so that they could be sung by groups of supporters. Of these, the most far-reaching was 'The Whig's Exaltation' (1682).[38]

The song was published in response to Shaftesbury's treason trial (see the Whig protest song 'The Subject's Hope').[39] The case was brought before a Whig-leaning London jury on 28 November and was found 'ignoramus' (no case to answer) to great acclamation by the London crowds. 'The Whig's Exaltation' was one of a flood of pro-Tory ballads (several published by Thompson's group) that parodied the voices and ambitions of the Whigs. The song was written by at least three hands at different times. Three verses had been written during the Civil War by cavalier poet Francis Quarles. These were amalgamated into a five-verse song by the court favourite, singer/songwriter Thomas D'Urfey, for his play *The Royalist*, which was pointedly set during the Civil War period and attacked the contemporary Whigs as traitors.[40] The broadside ballad market expected longer songs. Throwing all caution to the wind, two further verses appeared on Thompson's broadside version, which explicitly protested that the Popish Plot allegations were nothing more than a Whig lie, while the imprint boldly stated Thompson's full name. Moreover, to encourage more people to sing it, the ballad was headed up with accurate music notation, and the sheets were sold for half the usual price of a musical sheet at a halfpenny. Inevitably, Thompson was arrested, imprisoned, tried, and sentenced to be pilloried by the Whig city authorities.

Though no evidence has (so far) come to light of the song being performed, we do know that 'The Whig's Exaltation' had an impact. It sold so well that it was pirated by another printer (though without the music). At the same time, it was adapted for the popular market by Philip Brooksby, a Tory sympathiser and the biggest publisher of new retail songs at the time; it ran to yet another two editions. Needled Whig writers issued two separate answers to the song, while Thompson's punishment was celebrated in a parody entitled 'The Knight of the Wooden Ruffs Exaltation'.[41]

Importantly, although Thompson was publishing in support of the Tory interest, he was not part of the official print campaign described by historians as the 'Tory Reaction'.[42] A perennial outsider, Thompson's pro-Catholic views were neither widely shared nor appreciated. For example, one song published by his group expressly praised Thompson's role in promoting the duke of York's cause through the press. Though the song was popular enough to be reprinted by Philip Brooksby for the retail market, Brooksby removed all references to Thompson from his mainstream edition.[43]

Thompson's campaign of protest and persuasion involved huge personal and reputational risks. In 1681, he was attacked in the street, much of his house was torn down, and his figure was burned in effigy in London's massive pope-burning parade. In 1682, he was pilloried and mercilessly pelted by the crowd. He was also subjected to defamation in the Whig press: dubbed 'Popish Nat', several songs accused him of coordinating a papist plot. In his own words: 'the malice of the Factious Party [the Whigs] … caused me to be imprison'd six times, so that for near five years I was never free from Trouble, having seldom less than 3, or 4 Indictments at a Sessions against Me; at other times Information upon Information in the Crown-Office, which villainous contrivances of their Agents, cost Me at last £500 in Money, besides the loss of My Trade and Reputation'.[44] Yet Thompson apparently received no direct help from Tory leaders with his fines (as frequently happened for others) and was forced to mortgage his share of Stationers' Company stock in 1682.[45]

In 1685, Thompson's wishes came true: James II ascended to the throne. The Popish Plot was universally discredited, and those who had promoted it were disgraced. Steps were taken to lessen discrimination against both Catholics and Nonconformists. Thompson brought out an anthology of more than 180 songs that, he claimed, had persuaded those who were unpersuadable by any other rhetorical form: 'The misinform'd Rabble … Those that despise the Reverend Prelate in the Pulpit, and the Grave Judge on the Bench; that will neither submit to the Laws of God or Man, will yet lend an itching Ear to a New SONG, nay, and often become a Convert by It, when all other means prove ineffectual … [bringing them] under the Discipline of Obedience or Government'.[46]

Thompson ceased to print protest songs and turned, instead, to producing Catholic books. He died in 1687, at a high point for religious toleration (and song censorship) leaving his business to his wife. A year later, the revolution of 1688–89 reversed all those gains. James II fled, the chief instigators of the plot were restored, Thompson's printing business collapsed, and a new battle between Williamite and Jacobite songs filled the streets.

Thompson's career illustrates how the politics of intermediaries could play a significant role in the content and reach of the protest song, especially at a time when song authorship was commonly multi-handed and lyrics were mutable. In the case of 'The Whig's Exaltation', it was 'popish Nat' Thompson, the printer/publisher – not the songwriters – who introduced the idea of questioning the veracity of the Popish Plot in song. Moreover, though Thompson produced his songs in the context of competing political ideologies, his campaign of protest took an independent course. It was Thompson's own political agenda that facilitated the production and adaptation of hundreds of songs arguing his case; it was Thompson who faced the consequences, and Thompson who experienced the satisfaction and benefits of a successful campaign of protest.

Case Study

John Freeth – Pubs and Public Spaces

John Freeth stands for the importance of the pub, the theatre, and the coffee house to the genesis of English protest songs. In the 420 years this book covers, John Freeth (1731–1808) is as near as we come to someone embodying the spirit of their age – in this case, the eighteenth century. The son of Birmingham tavern-keepers, Freeth tried his hand at brass founding and geography teaching before turning to poetry, inheriting his parents' business at some date before 1768. This hostelry, the Leicester Arms on the corner of Bell Street and Lease Lane, Birmingham, soon became famous as Freeth's Coffee-House, which he 'ran' until his death in 1808. The inverted commas are in acknowledgement that it was really Freeth's wife and daughters who operated the business; Freeth was succeeded by his eldest daughter Elizabeth. Yet this coffee-house-cum-pub-cum-tavern and its proprietor's nominal role as tavern host are absolutely crucial in understanding Freeth's primary claim to both local and national fame as a writer of topical, political, and protest songs.[47]

Politically, Freeth was no insurgent. Rather, he embodied a very typical sort of independent liberalism. A lifelong Whig, he supported American independence and opposed slavery. Detesting the Tory administrations of Lord North and William Pitt the Younger, idolising

5.2 • Johannes Eckstein, *John Freeth and his Circle or Birmingham Men of the Last Century*, oil on canvas, 1792.

John Wilkes, and decrying the more extreme phases of the French Revolution and the tyranny of Napoleon, he proved equally scornful of the loyalist reaction and what he saw as the faintly absurd and illiberal excesses of anti-Napoleonic patriotism. He believed in free trade, a strictly limited constitutional monarchy, and the inalienable rights of the freeborn Englishman – all of which sound if anything rather right wing today but which placed him at the time much closer to the radical camp and meant that he spent most of his life in trenchant opposition. Five of his songs have made our longlist of 750, qualifying as subversive acts of protest on different grounds. 'The Rights of Mankind all the World Over' was written in 1790, in a moderate but nonetheless revolutionary spirit; 1774's 'American Contest' uses a domestic allegory to advance the US cause; 'On the Intended Bill' (1778) opposes enclosure; and 'The Dog Act' (1770) complains that dogs are better protected by law than free-speaking Englishmen. He is at his most provocative in 'The Old King's Ghost' (1768), an attack on the conduct of the new king George III that is at once traditionalist and rather scandalous in that it dares to raise the spectre of regicide, albeit in a self-censoring couplet: 'Be Cautious for Fear lest you split on that Rock, / Which brought the unfortunate Charles to the — [i.e., block]'.

As interesting as Freeth's output, however, are the networks of dissemination. More than this: in interrogating Freeth's networks, we gain fresh insights into those outputs. Technically, Freeth self-published – one marked-up manuscript copy of his *Modern Songs* (1782) survives, showing his edits – thereby taking upon himself both the financial and the legal responsibility for his output.[48] But he worked with a succession of local printers, all save one operating out of the same printing house on Birmingham High Street, known for their high production values and good reputation. The one exception was the 1771 edition of his much-reissued and -reworked *Political Songster*, printed by the same John Baskerville to whom we owe that font, a prestigious partner indeed. An influential and respectable local printer was key to his operation, resulting in covetable bound songbooks, rather superior to the competition at the price point of sixpence and upwards, containing anywhere from 23 to 150 songs. For the latter works, more ambitious and expensive, Freeth turned to the subscription model, allowing him to raise the capital in advance of publication and print secure in the knowledge that he was taking no risk. For the 1790 edition of the *Political Songster*, 516 copies were subscribed for by 396 individuals at a cost of 3s 6d each – giving a total of more than £90, twice the annual wage of a skilled artisan. The subscribers included a duke and three earls, all of which made for good promotion, given that Freeth could print the subscription list at the start of the volume. A Mr Tankard of Birmingham took twenty copies: we can only hope that, by his name, he was another publican.[49] But there was a second benefit to his regular printers: they also produced *Aris's Birmingham Gazette*, and at least eleven of Freeth's songs are known to have received their first airing in this newspaper prior to anthologising.[50] One now-lost 1770 work, an ode titled 'Wilkes' Enlargement', was written and printed in order to coincide with Wilkes's release from prison. When that release was brought forward by a day, Freeth was able to bring the publication forward a day as well – and to advertise its debut performance in the local paper: 'An entertainment will be provided by the Author on Wednesday the 18th, who is fitting up a commodious Room for the Reception of those Friends of the Cause that think proper to attend. — Dinner to be ready at One o'Clock'.[51]

The print market, then, in all its guises, was a key network for Freeth's songs. His price points and the material forms of his songs indicate a middling and even elite listenership – broadly speaking, the electorate and those engaged in public discourse – all of which is reflected in the songs themselves. Freeth makes free use of literary references, his lyrical tone can be similarly elevated, and his topical songs are often tied to the sort of official political process – acts of parliament, elections, decisions by the city corporation, foreign affairs – in which his wider readership took an active, participatory interest. Yet as that advertisement in the local *Gazette* reminds us, this was the mid-eighteenth century, when the cult of sociability was at its height – and Freeth's success as a protest songwriter was facilitated, above all, by his *personal* networks. These included that other emblematic Georgian institution, the theatre: in 1774, Freeth was granted a Benefit Concert (a form of personal charity) by what was soon to become the Theatre Royal on Birmingham's New Street. Freeth himself penned the epilogue to the performance, which concluded with the blatant advertisement, 'Call at his House, you'll find ROAST BEEF tomorrow'.[52] And it was this House that really provided Freeth with audience, reception, fame, status – and even security.

From 1771 to 1785, Freeth made use of a deliberately transparent alias, John Free, for both his business and his songs (in 1785, a *real* John Free set up business nearby, ruining the joke). This moniker stood at once for his political ideology and his commitment to hospitality, helping create a brand identity as a liberal host in all senses of the word – an identity attested to by thirteen likenesses, in which he usually appears seated at his ease, with pen and book before him but a long-stemmed pipe actually in his hand. He is at once the epitome of the respectable propertied Englishman and the convivial, sociable man of the world, placed at the centre of the most important political network of all: sociable conversation.[53]

The tavern, pub, or coffee house (and Freeth's seems to have been all three) was, of course, an ideal site for the dissemination of song. It allowed for the congregation of auditors and provided the ideal conditions for their receptiveness – sat down, comfortable, full, and slightly inebriated: in other words, perfectly prepared to find themselves in sympathy with the sentiments of a well-sung and entertaining argument. We see the effect of this performance context in Freeth's choices as a songwriter: his tunes are generally well-known, with simple melodies, often linked to drinking songs. 'On the Intended Bill' features a chorus that does little to advance the argument – but an awful lot to marshal its listeners in singing and drinking along to the earworm refrain. 'The Dog Act' is set to 'Roast Beef of Old England', a famed drinking song that celebrates the comforts of the table and is ideal for communal rendition by seated revellers clinking their tankards. This captive, contented audience – so different from the fragmentary, mobile listenerships to be fought for in the street or square – also allowed Freeth to compose more extended rhetorical arguments and elaborate lyrical conceits than many of his peers: 'The Old King's Ghost' riffs on *Hamlet* for the course of some seven minutes without ever returning to its original set-up: the entire premise relies on those hearing the later verses having been present and attentive from the beginning, rarely a given in other performance contexts.

Above all, it was Freeth's *ownership* – his control – of the site of reception that stands out as distinctive. He was able to direct the company and exert both moral and physical force, which was of no small importance in a turbulent age. Nearby, for instance, the local Tories kept a rival establishment, the Minerva Tavern on Peck Lane. In 1790, as the French Revolution gathered pace, they put up a sign reading 'No Jacobins Admitted Here' – a challenge that James Bisset, one of Freeth's circle, met publicly by entering the tavern, resulting in a fight, a bloodied nose, and a £5 fine for damages.[54] Freeth, by contrast, played up the welcome he afforded strangers to the town – and it is notable that his subscription lists numbered individuals from across the country, not just men of Birmingham. But he was also able to curate his audiences, issuing distinctive invitation cards for regular feasts and anniversaries on behalf of specific societies or causes.[55] If he chose, he had total control over the conditions in which his songs might be received. Most famously, his tavern was the meeting-place, in the 1790s, of Birmingham's own 'Jacobin Club' – twelve local worthies, all either professionals or businessmen, rich and influential enough to be able to commission a 48-guinea group portrait in oils by Johann Eckstein (fig. 5.2). It hung in the Coffee-House for several decades, itself constituting a significant local attraction.[56] Crucially, in a decade when Pitt's 'Terror' clamped down on freedoms of speech and assembly, and a series of trumped-up trials were designed to suppress the radical movement, Freeth's circle, secure in their property, their meeting-place, and their well-earned reputations for civic patriotism and good conduct, were able to meet, talk, sing, and publish without fear of persecution. In the 1760s, Freeth had felt secure enough to envisage a king's death in 'The Old King's Ghost'. Now, in the 1790s, he was confident enough to produce 'The Rights of Mankind all the World Over' – a pro-revolution, abolitionist, internationalist lyric that would have landed him in hot water almost anywhere else. Yet, unlike those of his contemporaries who were forced to emigrate, change their tune, or retire from public view, Freeth was able to continue singing and publishing in accordance with his own independent, radical perspective throughout the 1790s and 1800s, thanks to his propertied status, his local celebrity, his friends in high places, and the secure doors of his establishment. As chapter 6 shows, this was no small victory, and it was down in large part to the networks, resources, and credentials Freeth was able to leverage as a long-established pillar of the community in this rapidly expanding, industrial, and notably radical city.

Case Study

South Place – Press, Pulpits, and Politics

Religious spaces inspired the protest song. One such was South Place – later the South Place Ethical Society and now Conway Hall Ethical Society. It became a vehicle and home for protest song after the appointment of William Johnson Fox (1786–1864) as its minister in 1817. At that point it was, broadly speaking, a Unitarian organisation based around a chapel and congregation and, as such, fairly typical of England's many Dissenting (i.e., not Established) Christian communities. Whilst under Fox's leadership and thereafter, it became increasingly deistical, secular, and ultimately humanist. In the nineteenth century, its structure and ethos were recognisably similar to those of a committed Dissenting congregation. Music, and especially song, was central to its activities both internally and externally. The early decades witnessed major power struggles over repertoire, the use of the organ, and the relative participation of the dedicated choir and the whole congregation in devotional singing. Most significantly, South Place provided a remarkable and almost unique platform for politicised, female songwriters. In a later generation, this included the secularist-socialist Emily Josephine Troup (1853–1913), but pre-eminently the remarkable composer Eliza Flower (1803–1846) and the lyricists she worked with, including her sister Sarah (1805–1848) and her frequent early collaborator, Harriet Martineau (1802–1876), who would go on to be one of the leading political theorists and chroniclers of the century.

It is simplest to conceive of South Place's musical outputs as consisting of two categories – hymns and secular songs – though the distinction between the two is not always clear or especially helpful. In the 1830s and '40s – when Flower was active – the former category was a major vehicle of political protest, largely thanks to the role of Dissenting communities in organised radical demonstrations and the Chartist movement. As communal, respectable, anthemic (especially in the modern sense), and conducive to coordinated

5.3 • South Place Chapel. Drawn by Thomas H. Shepherd, from an engraving by J.F. Havell, 1827.

embodied action – mustering, singing, marching, occupying public space – the hymn was an ideal sonic vehicle for the orchestration of organised protest. Its lyrical field provided ample opportunity for the airing of radical ideology – enfranchisement, equality, liberation, levelling, redistribution – within the acceptable parameters of religious expression. Many hymns feature on our list of key songs from these decades. Externally, then, the hymn could be weaponised as part of protest: but it could also effect radical, politicised change when directed inwards. This was perhaps the one context in which 'preaching to the choir', in the realm of sacred song, could be a fraught and contested activity. Much as abolitionists had promulgated their argument through sentimental ballads a generation earlier, aiming to change hearts and minds within the private space of the middling and elite drawing-room or parlour, so Fox and Flower advanced both a radical political and religious programme through the hymns sung at South Place, primarily via the two-volume *Hymns and Anthems* they produced for the congregation in the final six years of Flower's life. Musically, the mix of Flower's own composition and extensive quotation of leading composers, often German, was a controversial step towards the secularisation and intellectualisation of devotional space and ritual. Lyrically this went still further: she not only set the lyrics of 'profane' writers, from Shakespeare to Shelley, but also words by contemporary radicals and Chartists such as Ebenezer Elliott, the famed 'Corn Law Rhymer', and texts by Martineau such as 'All Men Are Equal' (1842), which preached total equality in both a domestic and explicitly colonial context.[57]

In the realm of secular song, it was again Martineau and Fox who were Flower's most radical collaborators. Martineau's lyric 'The Gathering of the Unions. March and Song' (1832) was a seminal reformist anthem; the same year's 'Hymn of the Polish Exiles' was a major statement of internationalist solidarity in the face of Russian atrocities. Also in 1832, Fox's lyric 'The Barons Bold on Runnymede' was a rollicking argument for extending the franchise that referenced, rather daringly, the execution of Charles I. As late as 1845, he and Flower were producing works like 'The Day-Labourer's Song', a protest at casualisation of employment and the use of overseers.

In both realms, the creation and impact of songs of protest were enabled by networks of both print culture and personal influence. In the first instance, Eliza Flower and her sister Sarah were members of Fox's congregation. He became a family friend, and on the death of their single-parent father, Fox became their legal guardian, providing two otherwise precarious and legally vulnerable young women with resources, protection, time, licence, and opportunity. That late father, Benjamin, had been a leading radical journalist and editor, with spells in prison behind him, and brought both a reputation and connections to both family and congregation. South Place itself and its need for a revitalised and regular programme of music afforded an initial and lasting sphere of action, within which Eliza Flower was a known, respected, and even idolised presence. The personal networks around South Place, and its growing reputation as a well-endowed and innovative Dissenting community, helped it grow in influence, so that Flower's supporters, collaborators, and champions numbered not just Martineau and Fox but also the likes of Thomas Carlyle, John Stuart Mill, Robert Browning (who was besotted by her), Felix Mendelssohn, and leading music publisher Vincent Novello. Fox was editor of the *Monthly Repository*, an extremely successful organ of the progressive press, which afforded Flower a consistent platform, as in 1834, when each issue led with one of her 'Songs of the Months'. Individual works such as 'The Day-Labourer's Song' were self-published, subsidised by Fox's business, allowing the freedom to experiment with printing both lyrics *and* Flower's distinctive music in notation format, at the loss-leader price of a penny per sheet. Her protest hymns were given greater exposure by the commercial publication of *Hymns and Anthems*, along with a prestigious concert at London's Crosby Hall on 22 November 1845. A series of four 'Free Trade Songs' formed a key part of the 1845 Anti-Corn Law League Bazaar, a multi-day extravaganza somewhere between a jumble sale and the Great Exhibition, held at Covent Garden Theatre, one of the country's most significant cultural institutions. Fox was, of course, a key member of the league. And to counteract the impression that many of these networks and platforms were down to one man's patronage, it should above all be noted that Flower, as Fox's ward, acted not merely as his housekeeper and, for several years, the carer and educator of his children but also as his amanuensis and secretary. It was her extra-musical work that helped make the songs and their impact possible.

The fragility of these networks, founded in large part upon personal relations between key players in London's reformist and radical circles, was made clear when Fox broke with his wife and subsequently set up a separate household overseen by Flower in 1834. No evidence of a romantic relationship between the two exists, but this was the inevitable imputation put about at the time, as in an item of gossip entitled 'The Fox and the Flower' published in the *Sunday Times* on 7 September 1834. Martineau was among those who severed connections with Fox and Flower, bringing that key songwriting partnership to a premature end. South Place itself suffered a schism that threatened to be irreparable, Fox tendering his resignation, only to have it refused. Yet equally, the less personally dependent mechanisms of a national print culture were responsible, two years earlier, for the immense impact of the Flower-Martineau song 'Gathering of the Unions', distributed anonymously as one of several 'Reform Songs' in flysheets – effectively single-sided ballads but including notation – and taken up by multiple bodies of working-class reformers.[58] Over one hundred thousand demonstrators are reported to have sung this work at the Congregation of the Unions for the 'monster meeting' in Birmingham on 7 May 1832.[59] The song remained in radical songbook repertoires for the best part of a century – but as an anonymous production, associated with neither of its (middle-class, female) creators.[60] Martineau, whose account of the day includes extensive discussion of the song, does not claim authorship. That may be in part due to the break with Flower, but surely above all in order to allow the song to function as an 'authentic' piece of self-expression on the part of its singers, a cross-class alliance nonetheless mostly composed, on occasions such as the Birmingham monster meeting, of labouring and artisanal-class men. It is a familiar irony, common to more recent protest song, that a song's success may often depend on its actual mechanisms of creation and its ongoing mythology being kept entirely separate.

Case Study

The Critics Group and the Singers' Club – Mentors and Manifestos

In 1961, following a visit to the UK, the US protest singer Pete Seeger reported that there was a 'flourishing English political song movement'.[61] The movement was a product of individuals and groups, who between them gave voice to, and found an audience for, protest songs.

The most prominent figures were Ewan MacColl and Peggy Seeger. Greil Marcus described MacColl as the 'commissar of the British folk world, dictating through a network of folk clubs what songs could be sung and how'.[62] In the *New York Times*, Robert Shelton called MacColl 'the Charles de Gaulle of the British folk revival', over which he imposed his 'steel-grip esthetic'.[63] But while MacColl and Seeger were the figureheads – and, indeed, the ideologues – of a political song movement, it would be wrong to see its flourishing as simply the work of these two people, however driven, talented, and well-known. They were part, albeit an important part, of a larger network of performers, writers, and political activists.

Important nodes in the network were the Critics Group and the Singers' Club, both run by MacColl and Seeger. These two organisations were responsible for influencing the form of English protest songs in the early 1960s and for providing a venue in which they were performed. Bob Dylan was hosted by the Singers' Club in the early 1960s. Linked to the Group and the Club were other individuals and other bodies, without which the network would have collapsed. These others included the London Cooperative Society; the Communist Party of Great Britain (CPGB) and its newspaper the *Morning Star*; *Sing* magazine; Unity Theatre; the Workers' Music Association; the Broadsheet King (John Foreman); and Eric Winter, the music marshall of the Aldermaston marches.

The Critics Group, founded in 1964, functioned as a masterclass in the art of protest songwriting, attended by a select, but changing, cohort of musicians and performers. The Singers' Club resembled the more familiar folk club, providing a regular venue for musicians to perform. The Club had begun as Ballads and Blues in 1957, named after a BBC radio series that MacColl hosted in 1953.[64] It became the Singers' Club in 1961 and was held in a number of different London pubs, while the Critics Group met in MacColl and Seeger's home in Kent. Both followed MacColl and Seeger's strict views on what constituted the folk song and folk singing. In the first edition of the Singers' Club newsletter in 1965, Jim Carroll's editorial spelled out the party line. There were to be no performances by 'failed pop singers, navel contemplaters [*sic*], or professional alcoholics'.[65]

The Singers' Club was designed, according to MacColl in *Melody Maker*, 'to rescue a large number of young people, all of whom have the right instincts' from 'influences that are doing their best to debase the meaning of folk song'.[66] It was established as a regular event by Bruce Dunnet, who is described by Ben Harker as a 'well-connected promoter and manager' and a supporter of 'hard-line communism' who believed in '"real" folk music's political relevance'. Dunnet was to become one of the Singers' Club's 'principal backstage figures – promoter, organiser, accountant, bouncer, glass-collector'.[67]

The Club's income was generated by a small entrance fee (40–50p in 1973) and by support from the London Co-operative Education Committee, which in 1976 contributed £30 to the cost of a songbook. The money paid to visiting performers was capped to keep costs down (£14 in 1973). In 1967, those performing included well-known folk artists such as Anne Briggs, Frankie Armstrong, Trevor Lucas, and Sandra Kerr, as well as MacColl and Seeger. A.L. (Bert) Lloyd would sometimes give lectures on the history of folk music. Audience members were provided with song sheets, which were typically written just days before the concert and commented on current events. One such was 'Rogues Gallery' by MacColl and set to the tune of 'Oh Dear, What Can the Matter Be?':

5.4 • Bob Dylan performing at the Singers' Club in December 1962.

> They've privatised oil and the telephone system
> Gas and Rolls Royce, it takes too long to list 'em
> Water and coal's on the cards and they'll risk 'em
> But don't let them privatise air.

Dave Laing says of the Singers' Club that it was 'the most important institution for embodying MacColl and Seeger's vision of what the folk revival should encompass'.[68] It was a vision that placed protest at the heart of the revival.

The Critics Group followed the same agenda as the Singers' Club, in that its aim was to protect folk from commercialism and bourgeois takeover, and to place politics at its heart. It too benefitted from the sponsorship of the London Cooperative Society. Where the Singers' Club was about providing a place for the performance of folk protest, the Critics Group was about creating the songs. It was organised as a means of delivering 'classes', resembling those that are now standard practice for creative writing courses in higher education.[69] When it began in 1964, it issued its own 'Reading List and Bibliography' for the members of the 'Critics Group of Folksong Studies'. It listed 'Works of Reference, Criticism of Folksongs & Folkmusic' as well as 'Collections of English, Scots & Irish Songs With Music'.

The Group's meetings were used 'to develop ideas', which required members to give regular performances to their peers, and then to have their songs critiqued by the others and especially by the 'dictatorial' MacColl.[70] Laing describes MacColl's teaching style as resembling that of 'Marxist political parties'.[71] The effect was to both uplift and demoralise participants, who were often given a topic on which to deliver a song. In October 1966, the topic was 'Songs of Crime and Criminals'.[72] One occasional attendee, Jake Glanville, remembers being required to write a song about the Vietnam War. MacColl's comments suggested that it did not meet his mentor's exacting standards.[73]

The Critics Group was not just a folk song seminar group. It was responsible in 1966 for organising the Folksingers' Committee for Peace, which took part in the anti-war demonstrations of the period.[74] The Group also devised and performed the annual *Festival of Fools* at the Unity Theatre.[75] A Christmas show that satirised the year in politics, it was a source of protest songs. One of its most famous products was Peggy Seeger's 'I'm Gonna Be an Engineer' (1971):

> When I went to school I learned to write and how to read
> Some history, geography and home economy
> And typing is a skill that every girl is sure to need
> To while away the extra time until the time to breed
> Then they had the nerve to say, what would you like to be?
> I says, 'I'm gonna be an engineer!'[76]

According to Seeger, the song was written on the instruction of MacColl. It was needed for that year's *Festival*. Seeger explained to *Sing Out!* magazine: 'I did not write that because I had any tremendous feelings about the women's movement at the time. I was working with a group that was doing a political show [*Festival of Fools*] every year … Ewan, who usually did the writing, said, "Look, I just haven't got time to write this. And anyway, you should write it … We've got to have that song and we've got to have it in a week"'.[77] In her memoir, *First Time Ever*, she tells the story again, albeit with rather different emphasis. But it too downplays her own personal views and the social movement that might have explained the song's genesis: '"I'm Gonna Be an Engineer" was one of those songs that just appear. Standing unbeknownst on the threshold of feminism and never having wanted to be an engineer, I wrote it in two hours and took it upstairs to Ewan's cubicle in the cistern room. He was brisk. *The last verse is depressing, Peg. You need some hope.* Downstairs again, rewrote the verse, Mabel's Your Auntie and back to doing the accounts'.[78] Whichever story is the more accurate, the lesson is similar: the process of songwriting is contingent on many factors, in which conscience and context may be just two, and not necessarily the most important two.

Beyond the Singers' Club and the Critics Group, there were other actors, without whom protest songs would remain unknown and unheard. One of these was John Foreman, who went under the name of the Broadsheet King. In this guise, Foreman assumed responsibility for publishing (and illustrating) the song sheets used in various protests. This role was the result of his involvement with the Unity Theatre, another key player in the protest song process. Unity, writes Mike Butler, 'turned working-class experience into drama that was fresh, visceral and often funny'.[79] It produced plays, revues, and pantomimes. Its *Babes in the Wood* 'mocked Hitler and Mussolini'. Unity also provided a venue for music, which was where Foreman played in a jazz band and a skiffle group. He also helped to reproduce Unity's theatre programmes. He used Unity's duplicator in the early days to produce the original song sheets, only later using more sophisticated methods. The Unity Theatre, Foreman recalls, was a 'melting pot' through which he got to know Karl Dallas, Ewan MacColl, Peggy Seeger, and John Brunner, all of whose songs he published. The Aldermaston marches, organised by the Campaign for Nuclear Disarmament (CND),

5.5 • A songbook distributed to Campaign for Nuclear Disarmament marchers, n.d. Design by Kit Cooper and John Foreman (The Broadsheet King).

were key to his publishing career. Working with Eric Winter, the music marshall, and John Hasted who ran the London Youth Choir that performed on the marches, Foreman produced the booklets of songs that were distributed to the demonstrators.[80] The first of the CND songbooks was called *Sing your Protest*, and opened with 'Study War No More', set to the tune of 'Down by the Riverside': 'I'm gonna talk with my brethren / I'm gonna shout the call of peace / I'm gonna lay down that atom bomb'.

The work of the Critics Group and the Singers' Club was intimately linked to that of the Broadsheet King and Unity Theatre, and beyond that to the Workers' Music Association (WMA), Topic Records, the Communist Party of Great Britain, and CND. The contributions of these were financial, organisational, creative, and ideological. The WMA was Communist funded, and run by composer Alan Bush, who worked to create a repertoire of protest songs and to teach choirs to sing them. CND provided a movement, a context, and a role for the songs. And Topic produced the recordings.

The Critics Group was dissolved in 1972, and the Singers' Club hosted its final event in 1991. While no one would claim that they were responsible for all the many protest songs that characterised the decades of their existence, they illustrate one of the routes by which those songs came into existence, the particular form they took, and the audience that they reached. As Bert Lloyd once reflected: 'the organisation of folk song clubs has provided here and there a platform for directly political and agitational song'.[81] MacColl and Seeger's initiatives serve to illustrate the practical and political networks and dependencies that made possible the creation, production, and dissemination of the protest song in the late 1950s and 1960s. These processes owed a great deal to movements such as CND, individuals such as John Foreman and Eric Winter, and organisations such as the Critics Group and the Singers' Club. Of course, without them, there would still have been protest songs, but those would have sounded, travelled, and been heard differently.

Case Study

Dial House – Place, Praxis, and Punk

From 1977 to 1984, Dial House in Essex served as a hub for British punk, giving it a very distinctive political character. It was where songs such as 'They've Got a Bomb' (1978) and 'How Does It Feel (To Be the Mother of a Thousand Dead)?' (1982) began life. The band Crass formed and worked there, setting – along with Poison Girls – the template for what became known as anarcho-punk. Hundreds of young acolytes visited, bringing with them questions and aspirations inspired by the band's approach and politics. These visitors, more often than not, found a creative outlet in the spaces opened up by Crass as they endeavoured to circumnavigate the music industry and provide an alternative way of being for those resistant to 'the system'. Not only did Crass run their own record label, issuing debut singles from a range of like-minded artists, but they also generated countless pamphlets, posters, and flyers outlining their position on everything from intra-punk disputes to geopolitics and the Cold War. In their songs, moreover, Crass articulated a relatively coherent opposition to the prevailing socio-political currents of the twentieth century. Be it the horrors of the Holocaust or the patriarchal underpinnings of Christianity, Crass dissected and demonstrated against the perpetrators of violence and oppression.[82] 'Be exactly who you want to be, do what you want to do', they sang on 'Big A Little A' (1980), 'I'm he and she is she, but you're the only you'.[83] Their message was summed up neatly in a three-word equation: 'anarchy + peace = freedom'. The development of their ideas and their music owed much to the opportunities provided by their shared space.

Dial House itself dated back to the sixteenth century: a farm cottage located on the edge of Epping Forest. Penny Rimbaud (Jeremy Ratter) – later the drummer in Crass – moved there in the late 1960s, restoring the derelict building to create an open house for people to drop in, live, and create. 'I loved that idea of somewhere where people could stop to tell their story with a comfortable bed for the night and go on their journey', Rimbaud later recalled. 'My original dream was that if I created one of those, then everyone who visited would then go off and do something similar … Creating a workable community within society'.[84] People came and went, including future Crass members and collaborators Gee Vaucher, Mick Duffield, Pete Wright, and Dave King. As well as Crass's output, art was made and experimental music played under the guise of Exit.[85] In effect, the countercultural politics of the 1960s found creative expression through Dial House, before punk's intervention inspired a change of mood and tone.

The space afforded by Dial House was essential to Crass. Lead singer of the band Steve Ignorant remembers it as being 'like a maze': 'You'd

5.6 • Dial House, home to Crass, as it is today.

go through the garden gate and up the brick path past the vegetable patch and in through the back door. To your immediate left was the hallway. To the right was the fridge, a telephone and self-made dark room'.[86] Inside, space was given over to the usual bathroom, kitchen, and bedrooms, but the dark room was further complemented by a print room, a music room to listen to records in, and a 'library' where the band talked and read. Round corners, along pathways, up and then down stairs found Penny Rimbaud's studio and artistic spaces for Vaucher, King, and others to work in. There was also a small rehearsal room, about 20 feet by 20 feet, where the band tried out material and toiled at songs. Over time, the layout of the house changed as walls were repositioned and rooms swapped hands and usage.

5.7 • Steve Ignorant (left) and Crass performing at London's Zig Zag Club in 1982.

The kitchen was where Crass gathered to eat, drink, and chat long into the early hours of the morning. Ideas were swapped and songs inspired by debate, with Ignorant remembering one instance when singer Joy de Vivre disappeared upstairs mid-discussion to return about two hours later with the lyrics for 'Upright Citizen' (from 1979's *Stations of the Crass* album). In fact, their environment led Crass to produce a formidable arsenal of songs. Rimbaud, in particular, wrote lyrics of some length – essays almost – set to music and delivered by Ignorant in a Dagenham-inflected howl. Ignorant's own songs were shorter. Where Rimbaud and others dissected the power structures in front of them, Ignorant tended towards a venting of spleen: an angry exposition of his feelings and frustration ('do they owe us a living? / course they fucking do!').[87]

Songs and music were typically worked out collectively, experimented with, and tested in the small rehearsal room. 'When I first arrived at Dial House', Ignorant remembers, 'Penny was in the middle of writing a pamphlet with Eve Libertine [Bronwyn Lloyd Jones] called *Christ's Reality Asylum and Les Pommes Des Printemps*. Eve never wrote her bit, so it was really just *Christ's Reality Asylum*, which became the lyric to "Reality Asylum" on *The Feeding of the Five Thousand*. So Penny already had his way of doing things. My direction was that I'd never written anything before, so I just wrote down what I was feeling at the time'.[88]

Not all songs were accepted, though the reasons for this were sometimes practical, sometimes aesthetic, and sometimes political. Ignorant provided examples of each. A practical consideration was what could be sung. Of one proposed song, he reported: 'Some bits were so long they'd be just impossible to say. Other times, the lyric was just so difficult that I'd have to clip the words. So the "hands" in Eve Libertine's song "You've Got Big Hands" [about violence denying reason] became "'ands", then "big cans", then "be ca"'. Likewise, 'How Does it Feel?' proved difficult to sing before the chant comes in at the end: 'When you perform it, it feels such a plod. I'm thinking: is this ever going to end? The thing with Penny is, I don't think he ever learnt precis at school or wherever he went. He wanted to put everything into a song. Sometimes it works; sometimes it made me feel uncomfortable because he's not describing what he's on about'.[89] An example of an aesthetic criterion was 'Baader Meinhof', which, said Ignorant, 'was just bloody awful … It went: "It's 621984, Baader-Meinhof are dead / It's 621984, shot through the back of the head." I said, "I ain't fucking singing that!" Pete [Wright] also wrote one that was just too Frank Zappa; too jazzy. We all wasted lots of bits of paper on half-written songs'. Ignorant recalls another occasion when political judgements came into play. 'When Eve Libertine first came to Crass gigs, she'd shout "Where are the women?"', Ignorant explained. 'We tried to address that with women being in the band and releasing *Penis Envy* (1981). We also stopped using the word "cunt", turning it to "runt", which never quite had the same charge to it. But that was us trying to address those sorts of issues, which came out of us having conversations together and with people at gigs'.

Whatever the criteria being employed, the lyrics were the consequence of inhouse debate and discussion, a feature of Crass's collective approach, which extended into pooling resources to release their records. 'We'd barter', Ignorant recalls. To record the songs for what became *Feeding of the Five Thousand*, the band used 'some of Gee and Penny's artwork from college' to 'buy' time from John Loder at Southern Studio in London.[90] Small Wonder Records released *Feeding* as a 12-inch EP, allowing the band to start their own label from money made. 'We [sometimes] borrowed money', Ignorant remembers, but the band also lent it when they had it. 'If somebody has some money it gets lent, like what comes around goes around'.[91] In such a way, Crass proved able to finance early records by a number of bands and, from Dial House, to provide equipment to print fanzines, patches, T-shirts, and some record sleeves.

Living out their ethos at Dial House gave Crass's music an added political charge. 'Part of it', Ignorant insists, 'was that we could make as much noise as we wanted to. But it was also the people involved in it. Their various backgrounds, the books on the shelves. The backgrounds of Penny and Gee having been to art school. There was material to draw from. There were brains to pick. They and Pete Wright had all been through the 1960s thing. They brought that sense of rebellion, which wasn't just "fuck you". It was more considered. But, at the same time, the band wouldn't have been the same without me. It was Dial House that allowed Crass to happen. Without Dial House there wouldn't have been Crass'.[92] Ignorant's final assertion underlines the theme of this chapter: that the protest song is as much a product of place and space as it is a product of context and conscience. How songwriters and others involved in music and in politics come together, how they interact, and how they come to depend upon each other are key to understanding the creation and communication of protest songs.

CONCLUSION

The case studies focus on very different aspects of the business of producing protest songs and how, over time, that business was conducted. From Nathaniel Thompson's family connections, his deceptions with the

Stationers' Company, or his dealings with the authorities, to the past influences and daily routines in Dial House, to the guidance and mentoring of the Critics Group, to the space and religious musical traditions of South Place, and to the multiple creative, practical, and political contributions made by John Freeth: the differences are notable, but they all tell the story of how people and resources were brought together to enable the composition and distribution of protest songs.

Some of the routes taken in producing the protest song may seem mundane – exchanges between Seeger and MacColl at home or the domestic details of Dial House – but they form the practical basis by which music gets made. Equally, that music may depend on chance encounters and the travails of relationships as much as it does on more familiar forces of religion and politics. In focusing on case studies, we inevitably draw attention to the contingent and specific, but our approach is intended to establish a wider truth: that protest songs are the results of individuals and their networks, of institutions and resources, and of movements and their ideas. These elements do not just enable protest songs to be written: they shape the form they take, how they sound, and what say. We can see how religious beliefs were important to the protest songs of the earlier era, whereas versions of Marxism and anarchism were present in more recent times. These ideas and ideologies depended themselves on the organisations that propagated them, and the resources available. In his *Models of Musical Democracy*, Robert Adlington suggests that the modes of musical collaboration vary, according to whether the participants are brought together by friendship, religion, or education.[93] Our case studies cannot demonstrate causality of this kind, but they do offer examples of how this process might affect the form of the protest song.

No two protest songs will have the same biography, and the ones detailed here are just examples of what can lead to a protest song. They represent neither general types nor templates. There may be as many different stories as there are protest songs. What matters is that, in tracing the history and politics of the English protest song, we pay due attention to the processes of its production and distribution.

Focusing on these features of the making and circulation of songs is not to deny the importance of the wider social and political context in which they emerge, or of the movements that were forged in that context. Nor does it seek to deny the importance of the creativity and conscience of the individuals with whom the songs are most closely associated. Instead, it is to invite further reflection on how we understand the history of all protest songs, and the English variant in particular, a reflection that leads to consideration of those who seek to thwart the production and distribution of the protest song, rather than to facilitate it.

6

THE REGULATION AND REPRESSION OF THE PROTEST SONG

In June 2022, after a long struggle through the legislative process, the UK government's Police, Crime, Sentencing and Courts Act came into force.[1] Included in the law is a clause outlawing 'noisy' protest.[2] This restriction prompted Baroness Natalie Bennett to cite the protest song 'The March of the Women' (1911) in support of the House of Lords' attempt to amend the act.[3] Partly in consequence of the new law, and the debates surrounding it, Britain was reported to have fallen down the ranks of countries that promote and protect freedom of expression.[4] This decline serves to highlight the importance of time-specific contexts in the long history of the regulation and repression of the protest song. Far from a Whiggish narrative of continually increasing governmental toleration, the story to be told is that – despite D:Ream's (and New Labour's) claim to the contrary – things can't only get better, and certainly not for the protest song or its singers.

Scholars of every historical period have noted that the praxis of censorship (broadly defined) is a complex riddle that requires contingent unravelling.[5] Bans are typically applied to what is thought 'offensive' or 'dangerous', or other such terms. But the key issue is how a work of art or news story comes to be seen as offensive to those with the power either to ban existing works or to repress opportunities for oppositional expression. Censorship is about a *process* in which something comes to be deemed offensive or dangerous. In understanding why music, in particular, has been banned or restricted, we seek to observe the political processes and principles that are invoked in the business of regulation.[6]

In this chapter we argue that what was personally and politically at stake for both protest singers and authorities has changed radically from the outset of our period until the present day. However, the processes and principles that underlie the shifting regulatory and legislative frameworks provided by successive English governments, which have consistently sought to control protesting and oppositional voices in the popular music trade, have effectively remained the same.

For at least four hundred years, English states have employed two key processes of control. The first of these processes – licensing – has always been designed to limit freedom of expression, to create barriers to accessing technologies of production, and to restrict systems of distribution, venues for performance, broadcasting channels, and streaming platforms. Enforcement of these systems has been achieved through a strategic diffusion of powers from the state to local governmental and commercial agencies, who are thus coerced and conscripted into delivering the state's agenda of control. The second process has involved the creation of a 'hostile environment' for producers and oppositional singers by making them vulnerable to prosecution and violent or financially debilitating punishments. These have been meted out variously by the state – for contravention of capaciously defined capital crimes, such as sedition and treason, or for lesser crimes, such as riot or vagrancy; by the Church – for crossing ill-defined boundaries of 'Christian' taste and decency, supported by Church laws until the 1650s, and Blasphemy Acts from 1650–2008; and by social conservatives – through use of the civil courts or appeals to the 'court' of public opinion. It is in this second process, the creation of the hostile environment, that the long-standing principles driving oppression of protest songs become clear.

In this chapter, we first investigate the long-term continuities of processes and principles of regulation, showing how they have led to both direct and indirect repression of oppositional songs and singers, many of whom were engaged in protest. Secondly, we consider the competing strategies of resistance employed, on the one hand, by creators and producers determined to be heard and, on the other hand, by authorities seeking to counteract the unintended cachet of repression that gives oxygen to protest. Finally, we conduct three case studies to explore the complex and changing contingencies of risk and repression in the early-modern, modern, and contemporary periods, and show how, nonetheless, there are underlying continuities in the conflictual relationship between protest song and authority.

LICENSING

Throughout our period, state authorities have used multiple licensing systems to provide an almost infinite array of legal obstacles with which to stop politically critical or socially offensive songs of any kind from being published or performed. At the same time, to avoid being held directly responsible for restrictive licensing, governments have delegated authority for awarding and policing licences to a multitude of agencies. This has included commercial corporations with overarching public responsibilities, such as the Stationers' Company (still extant, but a regulatory authority only between 1557 and 1695) and the publicly funded British Broadcasting Corporation (BBC), or the British Board of Film Classification (responsible for regulating music videos, as well as other audiovisual material); local authorities (variously magistrates, army militias, police, and local councils); licence holders (including distributors, shop owners, managers of performance venues); and even the general public. This long-standing strategy has ensured that, by creating anxiety within the industry over gaining and retaining operating licences, censorship processes have successfully permeated every corner of the popular music marketplace.

'Protest songs' have never been singled out as a category within these systems of obstruction. However, the possibility of creating or performing them *has* been additionally restricted by laws that have controlled the kinds of activity that constitute acts of protest, such as crowds or marches. Nonetheless, how well a protest song could negotiate or avoid the licensing system was and is dependent on the scale of production required to reach the targeted audience, and the availability of skilled producers and materials. Handwritten songs, such as 'Come all you Farmers' (1603) (discussed in chapter 2) and the Jacobite 'Sir John Fenwick's The Flower Amang Them' (1701), required only pen and paper and were circulated to perhaps no more than a hundred people.[7] During the early era of musical print, unlicensed production of oppositional or protest songs on a larger scale could only be achieved by private sponsorship and the formation of a conspiratorial group including a stationer (to provide paper), a printer, and as many amateur or professional singers and sellers as possible. Many of the songs on our list were published in this way. For example, 'The Sale of Esau's Birthright', which protested the outcome of a corrupt election in 1679, was sponsored by a political organisation and was printed by an activist printer. However, while anonymous publication limited the risk of prosecution, it also restricted the scope of distribution. About five thousand sheets were printed across eight editions, but their distribution was limited – both socially, to luxury traders, wealthy county voters, and political elites, and geographically, to a few Buckinghamshire and Northamptonshire towns, London, and Oxford. Meanwhile, more than thirty people who had sung or distributed the song found themselves in court, although both author and printer escaped.[8] Fearful of discovery, distributors of privately printed protest songs might simply scatter the sheets in the streets, just as, several centuries later, a Crass record protesting the Falklands War, 'Sheep Farming in the Falklands' (1983), was reportedly slotted into the sleeves of unconnected albums.[9]

For a protest song to reach a socially broad national audience has always necessitated access to the commercial sector, to capitalised technologies of mass production and well-organised systems of distribution – all of which were subjected to licence regulation – and thus requiring some political alignment between creators and producers. Such relationships were particularly pronounced between 1600 and 1710, as commercial producers were responsible for acquiring the necessary permission to publish individual songs.[10] In this period, commercial publishers of protest songs often coordinated their co-composition, by personally editing and/or employing in-house writers to extend extant theatre or court songs into ballads for the popular market, while also fundamentally changing their original political stance.[11] After 1710, the power of producers was somewhat restricted since books of songs (though not individual sheets) came under the auspices of new copyright and intellectual property laws. These imposed obligations on publishers and creators, and determined the means by which revenue was distributed. Songwriters, such as John Freeth (see chapter 5), could publish books of their own songs without fear of being plagiarised, although most songs were published in anthologies, without mention of the various authors' names.

Similar rights were extended to music sheets by 1810, although they were nearly impossible to enforce.[12] But these benefits were soon undermined by the recording technologies developed in the late nineteenth century. By the twentieth century, recording and mass pressing of shellac and vinyl records, and later CDs, all required substantial capitalisation and specialist production skills, leading to renewed competition over music rights. The intellectual property of creators was defined by complex laws of copyright, which, as Simon Frith and Lee Marshall have argued, 'provide the framework for every business decision in the industry'.[13]

As the example of 'The Sale of Esau's Birthright' shows, a major stumbling block to *private* production of physical music objects is the limitations it imposes on distribution and marketing, especially if we compare it with the national coverage of 'The Parliament Routed' (1653), which was published for the *retail* market. Systems of mass distribution typically require a network of licensed businesses and access to appropriate modes of transportation. All of this depends upon licences of some sort – whether for a London publisher's team of ballad-singers, a pedlar and cart travelling to markets and fairs, or a van delivering to established and trusted record shops on behalf of a production company. Any or all of these licensed agents could refuse to stock songs they deemed too offensive or risky. In the early period of print products, licensing of distributors was patchy, and unlicensed distributors could usually be hired where licensed ones feared to tread.

Commercial producers have perennially dictated what and who should be published and to whom works should be marketed. However, these powers became even more pronounced as recording companies took over the marketplace, and creators as well as songs became commercial commodities. For example, Mike Jones, lyricist of Latin Quarter, recalls how his band, which enjoyed considerable commercial success with the song 'Radio Africa' (1985), 'suffered censorship *within* the commodification process through the indifference, bemusement, and hostility of individual members of various marketing departments'.[14]

Systems of control within the music industry have an impact both on what kind of music is produced and what kind of politics it gives expression to. The use of genre categories and methods of portfolio management have had an impact, as music scholar Keith Negus has shown, on how performers and their music are managed and marketed.[15] With the advent, first, of downloading and, latterly, of streaming platforms, copyright law has become a key site in the struggle for control.[16] Companies such as Spotify and YouTube now dominate the regulated market, and their systems of payment and of automatic takedown are, it is argued, restricting the diversity of performers and plurality of content available to consumers.[17] This new environment, while offering lower barriers to entry, also increases the challenge of garnering attention and, by implication, the prospect of songs of protest reaching an audience.[18]

A quite different set of regulations and practices served to restrict the reach and impact of protest songs throughout our period, by requiring live performers and performance spaces to be licensed. Until the nineteenth century, professional performers, from concert musicians to street ballad-singers, were, more often than not, formally required to obtain licences either from the Lord Chamberlain, the Master of the Revels, or local magistrates.[19] They provided only limited security, however, as a licence awarded by one authority could be summarily revoked by another. As court records make clear, by the eighteenth and nineteenth centuries, more and more of the performers who travelled from place to place were unlicensed. The range of legislation in play was daunting, enabling public singers to be persecuted on grounds such as disturbing the peace, drunk or disorderly conduct, indecency, begging in the wrong parish, causing an obstruction of the highway, or conniving with pickpockets.[20] City corporations were especially strict in their provisions. While the City of London was most notorious for its controls, the corporation of Birmingham issued an order for the removal of all ballad-singers in 1794. On a single tour, the subversive singer David Love was arrested by the authorities of Newcastle, Durham, and Hull on pretexts ranging from a breach of the peace to suspected burglary.[21] Specific regulations restricting the activities of travelling musicians and classing them as 'vagrants' or 'rogues and vagabonds' remained on the statute books from the reign of Elizabeth I onwards. They were later adapted to add new kinds of performer, as in the reign of George II, when minstrels with hurdy-gurdies and hand organs were added to the list. Seen as inadequate, this legislation was updated via successive Street Music acts in 1827 and 1864, which renewed the powers of the police (and their various predecessors) to detain, fine, and move on any musicians deemed to be causing a public nuisance.[22] In all these instances, the vagueness of the legal wording provided the authorities with a deal of interpretative latitude that extended their control of public space still further.

Alehouses, taverns, and inns have long been venues for public or semi-public musical performance, but by the 1670s, dedicated 'music houses' began to appear in London and elsewhere. These were largely controlled via the annual victualling licence system. In the long eighteenth century, most minor or 'illegitimate' venues were relatively safe spaces for unregulated performance, policed more by a consensus of the patrons and landlord than by external authorities. As we saw in chapter 5, John Freeth's tavern in Birmingham was a haven for radical expression even in the repressive 1790s. Meanwhile, successive theatre acts were designed primarily to protect the monopoly of the 'patent' houses, such as London's Covent Garden and Drury Lane, over spoken drama (such as Shakespeare). This meant that other theatres were positively *encouraged* to focus their efforts on song, dance, and other mixed media until 1843. Again, in London, play texts had to be cleared by the Licenser of Plays prior to performance – but only the spoken dialogue (which had to be balanced by song and music) was closely scrutinised. A writer could simply scribble 'insert song here' and thereby smuggle in an entirely uncensored lyric.[23] In 1843, the Theatres Act subjected public performance venues to new forms of licensing. Though song was not specified by the act, managers were responsible for policing the content of performances. Derek Scott notes that 'a contract offered to performers at Collins's Music Hall, in Islington Green, required them to present any new song to the management for approval seven days before it was to be sung'. In Middlesex, 'if a manager failed to restrain indecent performers, then London County Council could step in and, if it was deemed necessary, withdraw the hall's licence'.[24]

From the twentieth century onwards, similarly coercive control by licence has steadily increased thanks to the overlapping of copyright regulations, entertainment and alcohol licences, and health and safety laws.[25] This welter of regulation has left commercial live performances at least as – if not more – subject to sanction as at any time in the past, with the potential for censorship under another guise.[26] In 2003, the government introduced the Licensing Act, which restricted the public performance of unamplified music in pubs. A decade later, grime music performances were being cancelled on the orders of the Metropolitan Police.[27] While these initiatives might be justified on grounds of health and safety or law and order, they could also be seen – particularly given what was being targeted – as limiting what music could do and say.[28]

In sum, the long history of the music industry has seen an almost continuous elaboration of licensing systems, creating a chilling environment with the *potential* to restrict what oppositional and protest songs could say, who could sing them, where and to whom. It has also seen the increasing delegation of power to licensing and policing local or commercial authorities.[29] At the same time, the economics of the trade and the development of copyright laws have tended to take power from creators and put it into the hands of a few producers, distributors, venues, broadcasters, and streaming platforms.[30] These developments tend to strengthen the hand of governments too. The small number of producers, relative to the number of creators, reduces the scale of monitoring required and increases economic risk for non-compliant creators and producers.

LEGALISED HOSTILITY

The second consistent feature of state control over protest and political song has been to create a 'hostile environment' to silence words or behaviour considered threatening to (rather than merely critical of) government security or social stability. The level of hostility and risk of personal harm has lessened over time, in direct correspondence with government confidence in its systems of control. For much of our period, the greatest dangers faced producers and performers who fell foul of capacious (and frequently capricious) laws of treason and seditious libel, which carried punishments that threatened not only livings and freedoms but also lives. From the 1630s until the 1800s, capital laws of seditious libel cut directly to the creative heart of song-making by bringing within their purview songs deemed to have 'imagined' the monarch's death or 'alienated' the affection of his subjects.[31] In addition, the ancient (and still extant) law of *Scandalum Magnatum* broadened the scope of sedition to incorporate libelling the monarch's agents: ministers, privy councillors, local magistrates, and town corporations. Those found guilty faced indefinite imprisonment until impossibly huge fines (sometimes thousands of pounds) were either paid, forgiven by the libel victim, or pardoned by the monarch.[32]

Printers and publishers could avoid, or successfully defend themselves against, prosecution through anonymous or pseudonymous publication practices, or by pleading ignorance to the import of satirical song. Public performers were (and are) infinitely more vulnerable.[33] Performers faced laws regarding seditious libel as well as a raft of measures aimed at preventing 'unauthorised mobility', a 'breach of the peace', or loitering 'with intent'. These include vagrancy laws, initiated in 1572, renewed in 1824, and only theoretically repealed in 2022. The Police, Crime, Sentencing and Courts Act (2022) designed to replace it maintains the power to regulate noisy expressions of complaint, and at time of writing, its status relative to vagrancy remains a matter of intense political debate.[34]

Under these laws, performers of offensive songs could be arrested for vagrancy, tied to the back of a cart, and whipped as they were taken out of the parish. Repeat offenders were branded. If singing or selling songs were deemed by local magistrates to be spreading alarm or threatened disorder, performers could be bound over, fined, and pilloried on the common law basis of disturbing the 'King's peace'. These laws affected all travelling musicians, whether they performed outdoors – on streets, in fields, at fairs or markets – or indoors, in venues such as taverns, inns, or alehouses. The indoor performers were more likely to be reported by anxious licence holders or concerned members of the public. The terms of the offence were renewed and renamed as a 'breach of the peace' in a 1936 statute. From the 1970s until 1981, 'sus' laws, which were extensions of the 1824 act, permitted police to arrest anyone on suspicion that a crime *might* take place. In 1974, Dennis Bovell, then leader of the reggae band Matumbi and part of the soundsystem scene, found himself a victim of these laws and their susceptibility to corrupt and discriminatory policing. He was arrested for 'causing affray' at a soundsystem event that had been raided by the police. Bovell was accused of playing the song 'Burn Down Babylon' to provoke the crowd into resisting the officers. The record had been played, but not by Bovell; he refused to name the 'culprit'. After two trials, he was convicted of affray and given a custodial sentence of three years, though he was released on appeal after six months. The sus laws not only cost him eighteen months of his life but also almost deprived him of a long and fruitful musical career.[35]

PRINCIPLES OF CENSORSHIP

Licensing and legalised hostility have provided the main mechanisms for exercising censorship over the protest song. But, as we noted earlier, the story does not end there. It is also important to ask *why* such means were deemed necessary. What threat was the protest song thought to represent, and what principles were applied in identifying the danger posed? We highlight four themes that help answer these questions: diplomacy, disorder, disaffection, and disgust.

Diplomacy

States have consistently acted to repress songs that might disturb the UK's international standing or internal security at times of war. An early, often misunderstood act of censorship on this account took place after the Battle of Agincourt (1415), when – in order to build bridges and prevent outbreaks of violence – Henry V ordered that 'no Ballad or Song should be made or sung, more th[a]n of Thanksgiving to God for [the King's] happy Victory and safe Returne; but without words of either disgracing the French, or extolling the English'.[36] In the 1600s, the renowned ballad writer William Elderton was ordered to withdraw a 'well affected' song in case it offended a visiting ambassador, while Venetian and English ambassadors crossed swords (not literally) over mutually disrespectful songs.[37] In 1792, as Britain was preparing for war with France, issues of national security lay behind the Pitt government's proclamation against 'Seditious Writings and Publications' (which encompassed both printed song sheets and songbooks), in hopes of controlling campaigns by English radicals emboldened by the French Revolution. Similar wartime concerns prompted the draconian censorship of entertainments of all kinds during both world wars through a series of acts in 'Defence of the Realm'.

In more recent times, it is possible to read diplomatic fears into the BBC's 1967 decision to ban the Beatles' song 'A Day in the Life' (with its references to death and drug use) on the same day that the band was representing their country via the first-ever global-wide satellite broadcast of 'All You Need is Love'.[38] It may be that fears of 'political contamination' lay behind the US government's refusal to grant a visa to Ewan MacColl in 1964 and the investigation of John Lennon by the FBI in the 1970s.[39] By the 1980s, however, despite numerous songs protesting the war with Argentina, and widespread fear of the Cold War bringing about nuclear armageddon, the UK authorities felt unthreatened by protest songs and singers, even if they included leaked official material. Frankie Goes to Hollywood's anti-nuclear-war dance record, 'Two Tribes' (1984), was claimed by its producer to be 'the first genuine protest song for eight years, picking holes in the Official Secrets Act and firing at the two great world powers more than a pop record ever has'.[40] The song soared to success: it sold 1.5 million copies and topped the charts for nine weeks, featuring on all the mainstream chart shows. Though the song's effectiveness as a protest song was dismissed by critics, Dorian Lynskey argues that it 'translated the era's pervasive fear into crazed celebration' and provided 'thousands of young listeners [with] an unforgettable introduction to the whole concept of nuclear war'.[41]

Disorder

Songs that might promote uncontrollable public disorder have been of paramount concern to local and national governments. Active intolerance has emerged most often when the state's internal powers have been restricted to voluntary groups (parish constables and local militias) rather than professional forces (a standing army from *c.*1689 and a police force from *c.*1829) as well as limited communication systems.[42] Thus in 1596, when Thomas Deloney wrote a ballad warning of the risk of hunger in London, and advising the government how to act, both he and his song were seized for fear his song would spark uncontrollable food riots in the city. Deloney was held for a short time, and all copies of his ballad were burned by the hangman, but the government also took action to improve food supplies to the city.[43] Weakened governments could not combat the huge street protests in London, many of them incited, encouraged, and choregraphed by songs, that were central to the overturning of regimes in 1640, in 1660, or in 1688. In the case of the latter, one protest song was said to have prompted the majority of the army to desert the Catholic James II for the Protestant William of Orange (see chapter 4).[44] By contrast, strengthened but anxious governments brutally deployed their limited powers when crowds challenged their policies with songs and actions. In 1643, parliament's troops took action against a march for peace – called a 'tumult' at the time – by five thousand women: 'The

Trained-Band advised [the women] to come down [from parliament's door], and first pulled them; and afterwards to fright them, Shot Powder; But [the women] cry'd out, Not[h]ing but Powder; and having Brickbatts in the Yard, threw them apace at the Train-Band, who then Shot Bullets, and kill'd a Ballad-Singer with one Arm, that was heartning on the Women'.[45]

After 1707, the governments of a newly United Kingdom began to define and legislate against the threats that protesting crowds posed. Indeed, a song entitled 'The Gentlecrafts Complaint', written for the 'vast Multitude of Shoemakers' who presented a petition outside parliament on 26 May 1714, played its part in the passing of the Riot Act in 1714.[46] The petition begged the government to reduce exports of 'unworked' leather, which impoverished shoemakers at home by raising the cost of their raw materials. The song set out the shoemakers' case, and encouraged them to believe that their petition was well-received and that redress would be forthcoming. In the event, however, the parliamentary minutes described the peaceful protest as the 'Riotous Petition of the Shoemakers' and immediately passed an order reminding the city authorities of their responsibilities to prevent 'tumultuous assemblies'.[47] In the immediate wake of the shoemakers' mass petition and other crowd activities, a new Riot Act came into force in August 1715. It gave local officials power to read a proclamation ordering illegally assembled groups of more than twelve people to disperse or face the death penalty.[48] A sense of flickering government confidence in its controlling powers might be detected in the Seditious Meetings Act of 1795, which extended the size of an unlawful assembly to fifty and reduced the consequences of failing to disperse to transportation. If it did indicate confidence, it was only temporary: the act was repealed in 1817, leaving the more draconian Riot Act in place until 1967.

Songs that accompanied or encouraged mass protest have been relatively common over the centuries. There were those that petitioned over issues such as food supply, as in Lawrence White's campaign of songs and speeches or the 'Song of the Hunger Marchers' (1934).[49] Local environmental concerns inspired 'The Powte's Complaint' (1619), 'The Newgate Street Petition' (1823), and Extinction Rebellion's rewrite of 'A Nightingale Sang in Berkeley Square' (2019).[50] Where these were peaceful and respectful, they had long been considered an acceptable form of political communication.[51] However, songs that informed and helped to cohere mass protests seeking to undermine the constitution were a very different matter. They brought protestors, musicians, and singers into mortal danger, not least in 1819, when a mass meeting at Peterloo was brutally repressed by the military. Samuel Bamford, who survived the onslaught, recalled the destruction of his group's 'big drum' by a yeomanry horse, while many of those singing songs at the event were massacred.[52] Peterloo prompted the government of the day to pass the Six Acts, which together aimed to suppress both mass petitioning and radicalism. Nevertheless, far from being silenced, even more songs followed, protesting the government's murderous response to Peterloo and its renewed campaign of repression.[53]

More recent reaction to fears of music's disorderly effects were evident in government attempts to legislate against 'free festivals' and 'illegal raves' in the 1960s and 1980s.[54] In the 1970s, police and other authorities responded to the possibility of disorder caused by shops displaying the cover of the Sex Pistols' *Never Mind the Bollocks, Here's the Sex Pistols* album. The offenders were charged under the Vagrancy Act of 1824.[55] At the University of East Anglia, the vice-chancellor decided to cancel the first night of the Sex Pistols' Anarchy tour in 1976 because of the 'threat of violence' that he feared would result from their performance.[56]

In the early years of the twenty-first century, as mentioned earlier, London's Metropolitan Police assumed the role of direct and indirect censor. Their target was urban Black music, such as grime and drill. In 2010, for example, the Met caused a tour by the grime artist Giggs to be cancelled.[57] Their argument was that Giggs, who had served a prison sentence for gun offences, posed a threat to public order because of the audience he attracted and the celebration of violence that his music was believed to represent. These concerns were institutionalised by the introduction of Form 696 in 2008. This required venues to provide a detailed account of what was to be performed, and under what conditions, before they were granted a licence. Critics noted that it was used primarily to target Black venues and acts.[58] The form had a chilling effect on the performance of politically charged urban music. It was discontinued in 2017, but the Met continued to target grime and drill, insisting that videos be taken down from the Internet.[59] Lawyer Keir Monteith reported that 'the Met asked for 510 music videos to be taken down from YouTube in 2021. Only 3 per cent remain. This represents a year-on-year increase of video censorship of almost 300 per cent'.[60]

Disaffection

Just as concerning for the authorities has been the capacity of protest songs to encourage disaffection by bringing organs of state, figures of authority, or public policy into disrepute.[61] The clearest articulation of this concern first occurred in 1627, during legal debate between the great jurist Edward Coke and other privy councillors over what to do about a group of fiddlers who had performed a song for a private group in a tavern that was disrespectful to the king and his ministers.[62] Coke argued that 'political libels were seditious because they weakened the ties of respect that both constituted and naturalized hierarchical authority and that they therefore implicitly attacked the king even if they explicitly attacked only a royal servant or official'.[63] Another lawyer pointed out that 'such a thing which alienateth the subjects affection from their soveraigne is treason'.[64] It was decided to make an example of the men, who were subjected to multiple public whippings, brandings, and pillorying in Staines, where the song had been sung, and in London, the heart of government and the song trade.

Much harder for authorities to control were songs in which the ethos of the singer commanded popular respect – from the (often) anonymous 'tom-tell-troth' persona of the early modern balladeer to the trusted cultural commentators of the contemporary era, with access to the cultural and monetary capital required to mobilize protest regardless of authoritarian restraints.[65] See, for example, the ban imposed on Paul McCartney's 'Give Ireland Back to the Irish' by the BBC and other broadcasters. The record still reached number 16 in the charts.[66] As DJ John Peel pointed out: 'The act of banning it is a much stronger political act than the contents of the record itself'.[67]

Bringing the authority of the state to bear on the act of singing can have the effect of creating distrust and a sense of grievance. In July 1649,

6.1 • Greenham Common women singing as they block the gate at a United States Air Force base, 1982.

an old woman singing and selling songs that disparaged the parliament was attacked by soldiers, but she was defended by local shopkeepers, leading to a brawl. The affair became headline news in the royalist press.[68] Such attacks could last long in the memory. A demonstration by striking workers in 1842 was recalled in 1880 by writer Frank Peel, who, as a ten-year-old in Halifax, 'witnessed a very large crowd of women turn-outs standing "in front of the magistrates and the military" daring "them to kill them if they liked". "They then struck up [Samuel Bamford's] THE UNION HYMN … [and] defiantly stood in their ranks as the special constables marched up, but their music did not save them, for the constables did not hesitate to strike them with their staves"'.[69]

Sometimes, rather than using violence or suppression, governments have resorted to drowning out dissenting songs by encouraging the mass production of songs promoting loyalty and love for authority and the nation from committed or commissioned producers. This occurred, for example, during the Tory Reaction (1681–84), which saw hundreds of loyal songs being produced in support of the Stuart regime.[70] Another such episode occurred in the 1790s, as we describe in the '1793–1803 and the Creation of a Hostile Environment' case study below, and once again during the world wars. But whatever the tactics used, the government has found itself assailed by the sound of disaffection. Between 1981 and 2000, despite local opposition, frequent physical attacks, arrests and one death, hundreds of women, many of them middle-aged and middle-class and expressly legitimating their cause by emphasising their roles as mothers, set up peace camps at Greenham Common in protest against nuclear weapons. Their cause and coherence vitally sustained by singing songs from the Greenham Common songbook, in December 1982, thirty thousand women were inspired to join hands around the base in solidarity with the protest. In April 1983, about seventy thousand women formed a 14-mile human chain from Greenham to an ordinance factory in Aldermaston.[71] Notably, the powerful memory of these songs surfaced at our project's final concert. Several of the women in the audience knew by heart the Greenham Common song 'Brazen Hussies' and, unbidden, joined the performers by singing along.[72]

Disgust

A powerful means by which to counteract the power of the protest song – especially in the sphere of popular music – has been the use of terms such as 'lewdness', 'decency', and 'good taste'. Some of these emanate from the old church courts that policed morality and, subsequently, from the time of the British republic in the 1650s, enshrined in a long series of Blasphemy acts.[73] Striking parallels can be found in the language of disapproval elicited in response to Crass's 'How Does It Feel (To Be the Mother of a Thousand Dead)?' (1982) – described by a Conservative MP as 'the most vicious, scurrilous, and obscene record that has ever been produced' – and responses to 'The Parliament Routed' (1653) – described by a puritan divine as a 'base and scurrilous' ballad set 'in the most scummy and vilest Language conceivable'.[74] During the 1650s, religious conservatives used popular songs such as 'The downfall of women Preachers' to protest at the shocking activities of radical sects, some of whom (it was said) advocated free love and allowed women to preach.[75] These fears led to the first Blasphemy Act of 1650, a later incarnation of which would be used against music to great effect by moral campaigner Mary Whitehouse (although, in the case of 'How does it feel', the attorney general announced that he would not prosecute).[76] In 1984, a BBC DJ, acting alone as the guardian of public decency, decided that Frankie Goes to Hollywood's 'Relax' was 'obscene', prompting the broadcaster to ban it.[77]

Disgust as a cause for repression of protest could also come from people involved in the production process. In 1978, a Crass song, 'Asylum', which attacked religion, was to appear on the band's debut EP *The Feeding of the Five Thousand*, but the pressing plant refused to produce it until the track was removed. In protest, the record opened with two minutes of silence, entitled 'The Sound of Free Speech'.[78]

More viciously, disgust also prompted the public to act in defence of state authority, as in 1977, when members of the Sex Pistols were physically attacked by 'a mob', one of whom struck John Lydon (Johnny Rotten) with a machete, shouting as he did so: 'We love our queen, you bastard!'[79] Here, we are touching not only on state regulation but also on the effects of what John Stuart Mill famously called 'the tyranny of the prevailing opinion and feeling', or the ways in which liberty of thought and discussion can be limited by the threat of social sanctions for acting or speaking inappropriately. The flip side of this, however, is the ways in which (as we saw in chapters 2 and 3) this creates opportunities for disruptive dissent, for polemic intended to upset proprieties and so to call into question what can be talked about, in what way, and by what sort of person (see the discussion of Ian Dury's 'Spasticus Autisticus' (1981) in Case Study: The BBC and Corporate Censorship (1930–83) below).

SUBVERSIVE CENSORSHIP

So far, discussion of censorship has focused on the *direct* action of governments and their agents. But censorship can occur without interventions of this kind. It can take the form of self-censorship, or 'constitutive censorship'.[80] This is witnessed in decisions *not* to commission, create, or contract a performance, product, or publication. Such decisions may be hidden from view, or may even be unconscious. Here we might note the Stationers' Company ordering the burning of unlicensed ballads in their own hall; or HMV's decision not to sell Crass's *The Feeding of the Five Thousand*. Neither example might fit neatly as examples of censorship, being, on the one hand, a decision to uphold property rights and, on the other, exercising a retailer's freedom to choose what to sell – or to bin. Following the decision to destroy copies of the Crass/Poison Girls double A-side 'Persons Unknown'/'Bloody Revolutions', the managing director of HMV wrote to staff: 'The question is, does the commercial advantage of selling Crass records outweigh the risk of prosecution? I am not prepared to have HMV dragged through the courts'. This decision might be interpreted as an exercise of market freedom, or a form of censorship (deriving from fear of legal repercussions). There is a fine line between censorship by the self and by another.[81]

Aside from the complexities of self-censorship, commercial considerations do not themselves necessarily lead to a decision to withdraw a song from sale. There is a cachet to censorship that has persuaded producers to take risks on songs likely to cause a stir because of the benefits, either commercial or political, that can accrue. Censorship can boost sales. 'The Parliament Routed' was published by supporters of the Levellers for the commercial market and was performed all over the country, but after the printer was imprisoned, a new (anonymously published) edition appeared that was widely distributed both at home and to English exiles abroad.[82] The Sex Pistols' banned song 'God Save the Queen' reached number 2 (maybe even number 1) in the charts. Several of 'The Sale of Esau's Birthright''s eight editions were published after depositions began to be taken in preparation for a libel trial.[83] 'Relax' not only reached number 1 but also remained there for several months.[84] However, sales driven by the cachet of censorship are not the only criteria by which repression may help the effectiveness of protest songs: sometimes just one copy is enough to have an impact. Although all the copies of Deloney's 1586 song, mentioned earlier, were destroyed, the government authorities took its advice and acted to improve food supplies.[85] In 1984, when the South African arm of Chrysalis Records asked not to be sent copies of

'Free Nelson Mandela' by The Special AKA for fear of being closed down by the regime, a single copy of the song was used in broadcasts to large audiences over the public-address system at football matches.[86]

In order to counteract the alluring effect of action by government agencies in response to the provocations of artists, another long-standing strategy of government control has been to draw the teeth of protest songs by treating them as unimportant. Adorno described the process as the incorporation and neutralization of dissent.[87] This was the principle followed by Oliver Cromwell, who went no further in prosecuting singers or distributors after the printer of 'The Parliament Routed' was jailed. (Indeed, Cromwell was known for appreciating and laughing at witty songs that attacked him.[88]) This is a significant challenge to the power of protest songs. The sting is removed from works that can be recast as, in Tom Wolfe's mocking phrase, merely 'radical chic'. Today's governmental and commercial agencies may ignore the provocations of protest songs and singers, or may choose to re-frame or reinterpret them. Dave's song 'Question Time' (discussed in chapters 1 and 3) received an Ivor Novello Award. As radical critic Mark Fisher argued, it may be that acts of aesthetic protest are not merely impotent, but the very thing that keeps us in line: 'So long as we believe (in our hearts) that capitalism is bad, we are free to continue to participate in capitalist exchange'. For Fisher, protest can become nothing more than a 'carnivalesque background noise', hard to distinguish from corporatized forms of simulated politics – like 2005's Live 8, which presents poverty as something that can be willed away if people can just be nicer or more generous, without questioning the systematic forces that induce it, and with which we – and our protest – collude.[89]

Our concern so far has been with the general patterns, principles, and practices of censorship that were shared across four centuries. We have highlighted the continuities in both direct and indirect forms of censorship and have explored the politics of those who censor and those who are censored. Moving from these broad-brush accounts, the following case studies of censorship praxis, from the 1680s to the 1980s, exemplify how these processes worked and that many of the factors discussed above can be at play in any given instance.

Case Study

'A Ra-ree Show' and the Ultimate State Sanction

The risks faced by early-modern makers and performers of oppositional songs were immense. Producers were imprisoned and fined, their stock burned, and their presses seized and demolished. Performers not only suffered official (usually summary) imprisonment, whippings, and occasionally branding (if they were serial offenders) but also were subjected to violent attacks by soldiers and people in the street outraged by songs that scandalised the state and its governors. Producers and performers convicted of sedition were commonly sentenced to the pillory, where, pinned in place, they were targeted by largely unrestrained crowds who could inflict serious injuries. (Though some crowds protected victims deemed to have been tried unjustly.[90]) On top of their immediate losses and hurts, public punishments damaged the reputations and, crucially, the financial credit of producers, causing ongoing, sometimes lifelong penury for the families of those who openly protested against the state. Nevertheless, nothing compares to the severity of the treatment meted out to carpenter and Whig campaigner Stephen Colledge. He was condemned to death as a traitor for singing his protest song at the wrong time, in the wrong place, and to the wrong people in 1681.

A committed political activist, Stephen Colledge wanted Charles II's only legitimate heir, his avowedly Catholic brother James, Duke of York, to be prevented from succeeding to the throne. The prospect of a Catholic monarch was terrifying at a time when 'tyrannical' Catholic absolutism was well established in France and Spain. In England everyone knew that 'Bloody Mary' (the last Catholic monarch) had burned hundreds of Protestants in Smithfield. Fears were rife that, as king, James might reimpose 'popery' on England, enforce conversions, dispense with parliament's right to control taxation, and pass laws. In an effort to close down parliamentary opposition, Charles II had called no fewer than three general elections between 1679 and 1681. Yet despite the court's coaxing and bribing, the exclusionist Whigs, with their well-organised press campaign of songs and pamphlets, seemed to be growing in power and popularity. In a last-ditch attempt to stave off opposition, Charles ordered his third 'exclusion' parliament to assemble in ardently Tory Oxford, instead of London where Whigs reigned supreme. At this juncture, Stephen Colledge decided to join the Whig Lords and MPs as they rode to Oxford, intending to voice his political demands in song outside the parliament's meeting place.

The illustrated song that Colledge brought with him to Oxford had been prepared by a team of committed producers. Sporting a sophisticated satirical cartoon and eighteen verses, it had been refined after several outings in previous months, mainly for the entertainment of Whig supporters gathered in private houses. Colledge had also tested it out in a few London taverns, singing early versions of the song and showing first drafts of the image to men who later proved to be government informants.[91] The print version that travelled to Oxford had been amended to make it less prosecutable – it carried a false imprint, claiming it had been published by a well-known pro-Tory publisher.

Assisted by notorious Whig publisher and polemicist Francis 'Elephant' Smith, Colledge's plan was to win support for the Whig cause by performing the song, distributing the printed sheets, and handing out ribbons that carried the slogan 'No Popery, No Slavery' outside the doors where the MPs and Lords entered their meeting places.[92] In order to match his performance to the 'Ra-ree Show' title (referring to a spectacle or picture show), Colledge also dressed up: he wore a silk buff coat and a helmet covered in fine cloth, and carried a (near-useless) weapon.[93] Parliament's serjeant of arms, a protagonist in the song, stopped Colledge coming into the parliament's meeting place. He was forced to perform his scurrilous song out in the street for the parliament men as they exited and for the general population of Oxford.

The song was set in the form of a dialogue between Leviathan (the people) and Topham (parliament's serjeant of arms). Gary de Krey's succinct description tells how it depicted Charles II as a deceptive showman, as a master of political puppetry who held 'freeborn fools' [like the Whigs] in contempt, and who intended to substitute 'brave strong government' [i.e., absolutist rule] for the rule of king in parliament. The ballad also criticized the bishops and the clergy of the Anglican church as inclined to popery, and it recalled the punishment of Charles I 'for fleecing England's flocks'. It concluded with a call 'to pull down [the] raree show' (Charles's duplicitous political game), to preserve parliament, and to 'free … the nation', for 'the hunt's begun … like father, like son' … [In the cartoon] Charles II was shown being knocked over by agents of parliament, while bishops and courtiers were stuffed into the king's bag of political tricks.[94]

While outside, Colledge criticised the king and his ministers, inside, both Commons and Lords were coming to an agreement over an exclusion bill. However, just a week after parliament assembled, Charles II unexpectedly entered the house, dressed in his full regalia, and dismissed it. Colledge and his publisher Smith rode home with a cohort of Whig MPs, shocked but determined to continue singing and distributing 'The Ra-ree Show' as part of a campaign to force the king to hold new elections – if not something more revolutionary. But that is not how the story ended.

Following parliament's dismissal, an organised Tory press campaign deluged the country with propaganda in prose and song accusing the Whigs of wanting a new civil war. National opinion changed and the government took determined action. Six months later, one Whig leader, the Earl of Shaftesbury, was in prison awaiting trial for treason. Another, the Duke of Monmouth, was in exile. The song's Whig publisher Francis Smith had fled for New England. And on 31 August 1681, Stephen Colledge stood on a scaffold in Oxford where, to the delight of a jeering royalist crowd, he was hanged and quartered as a traitor. Prevented access to a lawyer (one who tried to help him was arrested), Colledge nonetheless, during his trial, vigorously denied being the author or engraver of 'A Ra-ree Show', but he was unable himself to persuade either judge or jury. In truth, his fate was decided by the king long before his case was heard by any court. Colledge's last letter warned his son against 'that folly of Riming, for … it will do you hurt'.[95] Charles II relented so far as to permit Colledge's family to bury his remains, rather than having them publicly displayed, but only in hope of preventing Colledge from becoming a Whig martyr.

'A Ra-ree Show' epitomizes our definition of a protest song. By means of its satirical dialogue, it promoted both a reasoned argument against the government's actions and an alternative political programme. But in doing so, it also transgressed three of the criteria that we identify as justifying censorship. In the first place, his prosecutors claimed, Colledge's performance incited disorder. It was a clear call to arms. Not only was he himself armed with sword and helmet during his performance outside the building where parliament and the king met, but his distribution of ribbons also suggested he was providing badges for followers to wear as soldiers in the field. Secondly, the song clearly promoted disaffection. It engaged in harsh ad hominem attacks on the king, who was described as being reduced to a 'Quaking King in a Hollow Oak' when he unsuccessfully invaded England with a Scottish army in 1651. Even more seriously, his prosecutors argued that it was treasonable, because both song and image had clearly 'imagined the King's death' by showing the king toppled over, and by suggesting he would be arrested. The latter, they said, was the equivalent of being killed, as arrest had resulted in the execution of the king's father in 1649 – an event to which the song also referred irreverently. Most importantly of all, however, the song provoked widespread disgust that aristocratic Whigs had permitted a lowly carpenter, dressed in a ridiculous costume, to humiliate the king and his brother in front of the assembled political nation. While it was acceptable for men of rank to demonstrate their position by wearing a sword, a lowly joiner could claim no such privilege. Colledge's costume presented a classic case of the 'mechanic' or 'leathern cap' attempting to subvert the natural social order as had happened during the Civil Wars. Disgust at such social subversion long permeated English society. As de Krey notes: 'Even Lord Macaulay, writing a century and a half later, judged Colledge from an aristocrat perspective, dismissing him as "a noisy and violent demagogue of mean birth and education"'.[96]

A RA-REE SHOW.

To the Tune of I am a Senceleſs Thing.

Leviathan.

COme hither, *Topham*, come, with a hey, with a hey,
Bring a Pipe and a Drum, with a ho,
Where e're about I go,
Attend my *Ra-ree ſhow*,
With a hey, Trany nony nony no.

Topham.

That monſtrous Foul *Beaſt*, with a hey, with a hey,
Has *Houſes Twain* in's Cheſt, with a ho,
O *Cooper*, *Hughs* and *Snow*,
Stop Thief with *Ra-ree Show*,
With a hey, Trany nony nony no.

For if he ſhould eſcape, with a hey, with a hey,
With *Halifaxes Trap* with a ho,
He'd carry good *Dom. Com.*
Unto the Pope of *Rome*,
With a hey, Trany nony nony no.

Levi.

Be quiet ye Dull Tools, with a hey, with a hey,
As other Free-born Fools with a ho,
Do not all Gaping ſtand,
To ſee my *Slight of Hand?*
With a hey, Trany nony nony no.

'Tis not to *Rome* that I, with a hey, with a hey,
Lugg about my *Trumpery*, with a ho,
But *Oxford*, *York*, *Carlile*,
And round about the *Iſle*,
With a hey, Trany nony nony no.

But if *they* would come out, with a hey, with a hey,
Let them firſt make a Vote, with a ho,
To yield up all they have,
And *Tower Lords* to ſave,
With a hey, Trany nony nony no.

Top.

Now that is very hard, with a hey, with a hey,
Thou art worſe than [illegible] *Guard*, with a ho,
And *Clifford*, *Danby*, *Hide*,
Hallifax does all outride,
With a hey, Trany nony nony no.

Holy Ghoſt in Bagg of Cloak, with a hey, with a hey,
Quaking King in hollow Oak, with a ho,
And *Roſamond* in Bower,
All Badges are of Power,
With a hey, Trany nony nony no.

And Popularity, with a hey, with a hey,
Adds Power to Majeſty, with a ho,
But *Dom. Com.* in Idle Eaſe,
Will all the World diſpleaſe,
With a hey, Trony nony nony no.

Levi.

Let 'um hate ſo they fear, with a hey, with a hey,
Curſt Fox has the beſt Chear, with a ho,
Two States in *Blindhouſe* pent,
Make brave ſtrong Government,
With a hey, Trany nony nony no.

Top.

But Child of Heathen *Hobbs*, with a hey, with a hey,
Remember old *Dry Bobs*, with a ho,
For Fleecing *Englands* Flocks,
Long Fed with Bits and Knocks,
With a hey, Trany nony nony no.

Levi.

What's paſt, is not to come, with a hey, with a hey,
Now Safe is *David's* Bm, with a ho,
Then hey for *Oxford* ho,
Strong Government *Ra-ree Show*,
With a hey, Trany nony nony no.

Ra-ree Show is Reſolv'd, with a hey, with a hey,
This is worſe than Diſſolv'd, with a ho,
May the mighty weight at's back
Make's Lecherous Loyns to crack,
With a hey, Trany nony nony no.

Me-thinks he ſeems to Stagger with a hey, with a hey,
Who but now did ſo Swagger, with a ho,
Gods-Fiſh he's Stuck i'th' Mire,
And all the Fat's i'th' Fire,
With a hey, Trany nony nony no.

Help *Cooper*, *Hughs*, and *Snow*, with a hey, with a hey,
To pull down *Ra-ree Show*, with a ho,
So, So, the Gyant's down
Let's *Maſters* out of *Pound*,
With a hey, Trany nony nony no.

And now you have freed the Nation, with a hey, with a hey,
Cram in the *Convocation*, with a ho,
With *Penſioners* all and Some,
Into this *Cheſt* of *Rome*,
With a hey, Trany nony nony no,

And thruſt in *ſix* and *Twenty*, with a hey, with a hey,
With *Not Guilty*, good plenty, with a ho,
And hout them hence away
To *Cologne* or *Breda*,
With a hey, Trany nony nony no.

Ha-loo the *Hunts* begun, with a hey, with a hey,
Like Father, Like Son, with a ho,
Ra-ree Show in *French*-Lap,
Is gone to take a Nap,
And *Succeſſor* has the Clap,
With a hey, Trany nony nony no.

London, Printed for *B. T.* and Sold at his Shop *Pauls* Church-yard: For the good of the Publick, 1681.

6.2 • 'A Ra-ree Show', (B. Tooke (pseud.) [F. Smith]), 1681. This single-sheet song and separate engraving were both attributed to Stephen Colledge. The image and song lyrics were sold together but were printed separately.

Case Study

1793-1803 and the Creation of a Hostile Environment

Perhaps no decade epitomises the contested nature of protest song's expression and repression more than the years 1793–1803. Bookended by two declarations of war by Britain upon France (the first following the execution of Louis XVI, the second ending the brief Treaty of Amiens), this was a period of revolutionary and counter-revolutionary fervour, characterised by fears of – and hopes for – insurrection from within and invasion from without. The government of William Pitt the Younger, in power throughout these years, launched its own 'reign of terror' against radicals of all kinds (including balladeers), suspending or revoking a series of rights and freedoms, and staging prominent trials of a number of writers. Below and alongside the official state, other forces – societies, individuals, spontaneous collectives – were also highly instrumental in the repression of protest song, and indeed enjoyed rather more success than the Tory government and its lawyers.

Pitt's 'Terror' hinged on the suspension of habeas corpus in 1794, allowing for arrest and imprisonment without charge or reasonable proof, a measure not unlike – but far more wide-ranging than – the notorious sus laws of the 1980s. Working through a system of local authorities, such as justices of the peace (often regional landowners) and with the connivance of an extensive state-run spy network, an increasingly centralised state engendered a climate of fear and suspicion that was as much about the possibility of surveillance as its actual implementation. In 1795, the Treasonable and Seditious Practices Act and the Seditious Meetings Act – commonly referred to as the Two Acts – effectively annulled all freedoms of assembly and expression. Yet even before these new official instruments, the effect of counter-revolutionary censorship had been felt.

In Sheffield, radical young printer James Montgomery was caught out by a technicality. In January 1795, he was charged with publishing the song 'A Patriotic Song by a Clergyman of Belfast'. Written in 1792 in support of the French Revolution by Thomas Stott of Dromore to a tune by loyalist composer Charles Dibdin the Elder, it contained the following verse, concerning the invasion of France by the Duke of Brunswick:

> Europe's fate on the contest's decision depends;
> Most important its issue will be;
> For should France be subdued, Europe's liberty ends;
> If she triumphs, the world will be free.[97]

Montgomery pointed out that several newspapers had published the song in 1792, without causing offence. But in 1792, Britain had not been at war with France. Now that the two countries *were* at war, the indictment set out to prove that Montgomery's printing of the song could only have served 'to degrade, vilify, and traduce our said Lord the King and his Government of this realm, and his conduct respecting the said War'. This was a landmark case, noteworthy in a number of respects. It was Montgomery, not the song's singer Joseph Jordan, who was prosecuted, and Montgomery chose to pair the song on a ballad sheet with Edward Rushton's anti-impressment song 'The Tender's Hold' (*c.*1792).[98]

Throughout Montgomery's trial, it was clear that he was a marked man. This was in no small part because he had featured in the more (in)famous Treason Trials of 1794, in London, as the author of a subversive hymn to be sung on the fast day of 28 February.[99] These were practically show trials, stage-managed by government to intimidate the radical cause into silence.

Songs also featured prominently in the evidence against Thomas Hardy, John Horne Tooke, and John Thelwall. We focus on the last of these as he was a notable songwriter. Since the trial took place *prior* to the passing of the Two Acts in December 1795, the prosecution transparently lacked confidence in their ability to condemn Thelwall's songs as treasonable. Though three of his works were produced in court, they were not read aloud – despite the repeated and at times jocular requests of Thomas Erskine, the defence counsel, that the songs be heard by the jury. Instead, as Thelwall contended in his account of the trial, other and more conclusively treasonable songs *were* read aloud, linked to Thelwall by implication, 'and thus the Court was left to suppose, and many persons, both in and out of Court did suppose that those bloodthirsty stanzas were the production of my pen'.[100]

The three unread songs, by contrast, *had* been previously published by Thelwall, and sung at meetings of the London Corresponding Society, the radical organisation of which Hardy was secretary. In the wake of his acquittal, along with that of his comrades, Thelwall took the provocative step of republishing the songs in his new journal the

Tribune, along with a commentary condemning the judicial process, in order 'that the public may see how far they support the character so insidiously given to them'.[101] At least a thousand copies of this three-penny journal were circulated, extending the reach of the songs, which were well calculated to find a wider audience, each being set to an appropriate and accessible melody.[102] 'A Sheepshearing Song' was set to the ubiquitous 'A-Hunting We Will Go'; 'Britain's Glory' to the tune of 'The Golden Days of Good Queen Bess' by the Birmingham journalist-cum-stand-up John 'Brush' Collins; and 'News from Toulon' to the enormously popular political tune of 'Bow Wow Wow'. [103] Fresh from his legal triumph, Thelwall capitalised on the publicity to extend the reach of his songs. Yet when the Two Acts came into force at year's end, he was forced to discontinue the journal in which they had been published, and even his public lectures thereafter were restricted to politically neutral topics.[104]

Thelwall's example bears out both the limitations and the effectiveness of different forms of legal censorship, and the extent to which songs were uniquely able to evade censure. Yet this was a decade defined as much by both constitutive and unofficial forms of censorship as by judicial process – all of which combined to determine the fate of the auctioneer and radical songwriter Robert Thomson, another member of the London Corresponding Society. In 1792, he produced his own contrafactum of 'God Save the King': 'God Save the Rights of Man'. The singing of this protest would later be scrutinised in the Treason Trials. However, Thomson also took the step of *printing* the work as a common slip song, with the set of lyrics given in a single column on a narrow strip of paper, for mass distribution. This was a highly inflammatory step, especially as the song was impertinent even at the level of typography: it printed the word 'King' in a miniscule font! For this act Thomson was censored, not by government, but by his own society, which passed a resolution on 23 August that any delegate who published, or sent to a newspaper, any such piece of writing, would be expelled from the society. Three weeks later on 13 September, three divisional delegates received an official reprimand from the central committee for reprinting his song.[105] The committee's caution was well founded: Thomson was under surveillance by the government spy George Munro, a fellow Scot. He sent Thomson's writings back to his paymasters as an example of 'corrupting the minds of the lower orders of the people by inflaming their imaginations with imaginary grievances, and working them up to com[m]it some great excess'.

Though he escaped imprisonment, Thomson was ultimately forced into exile and spent the next few years living as a bookseller in Paris on Rue Honoré (now Rue Saint-Honoré), opposite the Oratory.[106] He was driven out, however, not by the state but by a civilian organisation known as Reeves' Association.[107] In November 1792, John Reeves – a barrister, legal scholar, and pillar of the establishment who had previously held public office in England and Newfoundland – returned to London only to be dismayed at the extent of public disaffection. On 20 November, he founded and chaired a private society, the Association for Preserving Liberty and Property against Republicans and Levellers, beginning a movement that soon spread across the nation, with 'Reeves' Association' branches founded in numerous towns and cities.[108] These 'Loyalist' associations were committed to defending the monarchy and status quo against the threat of revolution. Their effect upon protest song was two-fold. The first was direct, serving to intimidate, harass, and threaten, enforcing a degree of normative conduct and expression among often small and closed communities.[109] Local printers were especially vulnerable, meaning that even before the Two Acts, radical ballads were far less likely to be published in areas where a printer could be held to account by rough, unofficial justice. As Thomas Holcroft wrote of protest singers in the capital: 'If but one of them dared to sing a stave in favour of any thing which looked like freedom, he or she was taken up and committed to the house of correction. I myself witnessed numberless scenes of this kind'.[110]

Whilst intimidation of this kind drove Robert Thomson from the country after his publication of *A Tribute to Liberty*, the second – and perhaps most significant – form of repression of protest song was indirect. Radical songs were simply drowned out by an avalanche of loyalist competition. Within three weeks of founding his association, Reeves was receiving letters from correspondents proposing that they publish loyal songs, since 'any thing written in voice & especially to an Old English tune ... made a more fixed Impression on the Minds of the Younger and Lower Class of People, than any written in Prose, which was often forgotten as soon as Read'. This anonymous writer suggested 'putting them ... by twenties into the hands of Ballad Singers who might sing them for the sake of selling them'.[111] Another female contributor concurred, writing that 'the lower class of people ... are incapable of reading or understanding any good or serious address to set them right; but through the medium of popular ballads surely much instruction might be convey'd and much patriotic spirit awakened'.[112]

Though Reeves had not envisioned any such measures, which themselves smacked rather too much of democracy in giving ordinary contributors a voice, the enthusiasm for loyal songwriting proved unbounded. Holcroft was convinced that the government was behind the campaign, citing the exceptional – and suspiciously expensive – production values of some of the songs.[113] Other societies, such as Hannah More's Cheap Repository Tracts organisation, followed suit. Upon the renewal of hostilities in 1803, when Napoleon's Army of England was known to be preparing to invade, the mass production of counter-revolutionary songs reached a height and ubiquity that recalled, and perhaps even surpassed, the Tory Reaction of 1681–84 (discussed in the previous case study).[114] Coupled with the legal risks of singing or publishing seditious material, the result was a near-total eclipse of songs of protest in England until after the final defeat of Napoleon in 1815.[115] Thus, when accounting for the forces levelled against protest song, we would do well to remember not just the potential of regulation and repression, such as the Treason Trials, the Two Acts, government surveillance, and the vigilantism of private societies, but also that song's greatest opponent could sometimes be song itself.

Case Study

The BBC and Corporate Censorship (1930-83)

While the state and its agencies may, in recent centuries, have exacted less extreme punishment on the writers, performers, and publishers of protest songs, this does not mean that protest songs have been free of interference. The advent of systems of mass communication introduced new anxieties (and new possibilities) for those in authority. For the UK government of the 1920s, new modes of communication were initially associated with military strategy (through the advent of wireless telegraphy, among other technologies), and their use became a matter of national security.[116] This in turn led to regulation as a 'public corporation', and content being regarded as a 'public good'.[117] In this guise, the BBC was required both to promote music that reflected the diversity of its audience and to educate that audience in music's possibilities, while at the same time taking responsibility for establishing standards of taste, decency, and (later) political impartiality. This is the context in which broadcast music was scrutinised and censored in the twentieth century.

The BBC made no secret of its practice of censoring of music. In 1943, gramophone director Graham Abraham wrote of the need for 'censorship' and of himself as 'Policy Censor'.[118] The Corporation's archives include lists of banned songs. One such list for the period 1938–54 identifies over 120 that were not approved, including 'I've Got an Invitation to the Royal Coronation', 'I Won't be a Nun', and 'Let's Get Lit Up'. There is also a three-CD compilation, *This Record is Not to be Broadcast*, that documents 75 examples of the BBC's musical bans between 1931 and 1957.[119] What is key, however, is the reason for these bans and how the BBC has interpreted its responsibilities over time. What is noticeable about both the CD collection and the longer lists is how few of the songs were banned for blatantly political reasons. Yet, as we shall see, the various criteria applied to the vetting of music did have the effect of censoring protest song.

In determining what was acceptable, the BBC operated (and continues to operate) an elaborate system of scrutiny and review. A series of committees reviewed all eligible records, most of which were approved. Those about which there were grounds for concern would be sent up to senior managers. Some records, as a result of this process, were banned from all airplay; others might be deemed suitable only for playing at certain times or in a particular programme. Or they might be approved only for specific purposes – for example, to illustrate a documentary.

The BBC's archives reveal that the policing of music was done in plain sight. On the list of songs released each week, some are marked NTBB ('not to be broadcast'). When Max Romeo's 'Wet Dream' was banned in 1969, assistant head of popular music Donald MacLean told presenters that they could acknowledge that it was a chart hit but should refer to it only as 'a record by Max Romeo'.[120] Bans of this kind were about fulfilling a *public service*. This service was understood to require judgement similar in some respects to that of earlier eras. One of the main criteria was that of 'taste' (and its corollary 'disgust'). What was perhaps different in the contemporary period was that, in judging taste, the BBC was anxious not to appear paternalist. The assistant director of sound broadcasting insisted that bans should be explained as breaches of 'general taste' rather than 'good taste', on the grounds that the latter suggested the BBC was superior in judgement to its listeners and the music industry.[121]

'Wet Dream' was deemed to offend against taste and decency, as was George Formby's 'With My Little Stick of Blackpool Rock' in 1939, Shirley Bassey's 'Burn My Candle' in 1956, and, as we have seen, Frankie Goes to Hollywood's 'Relax' in 1984. The policing of sexual content is, of course, a political act, and one that speaks to the idea of constitutive censorship, in the sense that it seeks to manage senses of self and relations between selves. It also sets limits to what music may be used to express, and what forms of music might be deemed acceptable. Sexual content in opera is allowed, while it is not in blues or reggae.

But ideas of decency and taste were not solely associated with sex. In 1966, head of popular music Kenneth Baynes issued a ban of all songs about 'deformed people'.[122] Several years later, Ian Dury wrote 'Spasticus Autisticus' (1981) as a protest against what the singer – who had contracted polio when a child – saw as the reductive and patronising representation of disabled people during the International Year of Disabled Persons. Its use of language thought to be offensive to disabled people caused the BBC to ban it, despite support for the song from polio charities.[123] The Dury ban was prompted – like that of 'Wet Dream' – by a concern for taste and decency rather than for any political sentiments that the song might represent.[124] Our inclusion of 'Spasticus Autisticus' in our 250 as a protest song recognises an unacknowledged consideration in the BBC's decision. The apparently apolitical nature of taste and decency can hide an ideological agenda, perhaps best illustrated by the fact that, some thirty years later, the song would be part of the Opening Ceremony of the 2012 Paralympic Games in London.

Political judgement is implicated even where the issue appears to be a matter of aesthetics. In 1953, the BBC's Central Music Advisory Committee, which had oversight of the system of vetting and selection, explained that the purpose of the Music Programme Advisory Panel, which considered each individual recording, should be 'to weed out from the works submitted [primarily records] those that are considered unworthy of performance'. Musical or aesthetic quality was almost as much a consideration as the 'message' that the recording was deemed to convey. As a result of this process, it was not until the 1960s that popular music was recognised as being 'capable of affording a degree of aesthetic satisfaction'.[125]

Taste offences of this kind included, according to BBC management, an excess of 'sentimentality'. This was the reason for the ban imposed on Chico Hamilton's 'God, Country and My Baby' in 1961.[126] Another form of taste offence was the popular use (or 'misuse', as it was seen) of classical music. In 1947, a memo reminded staff that 'there is a ruling in the BBC which forbids broadcasting of popular numbers based on the classical repertoire' – for example, 'I See Starlight', which was based on Grieg's Piano Concerto.[127] 'Jazz versions of serious traditional tunes' were also banned.[128] Taste was also given as the reason for the ban of a song by Marion Williams that was labelled as part of the 'Negro Gospel Tradition'. It was not deemed 'blasphemous', but in doubtful taste because of its repeated use of the words 'Jesus' and 'The Holy Ghost'.[129] This is another case of aesthetic judgement serving to chill forms of musical expression, and to recognise or marginalise the identities and interests of those who performed them.

Apart from the disgust elicited by sex and other matters, the BBC has also been exercised by the possibility that music might be linked to disorder. This was most evident in songs about drugs. Illegal drugs were seen as symptomatic or a cause of disorder. Well-known examples include, as we have mentioned, The Beatles' 'Day in the Life'.[130] Other instances include The Byrds' 'Have a Whiff on Me' (1971), which the controller of BBC2 worried 'might directly influence attitudes to drug taking'. Such songs led the controller of Radios 1 and 2 to remark that he and his colleagues 'were getting very tired of reputable companies allowing groups to record doubtful items without apparent supervision'.[131]

Examples of bans based on diplomatic concerns, as we have termed them, have been relatively rare in the BBC's vetting processes. One exception was Wout Steenhuis's 'Tevanj Boelan', which was banned because it was the Malaysian national anthem.[132] An important example, though, is to be found in our 250. It is Noël Coward's 'Don't Let's be Beastly to the Germans', released in 1943, and initially passed as suitable by the BBC scrutineers. Recorded at the height of World War 2, it anticipated Germany's defeat and spoke mischeviously of the German people: 'Let's give them full air parity / And treat the rats with charity / But don't let's be beastly to the Hun'. The BBC worried that there might be complaints from listeners, and the reply was to be: 'The BBC believes that most listeners would rather hear Mr Coward being himself than Mr Coward tied up in censorship from Broadcasting House'.[133] This decision caused considerable anxiety in the Corporation, with the director general becoming involved on the day of the first broadcast of the song, and being reassured by a report that Coward had sung the song to the prime minister (who had joined in the chorus).[134] It was still not a straightforward matter. There were discussions about who was allowed to sing the song, with the view being taken that it was not normally suitable for 'women [singers]' or for Dance Band Programmes.[135] It was also determined that, for those who were allowed to sing it, the word 'bloody' was to be replaced by 'blasted'.[136] Coward's original recording was to be exempt, however. This privileged exemption was allowed until 1958, when the song was banned – in a case of diplomatic censorship – in deference to improving relations with Germany.[137]

The final category of the BBC's censorship practice was disaffection. This was the most explicitly political criterion: it involved songs that promoted the cause of Britain's enemies or engaged with sensitive political issues. It went under the general heading in BBC memos of 'political propaganda or controversial material'. This led, at one point, to the assistant director of sound broadcasting suggesting that one party political song should be 'balanced' by another from a rival party.[138] Four songs by calypso artist Mighty Sparrow were reviewed in 1962 on grounds of taste and politics, even though the political references were described as 'indefinite'.[139] Ewan MacColl's 'The Colour Bar Strike', about a union facing down racial prejudice among its members, was referred upwards for approval, as was Leon Rosselson's 1962 EP *Songs for City Squares*, which included the song 'Battle Hymn of the New Socialist Party' as well as songs about John Profumo and Rab Butler. Sheila Hancock and Sydney Carter's 'Coming Down from Aldermaston' ('men and women stand together and ban the bomb') was another song that exercised the BBC censors.[140]

Ireland features prominently in this category. In 1962, a song by the Clancy Brothers and Tommy Makem, 'God Bless England', was labelled 'NTBB'.[141] It was a bitter satire on imperial rule: 'She gently raised us from the slime / Kept our hands from hellish crime /And sent us to Heaven in her own good time'. Three songs about Ireland by Kathleen Watkins were referred for review, of which 'On the One Road' was deemed 'NTBB', presumably because of its celebration of a united Ireland and its line: 'Singing a soldier's song'.[142] 'The Ballad of Roger Casement' was judged to offer 'no entertainment value'.[143] 'The Dying Rebel' and 'Sean South' were described as 'unsuitable for broadcasting in

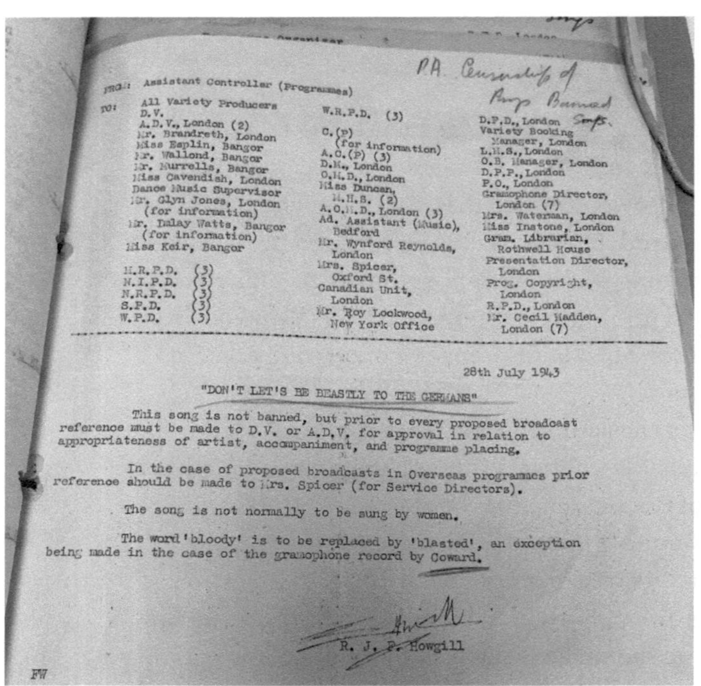
P.A. Censorship of Songs Banned Songs.

FROM: Assistant Controller (Programmes)

TO: All Variety Producers
D.V.
A.D.V., London (2)
Mr. Brandreth, London
Miss Esplin, Bangor
Mr. Wallond, Bangor
Mr. Murrells, Bangor
Miss Cavendish, London
Dance Music Supervisor
Mr. Glyn Jones, London (for information)
Mr. Dalay Watts, Bangor (for information)
Miss Keir, Bangor

M.R.P.D. (3)
N.I.P.D. (3)
N.R.P.D. (3)
S.P.D. (3)
W.P.D. (3)

W.R.P.D. (3)
C.(P) (for information)
A.C.(P) (3)
D.M., London
O.M.D., London
Miss Duncan, M.H.S. (2)
A.O.M.D., London (3)
Ad. Assistant (Music), Bedford
Mr. Wynford Reynolds, London
Mrs. Spicer, Oxford St.
Canadian Unit, London
Mr. Roy Lockwood, New York Office

D.P.D., London
Variety Booking Manager, London
L.M.S., London
O.B. Manager, London
D.P.P., London
P.O., London
Gramophone Director, London (7)
Mrs. Waterman, London
Miss Instone, London
Gram. Librarian, Rothwell House
Presentation Director, London
Prog. Copyright, London
R.P.D., London
Mr. Cecil Madden, London (7)

28th July 1943

"DON'T LET'S BE BEASTLY TO THE GERMANS"

This song is not banned, but prior to every proposed broadcast reference must be made to D.V. or A.D.V. for approval in relation to appropriateness of artist, accompaniment, and programme placing.

In the case of proposed broadcasts in Overseas programmes prior reference should be made to Mrs. Spicer (for Service Directors).

The song is not normally to be sung by women.

The word 'bloody' is to be replaced by 'blasted', an exception being made in the case of the gramophone record by Coward.

R. J. F. Howgill

FW

6.3 • Memo sent in 1943 approving the broadcast of 'Don't Let's be Beastly to the Germans', but specifying the conditions for its use, who was to sing it, and what words were to be sung.

general entertainment programmes' because they were 'laments for "volunteers" slain by the British'.[144] Similarly, 'The Irish Rover' was banned for its 'anti-British words'.[145] It was a decade later that the BBC banned Paul McCartney's 'Give Ireland Back to the Irish'.[146]

Looking back over the BBC's censorship, it is apparent that there were relatively few bans of songs for conventionally political reasons. However, this understates the Corporation's impact on voices of protest. Firstly, as we have pointed out, bans imposed for reasons of taste and decency (disgust, as we label it) can also contain a political dimension insofar as they affect claims of identity and forms of behaviour. Secondly, the known practices of the BBC may well have discouraged artists and record companies from risking political controversy (notwithstanding that a ban *could* be used as a marketing strategy). Finally, buried within all this is the BBC's understanding of what constitutes 'good radio' (or television). Judgements of this kind have tended to marginalise music such as metal, reggae, and, more recently, grime, and by implication the political content that might otherwise be expressed through them.

CONCLUSION

In English history, writing, producing, selling, or singing a protest song has frequently been met with violence from authorities, and even from audiences, but very rarely has it led to long-term imprisonment or capital punishment (probably only Stephen Colledge was actually executed for this crime and, even then, only as part of a broader political crackdown). Songs are more likely to decry the punishment of protest (for example, 'On Peterloo meeting' (1819)), while some brought a last-minute comfort of defiance for activists at the site of punishment. This occurred in 1820, when James Ings, a condemned Cato Street conspirator, sang 'Death or Liberty' upon the gallows, much as Vuyisile Mini, an African National Congress activist and composer of protest songs, did in 1964. The creators and producers of protest songs have avoided repression or control in myriad ways, through anonymity, or conspiracy, or by making the content of their songs sufficiently ambiguous to make them difficult to prosecute by using rhetorical devices such as allegory or satire, or by implicit contrasts.[147]

It has even been said that dismissing, denigrating, and refusing to recognise the status of the protest song is a form of soft censorship: part of the long-standing strategy of stripping song of its power by ignoring it. Specific musical responses to this have been made, such as in Grace Petrie's 'I Wish The Guardian Believed That I Exist' (2016). There is, on the other side, the scepticism expressed by Adorno and others about the significance of the protest song as a political act. Certainly, this view has been expressed by protest singers themselves. Rage Against the Machine believed that the change came when 'Live Aid removed the risk from politics' and advised would-be protestors: 'don't write a song – be an activist'.[148] Or in Billy Bragg's words, while performers of protest songs might raise awareness, 'only the audience can change the world'.[149]

Nonetheless, despite these calls to activism and the rare instances of draconian punishment of protest singers, the protest song in England has been subject to scrutiny and suppression throughout its long history. This has been the result of a complex process, in which multiple actors and ideas have been in play, and in which a 'hostile environment' has been as effective in silencing song as the action of courts and regulators. Our case studies serve to illustrate how, while the political context and political issues may change, the authorities in their various guises have consistently treated song as a form of political threat. In seeking to deny access to songs and the sentiments they express, those authorities have resorted to arguments that re-echo across the centuries. Censorship has been justified by reference to taste and disgust, to disaffection and disorder, and to the diplomatic relations between states.

Our longer perspective suggests that the subversive power of protest songs brings with it the risk of producing and performing them. Even in 2022, at a time of multiple global crises, the UK's Conservative government restored an element of personal danger to acts of noisy protest. In so doing, it perhaps sharpened the edge of protest songs, making them once again an important tool for communication – and a risk.

CONCLUSION

'When I started writing about music, in 1965', remembers Greil Marcus, 'music and politics – music as a form of the argument over the good, over how to make a commonwealth where all might find a way to see the good plain, but also the music in politics, the presence of harmony and dissonance as people argued over this election, that law, that speech, the crowd's response – was all I wrote about'.[1] This, it might be said, is what we have written about too. The difference is that our history reaches back some four hundred years.

Those centuries have revealed how the protest song, in its many different forms, has argued over the good and how to realise it, and has responded to the lives and experiences of people, faced with all manner of hardship and injustice. Our research began with three very simply premises. The first was that the history of the protest song had been, for the most part, wrongly confined to the twentieth and twenty-first centuries. The second was that, while the US version of the protest song was the main topic of the short history, there was a separate story to be told about the English variant. Our final premise was that the protest song was an important, but neglected, aspect of political communication, and deserved the same attention that has been given to speeches, pamphlets, adverts, manifestos, party election broadcasts, and the like.

Those simple premises, of course, yielded a wealth of problems as to how to research the long history of the protest song and how to understand it as a form of political communication. This book describes how we tackled these problems of history, definition, and methodology, and how we came to understand the protest song's particular qualities as political communication. Vital to these efforts has been the ambition to keep the long history always in view, in the range of our examples and in the choice of our case studies. We have also been mindful of not reading contemporary assumptions and categories into past events, whilst being sensitive to the multiple forms in which complaint was expressed in song over time. The idea of political thought and theory 'in the wild' has been central to this endeavour, as has our understanding of songs as political and musical rhetoric. But in focusing on how songs express political ideas and sentiments, we have attended to the means by which those songs and their singers came to claim the right to represent a cause or people and to speak with authority. Beyond this, we have asked – as anyone who studies political communication past or present must do – how those songs got made, distributed, and heard, and how they have been regulated and suppressed. And crucial to all this has been the mix of disciplines and specialisms that have contributed to the research. This book has been a team effort in all sorts of ways. Most significant has been the sharing of knowledge and perspectives, of questions and methods from across the humanities and social science.

We hope that readers have been persuaded both of the validity of our original premises and of the route we have taken in substantiating them. We are well aware, though, that the protest song is a subject that inspires passionate debate. One of the many pleasures of our research has been the discussions we have had with audiences at the talks, performances, and exhibitions that have been an important part of our project. Our list of 750 protest songs has prompted any number of responses, from endorsements for what appears to suggestions for what should have appeared.[2]

Those passionate discussions were underpinned by another argument: the value attributed to a protest song was often linked to a story about the difference that it had made to an individual or to the wider world. Certainly, this question of what protests *do* haunts the topic. It is explicit in those who deride or dismiss the protest song, just as it is for those who celebrate it. Looking back over its storied centuries, we would argue that the protest song can lay claim to have done many different, noteworthy things.

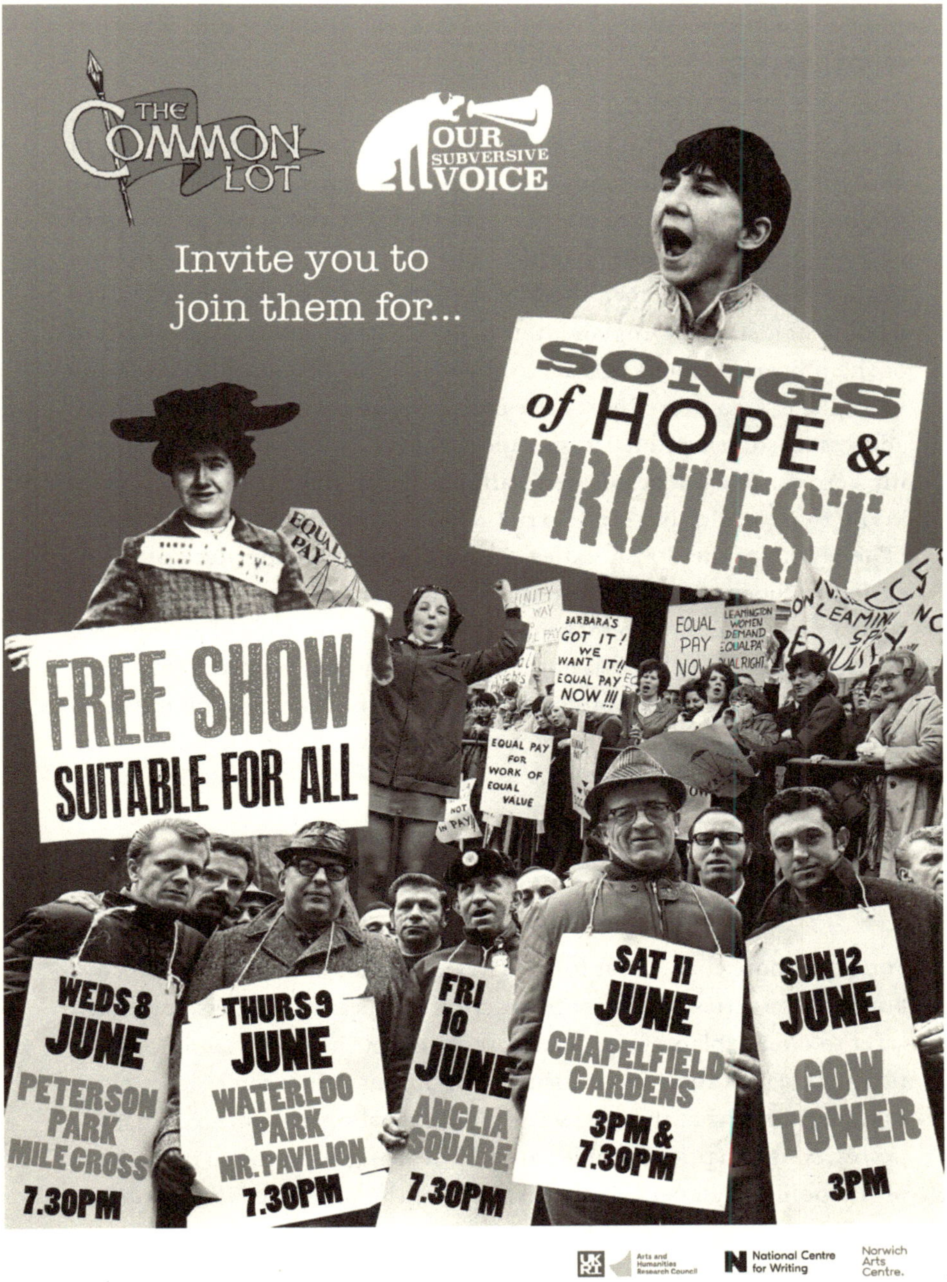

THE COMMON LOT

OUR SUBVERSIVE VOICE

Invite you to join them for...

SONGS of HOPE & PROTEST

FREE SHOW
SUITABLE FOR ALL

WEDS 8 JUNE
PETERSON PARK
MILE CROSS
7.30PM

THURS 9 JUNE
WATERLOO PARK
NR. PAVILION
7.30PM

FRI 10 JUNE
ANGLIA SQUARE
7.30PM

SAT 11 JUNE
CHAPELFIELD GARDENS
3PM & 7.30PM

SUN 12 JUNE
COW TOWER
3PM

7.1 • Poster for The Common Lot's performances of *Songs of Hope and Protest* in 2022.

INFORMING

The history of the protest song is also the history of the society from which it emerges. The songs on our list (and the many others that we might have included) are not mere footnotes to political, social, technological, and economic change. They are commentaries on those changes and on the experiences of them. Our 750 songs can be read as a political history of England, telling its listeners about the corruption of the powerful, about threats to the planet, or about injustices in the workplace. Chapter 1 charts the many issues that protest songs have addressed, some confined to specific events and moments, others speaking across time and across generations. These songs helped people to know their world. In 1833, Harriet Martineau and Eliza Flower wrote 'The Hymn of the Polish Exiles'. The song assumes the voice of a Pole exiled to Siberia to draw attention to Russia's harsh treatment of its Polish territories, and to make its British listeners aware of an injustice of which they have known nothing. Similarly, it is reported that Jerry Dammers learnt of the plight of Nelson Mandela from the music of South African Julian Bahula. This musical lesson led to Dammers writing 'Free Nelson Mandela'.[3]

EDUCATING

Songs do more than just inform. They educate too. The news informs, but only as a series of apparently discrete events and incidents. It is much rarer to offer explanations, putting those events in context or in connection with each other. Protest songs can do this. They can help listeners to understand what they are witnessing or feeling. And in so doing, the protest song can prime people to act. In drawing attention to the failings of the political class or to the dangers to the planet, to the inequities of power or the plight of the enslaved, protest songs attribute responsibility and blame. John Hasted, who wrote songs for the Aldermaston marches, says in his autobiography: 'I'd hardly spent a year at Oxford University, but my whole outlook on life was rapidly changing, not least of all due to the new songs and music that I was experiencing'.[4] In much the same way, Johnny Marr of The Smiths recalls encountering fans who became vegetarian because of 'Meat Is Murder' ('It's not natural, normal or kind / The flesh you so fancifully fry').[5]

MOVING

If all that protest songs did was inform and educate, they might be worth much less attention than we have given them. They offer not only facts and explanations; they also inspire feelings. They move their listeners. They make their audience care about people and causes. In 'Free Nelson Mandela', there is the line: 'shoes too small to fit his feet'; in 'Shipbuilding', the lines: 'A new winter coat and shoes for the wife / And a bicycle on the boy's birthday'.[6] These apparently mundane images, and the voices that sing them, elicit feelings of anger and empathy.

Protest songs, like all forms of political communication, act rhetorically. But their rhetoric is not identical to that of a political speech or pamphlet, just as lyrics are not poetry.

Protest song rhetoric is the product of words, music, and performance. Songs help to shape our feelings of injustice. No song can – or would aspire to – convey John Rawls's argument in *A Theory of Justice*, or what he meant by 'the original position' or 'the difference principle', but a song can evoke the moral intuition of 'justice as fairness', the central claim of Rawls's theory. In about 1860, the anonymous street ballad 'Lay of the Lash' addressed its appeal to women, arguing that 'If Eve's daughters but will it – the battle was won'. It is a compelling articulation of the need to effect legislative change:

> While, moreover, no doubt, 'twould be quickly found out
> By the knaves in high places, whom Europe should scout
> That all retrospective severe legislation
> 'Gainst rich or 'gainst poor, is abhored by the nation
> For these reasons, with others 'twere long I declare

I call on all women – just, fearless, and fair –
So raise the stern cry, nor till death let it fall: –
'The Lash be for none – or the Lash be for all!'[7]

UNITING

Protest songs, like national anthems, are often composed with the intention of audience participation, and the sense of unity that this engenders. Benedict Anderson, an expert on nationalism, noted many years ago that collective singing is a very effective means of summoning up the imagined community of a nation.[8] Explaining this phenomenon, cultural theorist Steve Connor writes that singing together 'is almost always concerned with the establishment of solidarity', and has a close affinity with both prayer and protest.[9] Whether in the form of choral singing or crowd participation, the protest song gives embodied and public form to a shared grievance or injustice, and anticipates a collective capacity to press for change. 'The Gathering of the Unions' (1832), sung by one hundred thousand protestors in Birmingham, not only registered a demand for freedom but also gave form to a movement, just as did 'Brazen Hussies' (1983) for the women protestors at the Greenham Common air force base.[10]

REPRESENTING

In calling communities into existence, the song and its performers are making a claim to representation. This claim may refer to an Other that is not present in the moment – the natural world, the foreign war, the future generation – or it may be those gathered to listen. In either case, the music and musicians act to represent the causes or peoples about which they sing. Lord Kitchener's 'If You're Not White, You're Black' (1953) gave voice to the experience of racial discrimination:

Your father is an African
Your mother may be Norwegian
You pass me, you wouldn't say goodnight
Feeling you are really white
Your skin may be a little pink
And that's the reason why you think
That the complexion of your face
Can hide you from the negro race
No! You can never get away from the fact
If you not white, you considered Black.

The 'you' and 'me' in this song both distinguishes and unites communities and experiences. It both evokes racial discrimination and makes abhorrent its practice.

ORGANISING

Protest songs are often sung as a demonstration is taking place. Sometimes this is about claiming public space and broadcasting a message; at other times it is about lifting morale or generating a sense of solidarity and defiance as the police move in.[11] The Extinction Rebellion movement used protest song in just such moments, but it also used song – and rhythm in particular – to choreograph the behaviour of its supporters in the act of demonstrating.[12] In his book *Music and Politics*, James Garratt writes of music organising time and space, and acting 'as a physical force, choreographing protest and annexing territory, translating political ideas into vividly felt experience'.[13] In January 1660, General Monck removed the military junta that had dissolved Richard Cromwell's Protectorate and restored the Long Parliament of 1640 in its entirety. Addressing 'both commons and peers', the song 'The Case is Altered, OR, Sir Reverence, The Rump's Last Farewel' played a part in renewed street demonstrations demanding free elections and urging people not to vote for members of 'that Reprobate "Rump"' parliament. These moments, as noted in chapter 5, depend on collaborations between a range of actors and institutions. These are important to the existence of the protest song, just as the song is important to the institutions and actors through its ability to organise protest both physically and imaginatively.

IMAGINING

Chris Waters, a historian of British socialism, quotes the *Keighley Labour Journal* of 1898 as saying of socialist choirs that they offered 'a first promise of what enjoyment may be obtained from life … under socialism'.[14] Here the suggestion is that the protest song helps in imagining the better world to which protests are directed. In some songs this is achieved by looking back and evoking a lost world to be recovered; in others, this is realised through speculation about a future not yet encountered. But as with all protest songs, this imagining is not confined to the lyrics alone. It is there too in the performance.

Informing, educating, moving, uniting, representing, organising, and imagining – these are some of the many ways in which protest songs might be understood to do things to and with people and their worlds. Together, they provide an answer to the question: do protest songs matter? Protest songs perform many roles, and their impact is felt in multiple ways, just as with other forms of political communication. And not all of them are equal in their effect, which leaves us with one, final question: is it possible to judge the quality of protest songs, to say that this one is better at performing these roles than others?

Even if you are tempted to say that the only good protest song is a successful one, there might remain – as with those to whom we talked during our project – a strong urge to pick out protest songs that were special, that did something other songs did not. For Garratt, 'the most effective protest songs' are those that 'break through the listeners' cynicism or force them to question their own prejudices'.[15] Even if 'Give Peace a Chance' has proved to be a successful protest song, you might argue that it posed no challenge to its listeners, either musically (a chant that anyone could sing) or politically (a cause that almost everyone would embrace).

Does a successful protest song need to entertain its audience?[16] For Simon Frith, the answer is 'no'. He argues that if culture is to change us, that culture 'must challenge experience, must be difficult, must be *unpopular*'.[17] This is not equivalent to 'unpleasant' or 'inept'. It is about distinguishing between the populist and the popular. The former refers to mass sales or mass support, earned by clever marketing or rhetoric. The popular here refers to the notion of a 'people', rather than a market or a mass. This distinction is present in some of the earliest writing about music, from Plato onwards. It is there, as we illustrate in chapter 4, in the competing ideas of England and Englishness with which protest songs have engaged. It is implicit in the work of Cecil Sharp who sought to identify the music of the everyday (of 'folk').[18] It is there in the Fabians' suspicion of commercial popular culture.[19] It is there too in Ewan MacColl's injunctions on how folk music should be performed and what it should address, and in the later writing of those who warned of the populist distortions of rock music.[20] All of these are examples of claims about what music can do politically, and how it can represent a cause or a constituency.

There are, of course, no scientific methods for resolving such arguments. There are no arts prize juries who offer some sanctioned view of what a good protest song is. There are no equivalents to the Pulitzer Prize, the Mercury Prize, or the Booker Prize, where a panel of expert judges pronounce on the best journalism, books, or music. Equally, there is no method by which the effect of any given protest can be measured. A judgement of the effectiveness of 'The Ballad of the Cloak', for example, would depend on whether it was appraised when it was first published in 1663 (zero impact) or when it took off as a protest song in 1679 and 1680. There are too many variables to control. None of this, of course, brings an end to the discussion. This was all too evident in the debates that our project alone prompted. What they brought home, though, is the fact that the protest song is a source of pleasure (and disdain), just like other forms of popular culture. It is also a source, and a product, of political argument and judgement. And these arguments and judgements are part of the pleasure and of the politics that give value to the protest song and enable it to make a difference.

Our Subversive Voice tells many stories, but a central one is that of songs *in* protest, and especially the ways in which direct action can appropriate or extemporise a song of protest from a non-political song or a mere phrase and do its work in real time. This has been the case throughout the long history of the protest song. Because, just as pop music did not begin with Chuck Berry or The Beatles, so protest song did not begin with Woody Guthrie or Ewan MacColl. And even if one's interest is in the contemporary or the recent, or the pre-modern past, it is surely helpful to step back sometimes. In hearing the whole song as well as the individual notes, you get a sense of the shapes and the stories. Even within England alone, that goes for narratives of feminist protest, counter-colonial struggle, environmental campaigning – the eco-protest of 'The Powte's Complainte' (1619) feels pretty profound, as do the anti-vaccination songs from the 1870s that could have taught public health scientists a lot about how to sort out their messaging in 2020. But more than the causes, it is the forms and processes of the protest song that we should attend to. Because such songs matter. They can *work*. Of course, as noted in chapter 1, they can be easily misunderstood and misrepresented, as with Neil Innes's 'Protest Song' from *Rutland Weekend Television* or Hugh Laurie's 'Protest Song' from *A Bit of Fry and Laurie*, or in the endless articles bemoaning the alleged disappearance of protest songs. But these prejudices and preconceptions are ably refuted by Grace Petrie in her song 'I Wish The Guardian Believed That I Exist' or by Oliver Anthony's 'Rich Men North of Richmond', which briefly topped the US charts in 2023.[21]

Sometimes the nature of protest songs is hard to perceive. What is apparent, though – as we look back over our research and the history it maps – is that the authority and the justice invoked and appealed to by protest songs is, and always has been, fundamentally *moral*, rather than based on first principles or empiricism. This takes us to the heart of what a good protest song can do: say what is wrong and what is right, and what needs to be done – and not just tell us, but make us feel, its truth.

Notes

In the case of multiple quotations from the same source in a passage, only one note number is inserted after the last quotation in the group.

Introduction

1 All these songs (bar one), together with their lyrics and a recording or a score, are to be found on the website oursubversivevoice.com. Where we discuss a song in detail, an endnote provides the link to it. The exception is 'Good Morning Mr Colston' by Reg Meuross, which can be found on Bandcamp at: https://regmeuross.bandcamp.com/track/good-morning-mr-colston; last accessed 29 April 2024.

2 Both incidents are discussed in chapter 6. See also John Rushworth, '1643 The Womens Tumult at the House of Commons, Aug. 7', *Historical Collections of Private Passages of State: Volume 2, 1640–1644* (London: D. Browne, 1721), Pt. 3, 357–8.

3 Keir Monteith, 'Ban rap and drill lyrics in the courtroom', *Popular Music* 41, no. 4 (2022): 556.

4 See chapter 1 for a full discussion of this claim.

5 Quoted in Dorian Lynskey, *33 Revolutions Per Minute: A History of Protest Songs* (London: Faber & Faber, 2010), 513–14.

6 Quoted in Greil Marcus, *Folk Music: A Bob Dylan Biography in Seven Songs* (New Haven: Yale University Press, 2022), 39. The folk singer Shirley Collins echoed these sentiments in 2023: 'For me, Pete Seeger bashing his bloody banjo and exhorting an audience to join the chorus of We Shall Overcome never seemed to advance any causes … I didn't quite trust the people writing protest songs because those I knew weren't, frankly, nice people' (Dave Simpson, 'Shirley Collins: "Is Folk Music a Political Tool? I Would Say My Arse"', *Guardian*, 18 May 2013; available at: www.theguardian.com/music/2023/may/18/shirley-collins-is-folk-music-a-potent-political-tool-i-would-say-my-arse).

7 David Hesmondhalgh, *Why Music Matters* (Chichester: Wiley Blackwell, 2013), 142.

8 Ibid., 146.

9 Michael Kenny, *The Politics ofEnglish Nationhood* (Oxford: Oxford University Press, 2014); Trish Winter and Simon Keegan-Phipps, *Performing Englishness: Identity and Politics in a Contemporary Folk Resurgence* (Manchester: Manchester University Press, 2013).

10 For a short summary of a new history of the trade, see Angela McShane, 'The Ballad Business', on the 100 Ballads website, available at: www.100ballads.org/page/Essays/the-Ballad-Business; last accessed 20 March 2024. For the longer version, see Angela McShane, *The Ballad Trade and its Politics in Seventeenth-Century Britain* (Woodbrige: Boydell and Brewer, forthcoming).

11 See Will Page, *Pivot: Eight Principles for Transforming your Industry in a Time of Disruption* (London: Simon & Schuster, 2023).

12 An example of a song with an explicitly English subject matter is 'Manchester Rambler' (1932), about the right to roam in the Peak District. An English song about elsewhere is 'The Slave Ship' (*c*.1848), advocating the abolition of slavery in the US.

13 See, for example, Holli A. Semetko and Margaret Scammell (eds), *The Sage Handbook of Political Communication* (London: Sage, 2012). Music receives scant attention in its forty-one chapters.

14 For example, see James Garratt, *Music and Politics: A Critical Introduction* (Cambridge: Cambridge University Press, 2019); the Special Forum on Music and Politics 1780–1850, edited by Oskar Cox Jensen and David Kennerley, *Journal of British Studies* 60, no.2 (2021); or the survey provided by Eric Drott, 'From Studies of Protest Music to Protest Music Studies: Mapping a Field that Doesn't (Yet) Exist', *Music Research Annual* 4 (2023): 1–23.

15 R. Serge Denisoff and Richard Peterson (eds), *The Sounds of Social Change* (Chicago: Rand McNally, 1972); Ian Peddie (ed), *The Resisting Muse: Popular Music and Social Protest* (Aldershot: Ashgate, 2006); Lynskey, *33 Revolutions Per Minute*; Noriko Manabe, *The Revolution Will Not Be Televised: Protest Music after Fukushima* (New York: Oxford University Press, 2015).

16 Ron Eyerman and Andrew Jamison, *Music and Social Movements: Mobilizing Traditions in the Twentieth Century* (Cambridge: Cambridge University Press, 1998); see also Rob Rosenthal and Richard Flacks, *Playing for Change: Music and Musicians in the Service of Social Movements* (Boulder: Paradigm Publishers, 2012); William G. Roy, *Reds, Whites, and Blues: Social Movements, Folk Music, and Race in the United States* (Princeton: Princeton University Press, 2010); John Street, *Music and Politics* (Cambridge: Polity, 2012).

17 Frank Esser and Jesper Strömbäck (eds), *Mediatization of Politics: Understanding the Transformation of Western Democracies* (Houndmills: Palgrave Macmillan, 2014); Kate Krenski and Kathleen Hall Jamieson (eds), *The Oxford Handbook of Political Communication* (Oxford: Oxford University Press, 2017).

18 See Liesbet van Zoonen, *Entertaining the Citizen: When Politics and Popular Culture Converge* (New York: Rowman and Littlefield, 2005) and John Street, 'Music as Political Communication', in Kenski and Jamieson, *The Oxford Handbook of Political Communication*, 885–96.

19 Oliver Anthony's protest song 'Rich Men North of Richmond' was number 1 in the *Billboard* charts, and featured in the first of the televised Republican presidential debates in summer 2023.

20 The song's author was Martin Parker, one of the best-loved ballad writers of the first half of the seventeenth century. In 1628, in contravention of the Stationers' Company's monopoly of printing and publishing, Thomas Symcocke obtained a potentially illegal patent to print ballads. He persuaded disaffected printers to publish a large number of new and old song titles, which carried the imprint: 'Printed by the Assigns of Thomas Symcocke'. These titles included 'Time's Alteration'. The Stationer's Company successfully challenged Symcocke's patent in the courts and in parliament, but not until 1631. See McShane, *The Ballad Trade and its Politics*, chapter 6.

21 Drott, 'From Studies of Protest Music to Protest Music Studies': 2.

22 See Dick Hebdige, *Subculture: The Meaning of Style* (London: Routledge, 1979); Jon Savage, *England's Dreaming: The Sex Pistols and Punk Rock* (London: Faber & Faber, 2005); and Matthew Worley, *No Future: Punk, Politics and British Youth Culture, 1976–1984* (Cambridge: Cambridge University Press, 2017).

23 We attempted to find one song from every decade and to give every period roughly equal weight.

24 Available at: https://ebba.english.ucsb.edu/ and http://ballads.bodleian.ox.ac.uk/.

25 On ballad collecting, see David Atkinson, *The English Traditional Ballad: Theory, Method and Practice*, Ashgate Popular and Folk Music Series (Aldershot: Ashgate, 2002); Tim Somers, *Ephemeral Print Culture in Early Modern England Sociability: Politics and Collecting*, Studies in the Eighteenth Century Series, 10 (Woodbridge: Boydell and Brewer, 2021); John C. Hirsh, 'Samuel Pepys as a Collector and Student of Ballads', *The Modern Language Review* 106, no. 1 (2011): 47–62; Patricia Fumerton, *The Broadside Ballad in Early Modern England: Moving Media, Tactical Publics* (Philadelphia: University of Pennsylvania Press, 2020); see also McShane *The Ballad Trade and its Politics*, chapter 4.

26 We should also acknowledge the disciplinary differences within the team, which, while a strength, have inevitably led to differences of emphasis in approach to research and selection within our various periods of expertise. In part mitigation of this, it is worth visiting the 'Song Suggestions' pages on our website, where we list further examples that have been sent to us (https://oursubversivevoice.com/other-voices/).

27 Our first protest song, written by Thomas Deloney to protest against food shortages, was in fact published in 1596, but all copies were destroyed by the London mayor on the orders of the crown (see https://oursubversivevoice com/song/11925/ and discussion in https://oursubversivevoice.com/case-study/the-subversive-voice-of-early-modern-hunger-1596-1774-songs-as-weapons-of-the-weak-or-ballading-the-badgers-in-times-of-dearth/).

28 Peter Manuel, 'World Music and Activism since the End of History [*sic*]', *Music & Politics* XI, no. 1 (2017); available at: https://quod.lib.umich.edu/m/mp/9460447.0011.101/--world-music-and-activism-since-the-end-of-history-sic?rgn=main;view=fulltext. We return to Manuel's argument in chapter 5.

29 Drott, 'From Studies of Protest Music to Protest Music Studies': 1.

30 Garratt, *Music and Politics*, xi.

31 F.R. Ankersmit, *Aesthetic Politics* (Stanford: Stanford University Press, 1996).

32 Quentin Skinner, 'General Preface', in *Visions of Politics, Volume 1: Regarding Method* (Cambridge: Cambridge University Press, 2002), vii (his emphasis).

33 Garratt, *Music and Politics*, 11.

34 See McShane, 'The Ballad Business' and McShane, *The Ballad Trade and Its Politics*, Chapters 6–7.

35 For 'The Whig Rampant', see https://oursubversivevoice.com/song/12009/ and (for the more popular edition) see https://ebba.english.ucsb.edu/ballad/33758/image; for the popular retail version of 'A New IRISH Song', see https://ebba.english.ucsb.edu/ballad/21974/image.

36 For 'The Sea Martyrs', see https://oursubversivevoice.com/song/12036/; for a discussion of the song, see https://oursubversivevoice.com/song/12036/. 'A Ra-ree Show' is the subject of a case study in chapter 6.

37 It should be noted that, in this period, far fewer people collected topical single-sheet ballads, and so it remains something of a historical blank.
38 Eyerman and Jamison, *Music and Social Movements*.
39 Michael Saward, *The Representative Claim* (Oxford: Oxford University Press, 2010).
40 Benedict Anderson, *Imagined Communities* (London: Verso, 1983).
41 Jennifer C. Lena and Richard A. Peterson, 'Politically Purposed Music Genres', *American Behavioral Scientist* 55, no. 5 (2011): 574–88.
42 Simon Frith, 'Representations of the People: Voices of Authority in Pop Music', *Revista de Musicologia* 16, no. 1 (1993): 528–32; Kalefa Sanneh, *Major Labels: A History of Popular Music in Seven Genres* (London: Canongate, 2021).
43 See, for example, Ukrainian Eurovision-winning entries such as '1994' by Jamala, about the deportation of Crimea tartars, or 'Stefania' by Kalush Orchestra, originally a tribute to the group's mothers that later came to be interpreted as a celebration of Ukrainian matriarchy in the wake of the Russian invasion. Back in 1980, the Norwegian entry, 'Sámiid ædnan', performed by Sverre Kjeldsberg and Mattis Hætta, protested at a proposed hydro-electric power station that threatened the local environment: see https://oursubversivevoice.com/voice/environmentalism-and-indigenous-rights-in-norwegian-protest-songs/.
44 Psalms were often set to ballad tunes to make them easier to sing.
45 Quoted in David Remnick, 'A Unified Field Theory of Bob Dylan', *New Yorker*, 31 October 2022.
46 Lyrics by Charlie Caine. Reproduced with permission. Available at: https://oursubversivevoice.com/song/13269/.

Chapter One

1 Available at: www.youtube.com/watch?v=aKBkOai1mAQ.
2 Available at: www.youtube.com/watch?v=Q8chs2ncYIw. In fairness, in a live performance for *Parkinson* in 2000, Laurie and his band also introduce a cod-reggae rhythm in the chorus.
3 These songs are also, in a sense, protest songs in that they protest protest music. They might also be read as promoting a certain kind of politics through a performance that implicitly highlights the alleged naivete, simplicity, or inauthenticity of '1960s' political revolt. They are thus an interesting example of how songs express and communicate politics through their form and through performative contestation of political style and genre – issues we address further in chapters 2 and 3.
4 Available at: www.oed.com/view/Entry/153191.
5 Eckhard John and David Robb, *Songs for a Revolution: The 1848 Protest Song Tradition in Germany* (Woodbridge: Boydell & Brewer, 2021), 13.
6 Carole R. Livingston, *British Broadside Ballads of the Sixteenth Century: A Catalogue of the Extant Sheets and an Essay* (New York: Garland Publishing, 1991).
7 Frederick J. Furnivall (ed), *Ballads from Manuscripts*, vol. 1 (London: Taylor and Co., 1868–72); Jenni Hyde, *Singing the News: Ballads in Mid-Tudor England* (Abingdon and New York: Routledge, 2018), esp. chapter 6.

8 At https://oursubversivevoice.com/case-study/the-subversive-voice-of-early-modern-hunger-1596-1774-songs-as-weapons-of-the-weak-or-ballading-the-badgers-in-times-of-dearth/.

9 For example, Roy Palmer, *The Sound of History: Songs and Social Comment* (Oxford and New York: Oxford University Press, 1988); Hyde, *Singing the News*; Angela McShane, 'Political Street Songs and Singers in Seventeenth-Century England', *Renaissance Studies* 33 (2019): 94–118; Kate Horgan, *The Politics of Songs in Eighteenth-Century Britain, 1723–1795* (London and New York: Pickering and Chatto, 2014); Ian Newman, *The Romantic Tavern: Literature and Conviviality in the Age of Revolution* (Cambridge: Cambridge University Press, 2019); Laura Mason, *Singing the French Revolution: Popular Culture and Politics, 1787–1799* (New York: Cornell University Press, 1996); Kate Bowan and Paul Pickering, *Sounds of Liberty: Music, Radicalism and Reform in the Anglophone World, 1790–1914* (Manchester: Manchester University Press, 2017).

10 Mark Philp, *Radical Conduct: Politics, Sociability and Equality in London, 1789–1815* (Cambridge: Cambridge University Press, 2020), especially 23–32.

11 oed.com/view/Entry/153191 and /153192.

12 oed.com/view/Entry/153191, definition 6a.

13 Oskar Cox Jensen, 'The Hymn as Protest Song in England and Its Empire, 1819–1919', *Yale Journal of Music and Religion* 8 (2022): 104–24.

14 James Garratt, *Music and Politics: A Critical Introduction* (Cambridge: Cambridge University Press, 2019), xi.

15 Oskar Cox Jensen, *Napoleon and British Song, 1797–1822* (Basingstoke: Palgrave Macmillan, 2015); Oskar Cox Jensen, David Kennerley, and Ian Newman (eds), *Charles Dibdin and Late Georgian Culture* (Oxford: Oxford University Press, 2018); Horgan, *The Politics of Song*; Isaac Land, *War, Nationalism, and the British Sailor, 1750–1850* (New York: Palgrave Macmillan, 2009); Mark Philp, 'Music and Movement in Britain, 1793–1815', *Journal of British Studies* 60 (2021): 403–15.

16 For further discussion of election songs, see Hannah Barker and David Vincent (eds), *Language, Print and Electoral Politics, 1790–1832: Newcastle-Under-Lyme Broadsides* (Woodbridge: Boydell & Brewer, 2001); Bowan and Pickering, *Sounds of Liberty*, esp. 140–64; Barbara Crosbie, 'Half-Penny Ballads and the Soundscape of Eighteenth-Century Electioneering', *Publishing History* 70 (2011): 9–32; and Oskar Cox Jensen, *The Ballad-Singer in Georgian and Victorian London* (Cambridge: Cambridge University Press, 2021), esp. 122–31.

17 Bruce R. Smith, *The Acoustic World of Early Modern England: Attending to the O-Factor* (Chicago: University of Chicago Press, 1999), 188, 196.

18 Jürgen Habermas, *The Structural Transformation of the Public Sphere: An Inquiry into a Category of Bourgeois Society* (1962, trans. Thomas Burger, Cambridge, MA: MIT Press, 1989). Habermas's theory has prompted so much debate and revisionism that even the core commentary has itself been superseded – e.g., Nick Crossley and John Michael Roberts (eds), *After Habermas: New Perspectives on the Public Sphere* (Oxford: Blackwell Publishing, 2004). Good places to start are perhaps Nancy Fraser, *Transnationalizing the Public Sphere* (Cambridge: Polity, 2014), and Hauke Brunkhorst, Regina Kreide, and Cristina Lafont (eds), *The Habermas Handbook* (New York: Columbia University Press, 2018).

19 Harriet Guest, *Small Change: Women, Learning, Patriotism, 1750–1810* (Chicago: University of Chicago Press, 2000); Anne Stott, *Hannah More: The First Victorian* (Oxford: Oxford University Press, 2003).

20 Wendy Hinde, *George Canning* (London: Collins, 1973), 109.

21 See especially Newman, *The Romantic Tavern*, 2019.

22 Nicholas D. Nace, 'The Author of Sodom among the Smithfield Muses', *Review of English Studies*, New Series, 68, No. 284 (2017): 296–321, 300.

23 https://charnwoodopera.wordpress.com/.

24 A possible exception to the first of these is Aphra Behn's 'Young Jemmy' (1681), in support of the Duke of York and future James II. Yet even here it may be significant that Behn's song adopts a thin veil of classic allegory rather than making its subject explicit, in contrast to related songs such as 'England's Darling', which makes our list – and that the single-sheet song was published anonymously, though it was also published in a collection of Behn's work.

25 David Atkinson, 'Folk Songs in Print: Text and Tradition', *Folk Music Journal* 8 (2004): 456–83, 457–8.

26 Undoubtedly, previous centuries had witnessed numerous songs aimed at moral reform, protesting cruelty to animals, women or children, and other such issues, but these had tended to be, if anything, top-down protests on behalf of the vulnerable, exemplified by Hannah More's *Cheap Repository Tracts* and the Society for the Promotion of Christian Knowledge in the 1790–1800s, represented on our list by 'The Plow-Boy's Dream' (1795).

27 David Kennerley, 'Strikes and Singing Classes: Chartist Culture, "Rational Recreation" and the Politics of Music after 1842', *English Historical Review* 135 (2020): 1165–94; Cox Jensen, 'The Hymn'.

28 This narrative is typically attributed to E.P. Thompson's *The Making of the English Working Class* (1963, revised ed., London: Penguin, 1991).

29 Erin Johnson-Williams, 'Musical Discipline and Liberal Reform', in Sarah Collins (ed), *Music and Victorian Liberalism: Composing the Liberal Subject* (Cambridge: Cambridge University Press, 2019), and 'Sonic Congregating: The Hymn as National British Spectacle', *Yale Journal of Music and Religion* 8 (2022): 125–47.

30 J.C. Hadden, 'Mainzer, Joseph (1801–1851)', *Oxford Dictionary of National Biography* (2004), https://doi.org/10.1093/ref:odnb/17814.

31 See, for example, Mark W. Booth, *The Experience of Songs* (New Haven: Yale University Press, 1981), 15–16, 22.

32 See oursubversivevoice.com/interviews for interviews with Sue Gilmurray, Kimwei, and Sam Lee.

33 David Kennerley, 'Music, Politics, and History: An Introduction', *Journal of British Studies* 60 (2021): 362–74.

34 Michael Braddick, 'John Hammond and the Explosion of Print in 1641: Commercial and Political Opportunities', forthcoming. We are grateful to Professor Braddick for allowing us to see a pre-publication copy of his essay.

35 The tune 'ragged and torn and true' was often used by Martin Parker (a royalist and an alehouse keeper) and Laurence Price (a parliamentarian); either could have provided this protest lyric to Hammond, who was not afraid to publish politically critical ballads.

36 Angela McShane, *The Ballad Trade and Its Politics in Seventeenth Century Britain* (Woodbridge: Boydell & Brewer, forthcoming), chapter 6. In the civil war years (1642–51), ballad traders, and indeed all publishers of entertainment literatures, were unable to either register or enforce their copyrights due to the more pressing need to register and license the many newsbooks that began to come out.

37 Ibid.

38 Bowan and Pickering, *Sounds of Liberty*, 235.

39 Harriet Martineau, *History of England during the Thirty Years' Peace, 1816–46*, 2 vols (London: Charles Knight, 1849–50), vol. 2, 58.

40 John Harkness of Preston would soon be sending his topical ballads down to London on the first train of the day. Gregg Butler, 'John Harkness: Reflecting the Northwest and Making a Living Out of It', paper given at Broadside Day conference, Chetham's Library, Manchester, 20 February 2016.

41 Alexandra Franklin and Mark Philp, *Napoleon and the Invasion of Britain* (Oxford: Bodleian Library, 2003); Mark Philp (ed), *Resisting Napoleon: The British Response to the Threat of Invasion, 1797–1815* (Aldershot: Ashgate, 2006); Cox Jensen, *Napoleon*.

42 Oskar Cox Jensen, 'The Ballad and the Bible', in James Grande and Brian Murray (eds), *Scripture and Song in Nineteenth-Century Britain* (London: Bloomsbury, 2023).

43 Cox Jensen, *The Ballad-Singer*.

44 Bowan and Pickering, *Sounds of Liberty*; Kennerley, 'Strikes and Singing Classes'.

45 Cox Jensen, *The Ballad-Singer*.

46 Kennerley, 'Strikes and Singing Classes'.

47 McShane, *The Ballad Trade and Its Politics*, chapter 10.

48 Kathryn Gleadle, *Borderline Citizens: Women, Gender, and Political Culture in Britain, 1815–1867* (Oxford: Oxford University Press, 2009).

Chapter Two

1 R.G. Collingwood, *The Idea of History* (Oxford: Clarendon Press, 1946).

2 See, for example, R. Serge Denisoff and Richard A. Peterson (eds), *The Sounds of Social Change* (New York: Rand McNally & Co., 1972).

3 See, for example: https://oursubversivevoice.com/song/11946/; see also Angela McShane, 'Puritans and Protest Songs in Revolutionary Britain', in Noriko Manabe and Eric Drott (eds), *The Oxford Handbook of Protest Song* (Oxford: Oxford University Press, forthcoming).

4 Theodor Adorno, 'On Popular Music', in S. Frith and A. Godwin (eds), *On Record: Rock Pop and the Written Word* (London: Routledge, 1990): 301–14.

5 Simon Frith and Angela McRobbie, 'Rock and Sexuality', in S. Frith and A. Godwin (eds), *On Record: Rock Pop and the Written Word* (London: Routledge, 1990): 371–89; Simon Reynolds and Joy Press, *The Sex Revolts: Gender, Rebellion and Rock 'n' Roll* (Cambridge: Harvard University Press, 1996).

6 See, for example, Danielle Fosler-Lussier, *Music in America's Cold War Diplomacy* (Oakland: University of California Press, 2015); James Garrett, *Music and Politics: A Critical Introduction* (Cambridge: Cambridge University Press, 2019); Ted Gioia, *Music: A Subversive History* (New York: Basic Books, 2019); Bruce Johnson and Martin

Cloonan, *Dark Side of the Tune: Popular Music and Violence* (Aldershot: Ashgate, 2009); John Street, *Music and Politics* (Cambridge: Polity, 2012).

7 See Oskar Jensen, *Vagabonds: Life on the Streets of Nineteenth-Century London* (Richmond: Duckworth, 2022); E. Wyn James, 'Painting the World Green: Dafydd Iwan and the Welsh Protest Ballad', *Folk Music Journal* 8, no. 5 (2005): 594–618; James Grande, 'London Songs, Glamorgan Hymns: Iolo Morganwg and the Music of Dissent', *Studies in Romanticism* 58, no. 4 (2019): 481–503; Paul Gilroy, '"Get Up, Get Into It and Get Involved" — Soul, Civil Rights and Black Power', in John Storey (ed), *Cultural Theory and Popular Culture: A Reader*, 4th ed., (London: Pearson, 2009): 355–64; Ian Biddle, 'Why We Should Listen to the Music of the Holocaust – and That of Syrian Refugees', *The Conversation*, 26 January 2016, available at: https://theconversation.com/why-we-should-listen-to-the-music-of-the-holocaust-and-that-of-syrian-refugees-53702; *Travellers: Songs, Stories and Tunes from English Gypsies* (Topic Records, TSDL395); Terry Moylan, *The Age of Revolution in the Irish Song Tradition, 1776–1815* (Dublin: The Lilliput Press, 2000).

8 Available at: https://oursubversivevoice.com/song/12393/.

9 Available at: https://oursubversivevoice.com/song/12251/.

10 Another part of the history of this kind of political song is the response of states, and of publishers, in the form of censorship and other ways of managing songs. This is something we consider in more detail in chapter 6.

11 But by contrast, see also James Epstein, *In Practice: Studies in the Language and Culture of Popular Politics in Modern Britain* (Stanford: Stanford University Press, 2003).

12 This sentiment is shared by Christian Lahusen, who writes that 'political songs … deliberately advocate for a new form of community and a new meaningful order'. See Christian Lahusen, *The Rhetoric of Moral Protest: Public Campaigns, Celebrity Endorsement and Political Mobilization* (Berlin: Walter de Gruter, 1996), 182.

13 Available at: https://oursubversivevoice.com/song/11926/.

14 Available at: https://oursubversivevoice.com/song/12446/.

15 Lyrics by Penny Rimbaud. Reproduced by permission.

16 A further correspondence between these two songs is that the Crass song represents Mrs Thatcher as the mother of the nation. This parental terminology was universally applied to early-modern monarchs before constitutional changes placed the king's power into the quasi-monarchical hands of the prime minister.

17 Angela McShane, '"Rime and Reason": The Political World of the Broadside Ballad', unpublished PhD dissertation, University of Warwick, 2005, 248.

18 Ibid., 249.

19 See also Brodie Waddell, *God, Duty and Community in English Economic Life, 1660–1720* (Woodbridge: Boydell and Brewer, 2012). See also Alan Finlayson, 'From "Come all you Farmers out of the Countrey" to "Question Time": Critique, Contempt and Ruling Classes in English Protest Songs since 1603', available at: https://oursubversivevoice.com/case-study/from-come-all-you-farmers-out-of-the-countrey-to-question-time-critique-contempt-and-ruling-classes-in-english-protest-songs-since-1603/.

20 Gerard A. Hauser and Erin Daina McClellan, 'Vernacular Rhetoric and Social Movements: Performances of Resistance in the Rhetoric of the Everyday', in Sharon McKenzie Stevens and Patricia Malesh (eds), *Active Voices: Composing a Rhetoric of Social Movements* (New York: SUNY Press, 2009): 39.

21 Kenneth Burke, 'Dramatism and logology', *Communication Quarterly* 33, no. 2 (1985): 89–93.

22 Hauser and McClellan, 'Vernacular Rhetoric', 39.
23 For example, J.G.A. Pocock, 'The Concept of a Language and the *metier d'historien*: Some Considerations on Practice', in Anthony Pagden (ed), *The Languages of Political Theory in Early Modern Europe* (Cambridge: Cambridge University Press, 1987), 19–38; Quentin Skinner, *Visions of Politics: Regarding Method* (Cambridge: Cambridge University Press, 2002); Gareth Stedman-Jones, *Languages of Class: Studies in English Working Class History, 1832–1982* (Cambridge: Cambridge University Press, 1983).
24 Pocock, *The Concept of a Language*, 21.
25 Elisabeth Robin Anker, *Orgies of Feeling: Melodrama and the Politics of Freedom*, (Durham, NC: Duke University Press, 2014), 20.
26 Skinner, *Visions of Politics*, 177–8.
27 Quentin Skinner, 'Rhetoric and Conceptual Change', *Finnish Yearbook of Political Thought* 3, no. 1 (1999): 67–8.
28 Stephen J. Pfohl, 'The "Discovery" of Child Abuse', *Social Problems* 24, no. 3(1977): 310–23; Ian Hacking, 'The Making and Molding of Child Abuse', *Critical Inquiry*, 17 (1991): 253–88.
29 Available at: https://oursubversivevoice.com/song/12648/.
30 Available at: https://oursubversivevoice.com/song/12385/.
31 Available at: https://oursubversivevoice.com/song/11972/.
32 Linda Colley, *Britons: Forging the Nation 1707–1837*, revised ed. (New Haven: Yale, 2009); Hugh Cunningham, 'The Language of Patriotism, 1750–1914', *History Workshop* 12 (1981): 8–33; Mary A. Favret, *War at a Distance: Romanticism and the Making of Modern Wartime* (Princeton: University of Princeton Press, 2010); Kevin Gilmartin, 'Popular Radicalism and the Public Sphere', *Studies in Romanticism* 33 (1994): 549–57; Kevin Gilmartin, '"Study to Be Quiet": Hannah More and the Invention of Conservative Culture in Britain', *ELH* 70 (2003): 493–540; Kevin Gilmartin, *Writing against Revolution: Literary Conservatism in Britain, 1792–1832* (Cambridge: Cambridge University Press, 2007); Mark Philp (ed), *Resisting Napoleon: The British Response to the Threat of Invasion, 1797–1815* (Aldershot: Ashgate, 2006); Mark Philp, 'Music and Movement in Britain, 1793–1815', *Journal of British Studies* 60, no. 2 (2021): 403–15.
33 Available at: https://oursubversivevoice.com/song/12106/.
34 Available at: https://oursubversivevoice.com/song/12128/.
35 Stuart White, '"We are fireworks": Anarcho-Punk, Positive Punk and Democratic Individuality', *Punk & Post-Punk* 10, no. 2 (2021): 187–200.
36 James Parkinson, *An Address to the Hon. Edmund Burke; from the Swinish Multitude* (Detroit: Gale Ecco, 2010).
37 Available at: https://oursubversivevoice.com/song/12113/.
38 As a means to convey political critique/protest, parodic ventriloquism can be found throughout our 250/750. See, for example, 'The Whigs Exaltation' and (the reply) 'The Popish Tories Confession'. And before that (though more sympathetically in this case) 'The World Turned Upside Down'. See also the case study of 'A New IRISH Song' in chapter 4.
39 Available at: https://oursubversivevoice.com/song/12114/.
40 Available at: https://oursubversivevoice.com/song/12095/.
41 Available at: https://oursubversivevoice.com/song/12285/.
42 Available at: https://oursubversivevoice.com/song/12381/.
43 Available at: https://oursubversivevoice.com/song/12401/.

44 Available at: https://oursubversivevoice.com/song/12634/.
45 Simon Frith, *Performing Rites: On the Value of Popular Music* (Oxford: Oxford University Press, 1998), 169.
46 J.L. Austin, *How to Do Things with Words* (Oxford: Clarendon Press, 1962).
47 Frith, *Performing Rites,* 164, 169.
48 As an interesting example of the complexity here, see Laurence White's 1674/5 'All Things Be Dear But Poor Men's Labour', which was produced as a song and as a pamphlet oration, *The Charitable Farmer of Somersetshire.* For more, see https://oursubversivevoice.com/case-study/the-subversive-voice-of-early-modern-hunger-1596-1774-songs-as-weapons-of-the-weak-or-ballading-the-badgers-in-times-of-dearth/.

Chapter Three

1 See also Simon Frith, *Performing Rites: On the Value of Popular Music* (Oxford: Oxford University Press, 1996); Timothy Hampton, *Bob Dylan: How the Songs Work* (New York: Zone Books, 2019); Christian Lahusen, *The Rhetoric of Moral Protest: Public Campaigns, Celebrity Endorsement and Political Mobilization* (Berlin: Walter de Gruyter, 1996); Keith Negus and Pete Astor, 'Songwriters and Song Lyrics: Architecture, Ambiguity and Repetition', *Popular Music* 34, no. 2 (2015): 226–44.
2 An obvious example of this approach is Christopher Ricks, *Dylan's Visons of Sin* (New York: Harper Collins, 2004). The present approach differs from that of Ricks, but it is notable that here too (as in our Chapter 2) a focus is on how songs represent vice and virtue.
3 See Roland Barthes, 'Myth Today', in *Barthes: Selected Writings* (London: Fontana, 1989), 93–149; Philip Tagg, 'Musicology and the Semiotics of Popular Music', *Semiotica* 66, 1–3 (1987): 279–8.
4 Terry Eagleton, *Literary Theory: An Introduction* (Oxford: Blackwell, 1986), 179 (italics in the original).
5 Lloyd Bitzer, 'The Rhetorical Situation', reprinted in John Lucaites et al. (eds), *Contemporary Rhetorical Theory* (London: Guilford Press, 1999), 217–26 (italics in the original).
6 James Martin, 'Situating Speech: A Rhetorical Approach to Political Strategy', *Political Studies* 63, no. 1 (2015): 25–42; James Martin, 'Capturing Desire: Rhetorical Strategies and the Affectivity of Discourse', *British Journal of Politics and International Relations* 18, no. 1 (2016): 143–60.
7 See Richard E. Vatz, 'The Myth of the Rhetorical Situation', *Philosophy and Rhetoric* 6, no. 3 (1973): 154–61; Scott Consigny, 'Rhetoric and Its Situations', *Philosophy and Rhetoric* 7, no. 3 (1974): 175–86.
8 Available at: https://oursubversivevoice.com/song/12502/; https://oursubversivevoice.com/song/12507/.
9 Different versions of 'Glad to be Gay' can be found at: www.gladtobegay.net/versions/.
10 Kenneth Burke, *A Rhetoric of Motives* (Oakland: University of California Press, 1969).
11 Michael Saward, *The Representative Claim* (Oxford: Oxford University Press, 2010). See also our discussion of performance and representation in chapter 4.

12 Richard B. Gregg, 'The Ego-Function of the Rhetoric of Protest', in *Philosophy and Rhetoric* 4, no. 2 (1971): 71–91.

13 Karlyn Kohrs Campbell, 'The Rhetoric of Women's Liberation: An Oxymoron', *Quarterly Journal of Speech* 59, no. 1 (1973): 74–86.

14 Gerard A. Hauser and Erin Daina McClellan, 'Vernacular Rhetoric and Social Movements: Performances of Resistance in the Rhetoric of the Everyday', in Sharon McKenzie Stevens and Patricia Malesh (eds), *Active Voices: Composing a Rhetoric of Social Movements* (New York: SUNY Press, 2009), 34.

15 David A. Carter, 'The Industrial Workers of the World and the Rhetoric of Song', *Quarterly Journal of Speech* 66, no. 4 (1980): 365.

16 Ralph E. Knupp, 'A Time for Every Purpose under Heaven: Rhetorical Dimensions of Protest Music', *Southern Journal of Communication* 46, no. 4 (1981): 382.

17 Charles J. Stewart, 'The Ego Function of Protest Songs: An Application of Gregg's Theory of Protest Rhetoric', *Communication Studies* 42, no. 3 (1991): 15.

18 Available at: https://oursubversivevoice.com/song/12272/.

19 Available at: https://oursubversivevoice.com/song/12157/.

20 For much more on this, see David Kennerley, 'Strikes and Singing Classes: Chartist Culture, "Rational Recreation" and the Politics of Music after 1842', *English Historical Review* 135, no. 576 (2020): 1165–94, and Oskar Cox Jensen, 'The Hymn as Protest Song in England and Its Empire, 1819–1919', *Yale Journal of Music and Religion* 8 (2022): 104–24. For the naval point, see Oskar Cox Jensen, 'Music to Some Consequence: Reaction, Reform, Race', *Journal of British Studies* 60, no. 2 (2021): 376–9.

21 Available at: https://www.youtube.com/watch?v=c9whWZHpdcw.

22 Kennerley, 'Strikes and Singing Classes'.

23 Available at: https://oursubversivevoice.com/song/12307/.

24 As an example of this sort of analysis, see Steven Griggs and David Howarth, 'A Transformative Political Campaign? The New Rhetoric of Protest against Airport Expansion in the UK', *Journal of Political Ideologies* 9, no. 2 (2004): 181–201.

25 See Alan Finlayson, *Making Sense of New Labour* (London: Lawrence and Wishart, 2003).

26 Available at: https://oursubversivevoice.com/song/12289/.

27 Available at: http://www.britishpoliticalspeech.org/speech-archive.htm?speech=202.

28 See 'Socialist Sunday Schools', Working Class Movement Library www.wcml.org.uk/our-collections/creativity-and-culture/leisure/socialist-sunday-schools/.

29 Theodore Matula, 'Contextualizing Musical Rhetoric: A Critical Reading of The Pixies' "Rock Music"', *Communication Studies* 51, no. 3 (2000): 218; Allan F. Moore, *Song Means: Analysing and Interpreting Recorded Popular Song* (Farnham: Ashgate, 2012).

30 Oskar Cox Jensen, *Napoleon and British Song, 1797–1822* (Houndmills: Palgrave Macmillan, 2015), 2, 21–2, 45–7.

31 Matula, 'Contextualising Musical Rhetoric': 218.

32 See Pierre Bourdieu, *Distinction: A Social Critique of the Judgement of Taste* (Cambridge: Harvard University Press, 1984), and Carl Wilson, *Celine Dion's Let's Talk about Love: A Journey to the End of Taste* (London: Continuum, 2008). See also: Holt N. Parker, 'Toward a Definition of Popular Culture', *History and Theory* 50, no. 2 (2011): 147–70; David Brackett, *Categorizing Sound: Genre and Twentieth-Century Popular Music* (Berkely: University of California Press, 2016); Theodore Gracyk, *Listening to*

Popular Music: Or, How I Learned to Stop Worrying and Love Led Zeppelin (Ann Arbor: University of Michigan Press, 2007).

33 See Dick Hebdige, *Subculture: The Meaning of Style* (London: Routledge, 1979); D. Simonelli, 'Anarchy, Pop and Violence: Punk Rock Subculture and the Rhetoric of Class, 1976–78, *Contemporary British History* 16, no. 2 (2010): 121–44; Matthew Worley, 'Shot by Both Sides: Punk, Politics and the End of "Consensus"', *Contemporary British History* 26, no. 3 (2012): 333–54.

34 See Frith, *Performing Rites*, chapter 4.

35 See Robert Shelton, Dave Laing, Karl Dallas, and Robin Denselow, *The Electric Music Revisited: The Story of Folk into Rock and Beyond* (London: Omnibus Press, 2021); and Rob Young, *Electric Eden: Unearthing Britain's Visionary Music* (London: Faber & Faber, 2010).

36 Simon Frith, '"The Magic That Can Set You Free": The Ideology of Folk and the Myth of the Rock Community', *Popular Music* 1 (1981): 160.

37 For further discussion, see Oskar Cox Jensen, 'The Ballad and the Bible', in James Grande and Brian Murray (eds), *Scripture and Song in Nineteenth-Century Britain* (London: Bloomsbury, 2023).

38 Available at: www.youtube.com/watch?v=aKBkOai1mAQ.

39 For a comic version of a punk political song, see Newtown Neurotics, 'Does anybody Know Where the March Is?' (1983). Available at: www.youtube.com/watch?v=ZjMF46oIy6I.

40 Available at: https://oursubversivevoice.com/song/12616/.

41 Alexander D. Great, an actual calypso musician, released an answer song that same year called 'Copycat Crime'. In one verse he adopts a mock RP English accent and sings: 'Mr Read there's something you should understand / English folk music accompanied by brass band / Is the music of which UKIP might approve / So for goodness' sake Mike, get OUT of the groove / Leave satirical singing to those who know / What it means to deliver a calypso'.

42 John J. Makay and Alberto Gonzalez, 'Dylan's Biographical Rhetoric and the Myth of the Outlaw-Hero', *Southern Journal of Communication* 52, no. 2 (1987): 165–80. Timothy Hampton writes of Dylan's three voices ('hobo', 'archaic', and 'college kid'), observing that 'the craft involved in creating his voice ... will in turn guarantee its authority to speak on the "folk" themes of proletarian experience and social injustice. Dylan is not primarily interested in writing songs that will be sung by factory workers on strike. He is interested in writing songs that will guarantee his success as a performer' (Hampton, *Bob Dylan: How the Songs Work*, 27).

43 Available at: https://oursubversivevoice.com/song/12630/.

44 Mark W. Booth, 'The Art of Words in Songs', *Quarterly Journal of Speech* 62, no. 3 (1976): 246–7 (italics in the original).

45 Dana L. Cloud and Kathleen Eaton Feyh, 'Reason in Revolt: Emotional Fidelity and Working Class Standpoint in the "Internationale"', *Rhetoric Society Quarterly* 45, no. 4 (2015): 308.

46 Deryck Cooke, *The Language of Music* (Oxford: Oxford University Press, 1954), 33.

47 Oskar Cox Jensen, *The Ballad-Singer in Georgian and Victorian London* (Cambridge: Cambridge University Press, 2021), 111; see also Cox Jensen, 'Music to Some Consequence': 375–9.

48 Quoted in Brian Vickers, 'Figures of Rhetoric/Figures of Music?', *Rhetorica* 2, no. 1 (1984): 5.

49 Simon Frith, 'Why Do Songs Have Words?', *Contemporary Music Review* 5, no. 1 (1989): 90.

50 David R. Dewberry and Jonathan H. Millen, 'Music as Rhetoric: Popular Music in Presidential Campaigns', *Atlantic Journal of Communication* 22, no. 2 (2014): 81–92.

51 Cox Jensen, *The Ballad-Singer*, 111.

52 Chaim Perelman and Lucie Olbrechts-Tyteca, *The New Rhetoric: A Treatise on Argumentation* (London: University of Notre Dame Press, 1969), 116–17.

53 The melody is illustrated on the Our Subversive Voice website at: https://oursubversivevoice.com/song/12113/.

54 Available at: https://oursubversivevoice.com/song/12230/.

55 Jennifer Maclure, 'Rehearsing Social Justice: Temporal Ghettos and the Poetic Way Out in "Goblin Market" and "The Song of the Shirt"', *Victorian Poetry* 53, no. 2 (2015): 154.

56 Available at: https://oursubversivevoice.com/song/12230/.

57 J. Edelstein, '"They Sang "The Song of the Shirt": The Visual Iconology of the Seamstress', *Victorian Studies* 23, no. 2 (1980): 184.

58 Available at: https://oursubversivevoice.com/song/12648/.

59 Jayna Brown, '"Brown Girl in the Ring": Poly Styrene, Annabella Lwin, and the Politics of Anger', *Journal of Popular Music Studies* 23, no. 4 (2011): 456. Lavinia Greenlaw recounts a similar experience in her memoir, *The Importance of Music to Girls* (London: Faber & Faber, 2007).

60 Ibid., 458–9.

61 Available at: https://oursubversivevoice.com/song/12629/.

62 Elizabeth J. Kizer, 'Protest Song Lyrics as Rhetoric', *Popular Music and Society* 9, no. 1 (1983): 4–5.

63 G.P. Mohrmann and F. Eugene Scott, 'Popular Music and World War II: The Rhetoric of Continuation', *Quarterly Journal of Speech* 62, no. 2 (1976): 156. See also David Hesmondhalgh, *Why Music Matters* (Chichester: Wiley Blackwell, 2013).

64 Available at: https://oursubversivevoice.com/song/11962/.

65 See James A. Knapp, *Illustrating the Past in Early Modern England: The Representation of History in Printed Books* (Aldershot: Ashgate, 2003); see also 'The Parliament Routed' (1653); available at: https://oursubversivevoice.com/song/11972/.

66 Lloyd Bitzer, 'Aristotle's Enthymeme Revisited', in Richard Leo Enos and Lois Peters Agnew (eds), *Landmarks Essay in Aristotelian Rhetoric* (London: Routledge, 2010 [1959]): 187, 188.

67 Max Black, *Models and Metaphor: Studies in Language and Philosophy* (London: Cornell University Press, 1962), 41.

68 For the songs referred to, see: https://oursubversivevoice.com/song/12100/; https://oursubversivevoice.com/song/12106/; https://oursubversivevoice.com/song/12377/.

69 Available at: https://oursubversivevoice.com/song/12989/.

70 Johanna Siméant and Christophe Traïni, *Bodies in Protest: Hunger Strikes and Angry Music* (Amsterdam: Amsterdam University Press, 2016), 122.

71 Cloud and Feyh, 'Reason in Revolt', 313.

Chapter Four

1 For Smith chiding his fellow band members, hear the live album *Totale's Turns (It's Now or Never)* (Rough Trade, 1980).
2 The Fall, 'N.W.R.A.' on *Grotesque* (Rough Trade, 1980).
3 Paul Morley, 'They Mean It M-a-a-a-nchester', NME, 30 July 1977, 6–7.
4 *Temporary Hoarding*, 5 (1978); Ian Penman, 'Between Innocence and Forbidden Knowledge', NME, 19 August 1978, 7–8.
5 Quoted in Penman, 'Between Innocence and Forbidden Knowledge', 7–8.
6 See, for example, 'Industrial Estate' (1978) or 'City Hobgoblins' (1980).
7 Sex Pistols, 'God Save the Queen' (Virgin, 1977).
8 James Garratt, *Music and Politics: A Critical Introduction* (Cambridge: Cambridge University Press, 2019); Timothy Hampton, *Bob Dylan: How the Songs Work* (Brooklyn, NY: Zone Books, 2019); and John Street, 'From Performance to Protest: The Sound of Political Representation', in Paula Diehl and Michael Saward (eds), *Bodies, Spaces, Claims: The Theory and Practice of Performing Political Representation* (Oxford: Oxford University Press, forthcoming).
9 We might also consider our own subjective response to a song: the researcher's reading of a song as protest – a problem that only becomes harder the further back in history you go.
10 Angela McShane, *Political Broadside Ballads in Seventeenth Century England: A Critical Bibliography* (Pickering and Chatto: London, 2011), No. 105; Keith Lindley, *Popular Politics and Religion in Civil War London* (Aldershot: Scolar, 1997), 30–2.
11 Tracey Thorn, *Bedsit Disco Queen: How I Grew up and Tried to be a Pop Star* (London: Virago, 2013).
12 https://oursubversivevoice.com/song/11956/.
13 Philip Auslander, *Liveness: Performance in Mediatized Culture* (London: Routledge, 2008).
14 Quoted in Lynskey, *33 Revolutions Per Minute: A History of Protest Songs* (London: Faber and Faber, 2010), 512.
15 Desperate Bicycles, 'The Medium Was Tedium' b/w 'Don't Back the Front' (Refill Records, 1977).
16 Angela McShane, *Ballad Trade and Its Politics* (Woodbridge: Boydell and Brewer, forthcoming), Chapter 8; Oskar Cox Jensen, *The Ballad-Singer in Georgian and Victorian London* (Cambridge: Cambridge University Press, 2021), 1–2, 81–131.
17 For example, Thomas Jordan, *A Royal Arbour* (London: E.Andrews., 1664); Matthew Taubman, *An Heroick Poem to His Royal Highness the Duke of York on His Return from Scotland with Some Choice Songs and Medleyes on the Times* (London:J. Smith, 1682); Thomas D'Urfey, *A New Collection of Songs and Poems* (London: J. Hindmarsh, 1683).
18 Samuel Bamford, *The Weaver Boy; Or, Miscellaneous Poetry* (Manchester: Observer Office, 1819), *Hours in the Bowers. Poems, etc* (Manchester: N.p., 1834), Poems (Manchester: N.p., 1843), and *Homely Rhymes, Poems, and Reminiscences* (London: A. Ireland & Co; and Manchester: Simpkin, Marshall & Co., 1864). See also Oskar Cox Jensen, 'Music to Some Consequence: Reaction, Reform, Race', *Journal of British Studies* 60 (2021): 375–88.

19 *Excellent New and Popular Songs on Queen Caroline of England Adapted to the Most Popular Tunes*, Bodleian Ballads Harding B 25(339), at ballads.bodleian.ox.ac.uk/view/edition/3454.

20 See, for example, David Brackett, *Interpreting Popular Music* (Berkeley: University of California Press, 2000); Allan F. Moore, *Song Means: Analysing and Interpreting Recorded Popular Song* (Aldershot: Ashgate, 2012); Philip Tagg and Bob Clarida, *Ten Little Tunes: Towards a Musicology of Mass* Media (New York: Mass Media's Music Scholars' Press, 2003).

21 The Smiths, 'Shakespeare's Sister' b/w 'What She Said & 'Stretch Out and Wait' (Rough Trade, 1985).

22 For the full text, see Criminal Justice and Public Order Act 1994; available at: www.legislation.gov.uk/ukpga/1994/33/contents/enacted.

23 https://extinctionrebellion.uk/2019/04/25/update-7-to-parliament-and-beyond/.

24 Interview with Kimwei. Available at: https://oursubversivevoice.com/interview/kimwei/.

25 Michael Denning, *Noise Uprising: The Audiopolitics of a World Musical Revolution* (London: Verso, 2015), 140.

26 Ibid., 155.

27 Simon Frith, *Performing Rites: On the Value of Popular Music* (Oxford: Oxford University Press, 1996), 187 (his emphasis).

28 Simon Frith, 'Representations of the People: Voices of Authority in Pop Music', *Revista de Musicologia* 16, no. 1 (1993): 529.

29 Rawiya Kameir, 'Rethinking Appropriation and Wokeness in Pop Music', *Pitchfork*, 19 October 2020; available at: https://pitchfork.com/features/article/rethinking-appropriation-and-wokeness-in-pop-music/.

30 Although in his 2024 London show, Springsteen wore a tie and waistcoat ... and jeans.

31 Greil Marcus, *Folk Music: A Bob Dylan Biography in Seven Songs* (New Haven: Yale University Press, 2022), 23.

32 'The truth is only known by guttersnipes', from The Clash, 'Garageland' (1977).

33 Cox Jensen, *The Ballad-Singer*, 81–112.

34 Charles Williams, 'Political Ballad-Singers' (London, 1805), at britishmuseum.org/collection/object/P_1868-0808-7359.

35 This might be considered part of a wider social change, happening from the mid-eighteenth century, that distinguished 'good music' from 'bad music' – in today's parlance, popular music from classical music. This could explain why protest songs appear in highly ornate and expensive volumes that were beyond the pockets of the 'masses' they are supposed to influence.

36 Oskar Cox Jensen, 'The Hymn as Protest Song in England and Its Empire, 1819–1919', *Yale Journal of Music and Religion* 8 (2022): 104–24.

37 See Ian Newman (ed), *The Francis Place Ballad Project*, at https://francisplaceballads.nd.edu/ and Mary Thale (ed), *The Autobiography of Francis Place* (Cambridge: Cambridge University Press, 1972).

38 Quoted in Daniel Rachel, *Walls Come Tumbling Down: The Music and Politics of Rock Against Racism, 2 Tone and Red Wedge* (London: Picador, 2016), 59–60.

39 For history of the song, its publication history, and a professional performance by the Carnival Band, see the 100 Ballads Website No: 8. On the ongoing use of the song, see

Katy Radford, 'Red, White, Blue and Orange: An Exploration of Historically Bound Allegiances through Loyalist Song', *The World of Music* 46, no. 1 (2004): 71–89.

40 This account draws on important new research by Kenneth Fergusson, 'Who Wrote Lillibullero? If Not Tom Wharton, What about Robert Ware and Henry Wharton?', *The Irish Sword : The Journal of the Military History Society of Ireland* 33, no. 131 (2021): 35–58.

41 Ibid., 42.

42 Fergusson makes this reasonable conjecture, given Ware's politics and social position, though he suggests only Henry Wharton as a co-writer. However, ballad writing frequently involved multiple hands and Thomas Wharton was later reported (by a political opponent) to have claimed authorship of the song: see Anon., *A True Relation ... of the Intended Riot and Tumult of Queen Elizabeth's Birthday* (London: J. Morphew, 1711), 5.

43 Louis XIV's Edict of Nantes (1685) threatened all Protestants with death unless they converted (or left the country).

44 For an interview on this complex topic with leading historian Professor Micheál Ó Siochrú, see www.rte.ie/brainstorm/2021/0209/1196035-irish-rebellion-1641/.

45 Deana Rankin, '"Shet Fourd vor Generaul Nouddificaushion": Relocating the Irish Joke, 1678–1690', *Eighteenth-Century Ireland / Iris an dá chultúr* 16 (2001): 47–72.

46 The song is most likely to have been performed as a jig after a play, but which play and when is uncertain: for playhouse performances in 1688, see the *London Stage Database:* https://londonstagedatabase.uoregon.edu/sphinx-results.php?sortBy=relevance&theatre=all&volume=1&date-type=1&start-year=1687&end-year=1688&performance=&author=&actor%5B%5D=&role%5B%5D=&keyword=&limit=25&p=2.

47 *Bishop Burnet's History of His Own Time*, https://archive.org/details/bishopburnetshis01burn/page/n9/mode/2up], edited by Martin Joseph Routh (6 vols., Oxford: Oxford University Press, 1823), vol. III, 319.

48 Linda Colley, *Forging the Nation 1707–1837* (New Haven: Yale University Press, 2009).

49 Bratton (ed), 1986, 2017.

50 Available at: https://oursubversivevoice.com/song/12307/.

51 Available at: https://oursubversivevoice.com/song/12304/.

52 A representative sample from our list might include: The Waterboys, 'Old England' and The Clash, 'This Is England' (both 1985); Cornershop, 'England's Dreaming' (1994); Coope, Boyes & Simpson, 'Jerusalem Revisited' (2004); Lady Sovereign, 'My England' (2006); Dizraeli, 'Engurland' (2009); Lowkey, 'Dear England' (2011); PJ Harvey, 'The Glorious Land' (2011); Riz Ahmed, 'Englistan' (2016); The Good, The Bad & The Queen, 'Merrie Land' (2018). Nor is this an exclusively contemporary phenomenon: mid-nineteenth-century songs such as 'The Emigrant's Farewell' (1850s) evince a similar disenchantment and critique of the nation.

53 Available at: https://oursubversivevoice.com/song/12458/.

54 Available at: https://oursubversivevoice.com/song/12597/.

55 Colin Irwin, 'Various Artists – Folk against Fascism', BBC website. Available at: bbc.co.uk/music/reviews/r3vh/. Robin Denselow, 'Show of Hands – review', *Guardian*, 14 November 2013. Available at: theguardian.com/music/2013/nov/14/show-of-hands-folk-review.

56 See discussion of 'Roots' at Songfacts: www.songfacts.com/facts/show-of-hands/roots.

57 Show of Hands, 'Roots'. Available at: youtube.com/watch?v=P5h4PFBuzvw.

58 Una McCormack, 'Welcome to the Cheap Seats', *The World's Own Optimist*, 3 August 2010. Available at: unamccormack.com/index_p_524.html.

59 Available at: https://oursubversivevoice.com/song/12666/.

60 Bob Vylan is, formally, a band of two people, both of whom take the name 'Bob Vylan', but in interviews it tends to be the singer whose experiences and views that are represented. See, for example, Jason Okunday, 'We Answer to Nobody': Duo Bob Vylan on Humility, Hell-raising – and Punk Hypocrisy', *G2*, *Guardian*, 4 April 2024, available at: www.theguardian.com/music/2024/apr/05/we-answer-to-nobody-duo-bob-vylan-on-humility-hell-raising-and-punk-hypocrisy; last accessed 8 April 2024.

61 See interviews with Bob Vylan in *Kerrang!* (www.kerrang.com/bob-vylan-if-you-feel-like-you-cant-say-something-on-an-elevated-platform-you-probably-shouldnt-have-said-it-in-the-first-place); *DIY* (https://diymag.com/interview/bob-vylan-presents-the-price-of-life-april-2022-interview); and *NME* (https://www.nme.com/news/music/bob-vylan-want-to-show-others-that-rock-music-is-an-ok-thing-for-black-people-to-do-3360793).

62 Joseph Mather, *The Songs of Joseph Mather: To Which Are Added a Memoir of Mather, and Miscellaneous Songs Relating to Sheffield*. With introduction and notes by J. Wilson (Sheffield: Pawson and Brailsford, 1862), viii.

Chapter Five

1 Oskar Cox Jensen, 'Lessons from the 750'; available at: https://oursubversivevoice.com/case-study/lessons-from-the-750/.

2 Available at: www.beatlesinterviews.org/db1971.0121.beatles.html.

3 Available at: www.glamourmagazine.co.uk/article/lily-allen-interview-2023.

4 See the *Philadelphia Weekly*, 27 October 2021, https://philadelphiaweekly.com/where-have-all-the-protest-songs-gone/; and BBC News Online, 24 February 2003, http://news.bbc.co.uk/1/hi/uk/2788263.stm.

5 Tim Cooper, 'Pete Townshend: 'Music Has Always Suffered from Being Tied to Politics or Religion', *Guardian*, 2 July 2015. Available at: www.theguardian.com/music/2015/jul/02/pete-townshend-the-who-interview-symphonised-quadrophenia.

6 Dave Simpson, 'Johnny Marr on the Smiths, Morrissey and Putting Politics Back in Pop', *Guardian*, 11 January 2013. Available at: www.theguardian.com/music/2013/jan/11/johnny-marr-smiths-morrissey-politics-pop. The US magazine *Broadside*, which published the early songs of Bob Dylan, Phil Ochs, Peggy Seeger, and others, reported that it would receive song submissions, accompanied by the newspaper clippings that had inspired them. See Jeff Place and Ronald D. Cohen (eds), *The Best of Broadside 1962–1988: Anthems of the American Underground from the Pages of Broadside Magazine* (Washington: Smithsonian Folkways, 2000) 22.

7 Brian Eno interview, 'Taking the World by Storm', *Independent*, 25 November 2005.

8 Greil Marcus, *Folk Music: A Bob Dylan Biography in Seven Songs* (New Haven: Yale University Press, 2022), 7–8.

9 Ibid., 12.

10 Paul Friedlander, *Rock and Roll: A Social History* (Boulder, CO: Westview Press, 2006); Sean Kay, *Rockin' The Free World: How Rock & Roll Revolution Changed America and the World* (New York: Rowman & Littlefield, 2017).

11 Peter Manuel, 'World Music and Activism since the End of History [*sic*]', *Music & Politics* XI, no. 1 (2017). Available at: https://quod.lib.umich.edu/m/mp/9460447.0011.101/--world-music-and-activism-since-the-end-of-history-sic?rgn=main;view=fulltext.

12 Ibid.

13 Beate Kutschke, Noriko Manabe, and John Street, 'Responses to Peter Manuel's "World Music and Activism since the End of History [*sic*]"', *Music & Politics* XI, no. 1 (2017). Available at: https://quod.lib.umich.edu/m/mp/9460447.0011.102/--responses-to-peter-manuels-world-music-and-activism-since?rgn=main;view=fulltext.

14 Even in the age of the Internet, this remains a problem. Spotify, to take one example, has no means of identifying, or making searchable, the 'protest song' on its platform.

15 Noriko Manabe, 'The Unending History of Protest Music', *Music & Politics* XI, no. 1 (2017). Available at: https://quod.lib.umich.edu/m/mp/9460447.0011.102/--responses-to-peter-manuels-world-music-and-activism-since?rgn=main;view=fulltext.

16 Stanley Lieberson, *A Matter of Taste: How Names, Fashions and Culture Change* (New Haven: Yale University Press, 2000); Richard A. Peterson, 'Why 1955? Explaining the Advent of Rock Music', *Popular Music* 9, no. 1 (1990): 97–116.

17 Lieberson, *A Matter of Taste*, 274.

18 Peterson, 'Why 1955?': 98.

19 Nick Crossley, *Networks of Sound, Style and Subversion: The Punk and Post-Punk Worlds of Manchester, London, Liverpool and Sheffield, 1975–80*, (Manchester: Manchester University Press, 2015), 87–8, 80 (his emphasis).

20 Ron Eyerman and Andrew Jamison, *Music and Social Movements: Mobilizing Traditions in the Twentieth Century* (Cambridge: Cambridge University Press, 1998); Kevin McDonald, *Global Movements: Action and Culture* (Oxford: Blackwell, 2006); Mark Mattern, *Acting in Concert: Music, Community, and Political Action* (New Brunswick: Rutgers University Press, 1998); Rob Rosenthal and Richard Flacks, *Playing for Change: Music and Musicians in the Service of Social Movements* (Boulder, CO: Paradigm Publishers, 2012); and William A. Roy, *Reds, Whites, and Blues: Social Movements, Folk Music, and Race in the United States* (Princeton, NJ: Princeton University Press, 2010). A particular debt is owed to Christian Lahusen's *The Rhetoric of Moral Protest: Public Campaigns, Celebrity Endorsement and Political Mobilization* (Berlin: Walter de Gruyter, 1996), in which he writes in detail about the importance of organizations to harnessing music to political protest.

21 Eyerman and Jamison, *Music and Social Movements*, 23–4; see Kate Nash, 'The "Cultural Turn" in Social Theory: Towards a Theory of Cultural Politics', *Sociology* 35, no. 1 (2001): 77–92.

22 Scott Saul, *Freedom Is, Freedom Ain't: Jazz and the Making of the Sixties* (Cambridge, MA: Harvard University Press, 2003); Suzanne E. Smith, *Dancing in the Street: Motown and the Cultural Politics of Detroit* (Cambridge, MA: Harvard University Press, 1999); Brian Ward, *Just My Soul Responding: Rhythm and Blues, Black Consciousness and Race Relations* (London: UCL Press, 1998).

23 Ian Goodyer, *Crisis Politics: The Cultural Politics of Rock against Racism* (Manchester: Manchester University Press, 2009); David Widgery, *Beating Time: Riot 'n' Race 'n'*

Rock 'n' Roll (London: Chatto and Windus, 1986); Rick Blackman, *Babylon's Burning: Music, Subcultures and Anti-Fascism in Britain 1958–2020* (London: Bookmarks Publications, 2021).

24 John Sinclair, manager of the MC5 rock band and founder of the White Panther Party, did something similar with the Detroit Artists Workshop, which he set up to forge a connection between music and politics. See *John Sinclair Presents Detroit Artists Workshop: Community, Jazz and Art in the Motor City, 1965–1981* (Berlin: Strut/Art Yard, 2022).

25 Trish Winter and Simon Keegan-Phipps, *Performing Englishness: Identity and Politics in a Contemporary Folk Resurgence* (Manchester: Manchester University Press, 2013). In the US, *Broadside* performed this role. It published the early songs of Bob Dylan and Phil Ochs (and Peggy Seeger and Ewan MacColl). Songwriter Eric Andersen said that *Broadside* 'lent a forum for discussions and an outlet for honing our skills' (Place and Cohen, *The Best of Broadside*, 149).

26 Stewart Duncan, 'English Choral Music and Politics in the 1930s' (unpublished PhD dissertation, Indiana University Bloomington, 2022), 52.

27 Duncan, 'English Choral Music', 57, 61.

28 Stewart Duncan, 'Bringing Political Song to the Masses: The 1938 Left Song Book'. Available at: https://oursubversivevoice.com/voice/bringing-political-song-to-the-masses-the-1938-left-song-book/. Many years later, the leader of the National Union of Miners, Arthur Scargill, was to feature in the vocals for the protest song 'Strike!' (1984). See: https://oursubversivevoice.com/case-study/strike-the-story-of-a-protest-song/.

29 The information reported here is derived from the WRPM archive held at Goldsmiths College, University of London.

30 Dave Laing, 'Introduction', in Robert Shelton, Dave Laing, Karl Dallas, and Robin Denselow, *The Electric Muse Revisited: The Story of Folk into Rock and Beyond* (London: Omnibus, 2021), x.

31 For Thompson's life history see G.M. Peerbooms, 'Nathaniel Thompson, Tory Printer, Ballad-Monger and Propagandist', unpublished PhD dissertation, Instituut Engels-Amerikaans, Katholieke Universiteit, Nijmegen, 1983; and William E. Burns, 'Thompson, Nathaniel (d. 1687), printer', *Oxford Dictionary of National Biography* (Oxford: Oxford University Press, 2004).

32 Past Catholic outrages were continually replayed in every form of media from sermons to songs; 'Bloody Mary's' burnings at Smithfield in the 1550s were immortalized in Foxe's Book of Martyrs (a book owned by every parish); the providential 'Protestant wind' that helped defeat the Spanish Armada of 1588 was celebrated at every opportunity; the Gunpowder Plot of 1605 was memorialised with national festivities and 'pope burnings' every 5 November. Laws enforced all the king's subjects to take oaths of allegiance to the king and to prove their allegiance to the Protestant Anglican Church by publicly taking communion.

33 Shortly before Thompson had arrived in London, French Catholics were held responsible for starting the Great Fire of 1666. One man was executed (he confessed but no one really believed he was guilty), while in 1671, London's Monument not only celebrated the city's survival but also displayed a plaque declaring that 'papists' were guilty of starting the fire. It was removed in 1689. Today the Monument is largely, but not entirely, free of its original anti-papist sentiment.

34 Two loosely organised political 'parties' emerged both in and outside parliament. 'Whigs' argued that, as a Catholic, the duke of York should be excluded from the succession and replaced by a protestant heir, that all papists should be controlled, and that parliaments should have more power. 'Tories' believed the succession was sacrosanct and argued that Protestant Nonconformists were just as, if not more, dangerous than Catholics: after all, it was a republican government led by Nonconformists who had executed Charles I in 1649. The literature on this period is extensive. For a good overview, see Tim Harris, *Restoration. Charles II and His Kingdoms, 1660–1685* (London: Penguin, 2005); idem, *Revolution. The Great Crisis of the British Monarchy, 1685–1725* (London: Allen Lane, 2006).

35 For a full catalogue, see Peerbooms, 'Nathaniel Thompson, Tory Printer, Ballad-Monger and Propagandist', 175–267.

36 Those we know of were former apprentices, such as Allen Banks (a bankrupt), unlicensed bookseller and political songwriter James Dean, and Catholic writer and astrologer John Gadbury. See Peerbooms, 'Nathaniel Thompson, Tory Printer, Ballad-Monger and Propagandist'.

37 Angela McShane, *The Ballad Trade and Its Politics* (Woodbridge: Boydell and Brewer, forthcoming), chapters 7 and 8.

38 Available at: https://oursubversivevoice.com/song/12009/. For the full publication history and a performance of the song by the Carnival Band see the 100 Ballads Website No. 27.

39 Available at: https://oursubversivevoice.com/song/12008/.

40 Thomas D'Urfey, *A New Collection of Songs and Poems* (London: J. Hindmarsh, 1683), 33.

41 Printed in *Trincalo Sainted* (London: J. B., 1682), an anthology of Whig songs.

42 Tim Harris, *London Crowds in the Reign of Charles II. Propaganda and Politics from the Restoration until the Exclusion Crisis* (Cambridge: Cambridge University Press, 1987); idem, 'Was the Tory Reaction Popular?: Attitudes of Londoners towards the Persecution of Dissent, 1681–1686', *London Journal*, 13.2 (1987–8): 106–20; Mark Knights, *Politics and Opinion in Crisis, 1678–81* (Cambridge: Cambridge University Press, 1994).

43 Compare *The Loyal Health* (London: A. Banks, 1682), printed by Thompson's supporter Allen Banks, and *The Oxford Health* (London: P. Brooksby, 1682), published by the retail ballad specialist Philip Brooksby. See McShane, *Ballad Trade and Its Politics*, chapter 7.

44 Nathaniel Thompson (ed), *A Choice Collection of 180 Loyal Songs* (London: N. Thompson, 1685), Introduction.

45 Burns, 'Thompson, Nathaniel (d. 1687), printer'.

46 Thompson, *Choice Collection of 180 Loyal Songs*, Introduction.

47 John Horden, *John Freeth (1731–1808): Political Ballad Writer* (Oxford: Leopard's Head Press, 1993), 2–4, 18.

48 Ibid., 11.

49 Ibid., 21.

50 Ibid., 10.

51 Ibid., 5–6.

52 Ibid., 14.

53 Recent studies of this phenomenon are legion, but the best place to begin is perhaps Jon Mee, *Conversable Worlds: Literature, Contention, and Community 1762–1830* (Oxford: Oxford University Press, 2013).

54 Horden, *John Freeth*, 25–6.

55 Ibid., 27–30

56 Ibid., 23–5.

57 Oskar Cox Jensen, 'The Hymn as Protest Song in England and Its Empire, 1819–1919', *Yale Journal of Music and Religion* 8 (2022): 104–24, 119–20.

58 British Library Music Collections H.1917, 105–14.

59 David Kennerley, 'Music, Politics, and History: An Introduction', *Journal of British Studies* 60 (2021): 362–74, at 362–4.

60 Kate Bowan and Paul Pickering, *Sounds of Liberty: Music, Radicalism and Reform in the Anglophone World, 1790–1914* (Manchester: Manchester University Press, 2017), 235.

61 Place and Cohen, *The Best of Broadside*, 12.

62 Marcus, *Folk Music*, 183. Even the Special Branch thought MacColl was important; they monitored his movements and mail, according to Rob Young, *Electric Eden: Unearthing Britain's Visionary Music* (London: Faber & Faber, 2010), 114–15.

63 Robert Shelton, 'Britain's Folk Scene: "Skiffle Craze" to Clubs in Pubs', *New York Times*, 6 March 1966. Singer Shirley Collins, speaking in 2023, recalled that 'the folk scene in England in the '50s and '60s was very left wing; it was sort of bullied into it by Ewan MacColl' (quoted in Jim Wirth, 'The Mojo Interview', *Mojo* 357 (August 2023): 28). Musician Bob Pegg says of seeing MacColl and Seeger: 'When he [MacColl] was on form he was brilliant … He held a room … And Peggy could play any bloody thing under the sun', according to Mike Butler, *Sounding the Century: Bill Leader & Co., Vol. 2 – Horizons for Some: 1956–1962* (Market Harborough: Matador, 2022), 27.

64 Young, *Electric Eden*, 142–4.

65 The newsletter was called *The Lark*. It – and some other material referred to here – was held in the Ewan MacColl and Peggy Seeger archive at the Ruskin College library in Oxford. The archive is now held in the Library of Congress, Washington, DC.

66 Quoted in Ben Harker, *Class Act: The Cultural and Political Life of Ewan MacColl* (London: Pluto Press, 2007), 159. Brian Shuel, who took the photograph of Bob Dylan at the Singers' Club, says that MacColl made Dylan audition before he was allowed to perform at the club. Private correspondence, 16 December 2021.

67 Ibid., 158–9.

68 Dave Laing, 'MacColl and the English Folk Revival', in Allan F. Moore (ed), *Legacies of Ewan MacColl* (London: Taylor & Francis, 2014), 158.

69 Harker, *Class Act*, 185.

70 Young, *Electric Eden*, 144; see also Harker, *Class Act*, 186–90.

71 Laing, 'MacColl and the English Folk Revival', 162.

72 *The Lark*, No. 6.

73 Interview with Jake Glanville. Available at: https://oursubversivevoice.com/interview/jake-glanville/. One of our anonymous reviewers reported that they found the attitude of the Critics Group 'utterly insufferable' and that they toasted the news of its demise.

74 Harker, *Class* Act, 198–9.

75 Ibid., 196–9, 209–11.

76 Available at: https://oursubversivevoice.com/song/12372/.

77 Quoted in Lisa Garrison and Sarah Plant, 'Honing, Polishing, Casting Out: Peggy Seeger Talks about the Folk Process', *Sing Out!* 28, no. 2 (1980): 2–11.

78 Peggy Seeger, *First Time Ever: A Memoir*, (London: Faber & Faber, 2017), 265–6.

79 Mike Butler, *Sounding the Century: Bill Leader & Co., Vol. 1 – Glimpses of Far Off Things: 1855–1956* (Market Harborough: Matador, 2022), 66.

80 Foreman did not publish just CND protest songs. One of his first was Karl Dallas's song, 'The Greedy Landlord', in support of the London Rent Strike of 1960. He sold his sheets in places like Portobello Market. Interview with John Foreman, 31 March 2022.

81 Quoted in Dave Arthur, *Bert: The Life and Times of A.L. Lloyd* (London: Pluto Press, 2012), 372.

82 For example: https://oursubversivevoice.com/song/12446/.

83 Crass, 'Big A Little A' b/w 'Nagasaki Nightmare' (Crass Records, 1980).

84 Rimbaud quoted in George Berger, *The Story of Crass* (London: Omnibus, 2006), 24.

85 Exit was a mid-1970s performance art group, influenced in part by Fluxus, to which Yoko Ono belonged.

86 Interview with Steve Ignorant, 14 March 2023.

87 Crass, 'Do They Owe Us a Living', on *The Feeding of the Five Thousand* (Small Wonder, 1978).

88 Interview with Steve Ignorant, 17 February 2023.

89 Ibid.

90 Loder had also been a member of Exit with Rimbaud and others.

91 Interview with Steve Ignorant, 14 March 2023.

92 Ibid.

93 Robert Adlington, *Musical Models of Democracy* (Oxford: Oxford University Press, 2024), 162.

Chapter Six

1 https://www.legislation.gov.uk/ukpga/2022/32/contents/enacted.

2 Barry Dufour and Nick Brown, 'Street Protests from Peterloo to Just Stop Oil and Public Sector Strikes', *Guardian*, 19 January 2023.

3 During the House of Lords debate on the Bill, Natalie Bennett tweeted: 'Noise amendments – I just quoted 'March of the Women'. "Shout, shout your song"'. @natalieben, 26 April 2022. Bennett slightly misquotes the chorus, which is 'Shout! Shout! Up with your song!': https://oursubversivevoice.com/song/12310/.

4 Ben Quinn, 'UK Placed in Third Tier in Global Index of Free Expression', *Guardian*, 25 January 2023.

5 See, for example, Robert Ingram, Jason Peacey, and Alex W. Barber (eds), *Freedom of Speech, 1500–1850* (Manchester: Manchester University Press, 2020); Cyndia Clegg, *Press Censorship in Jacobean England* (Cambridge: Cambridge University Press, 2001); Cyndia Clegg, *Press Censorship in Caroline England* (Cambridge: Cambridge University Press, 2008); Benjamin Woodford, 'Developments and Debates in English Censorship during the Interregnum', *Early Modern Literary Studies* 17, no. 2 (2014): 1–21; Jason McElligott, *Royalism, Print and Censorship in Revolutionary England* (Woodbridge: The Boydell Press, 2007).

6 John Street, *Music and Politics* (Cambridge: Polity, 2012); see also Martin Cloonan and Reebee Garolfalo (eds), *Policing Pop* (Philadelphia: Temple University Press, 2003).

7 https://oursubversivevoice.com/song/12044/.

8 Angela McShane, *The Ballad Trade and Its Politics in Seventeenth Century Britain* (Woodbridge: Boydell and Brewer, forthcoming), chapter 9.

9 Dorian Lynskey, *33 Revolutions Per Minute: A History of Protest Songs* (London: Faber & Faber, 2010), 445.

10 Nathaniel Thompson, who appears in a chapter 5 case study, licensed only his music books and none of his music sheets. On the 1710 act, see Martin Kretschmer and Friedemann Kawohl, 'The History and Philosophy of Copyright', in Simon Frith and Lee Marshall (eds), *Music and Copyright* (Edinburgh: Edinburgh University Press, 2004), 21–53.

11 See, for example, 'The Whigs Exaltation' at: https://oursubversivevoice.com/song/12009/ and the discussion in chapter 5.

12 Ephemeral printers constantly flirted with criminality, falling foul of laws against libel or sedition. After 1695, when both the licensing act and the Stationers' Company printing monopoly came to an end, the social and financial instability of such publishers offered them some protection against the most common threat: a prosecution for piracy. Charles Dibdin the Younger was advised against legal action by his own printer (a man who knew better than most) on the grounds that he would fail to recoup his costs from the impoverished culprits. Even when the relevant act against piracy was updated to account for broadsides in 1810, it merely prohibited using an author's name without permission: their lyrics could still be printed without fear of reprisals. The margin this left for illegality naturally encouraged the spread of songs across different social contexts, particularly the illicit appropriation of elite publications by popular printers. See Oskar Cox Jensen, *Napoleon and British Song, 1797–1822* (Basingstoke: Palgrave Macmillan, 2015), 25; George Speaight, *Professional and Literary Memoirs of Charles Dibdin the Younger* (London: Society for Theatre Research, 1956), 47; *The Statutes of the Realm*, 11 vols. (London: Dawsons of Pall Mall, 1810), vol. 5, 430.

13 Simon Frith and Lee Marshall, 'Making Sense of Copyright', in Frith and Marshall (eds), *Music and Copyright*, 1.

14 Mike Jones, 'Marxists in the Marketplace', in Martin Cloonan and Reebee Garofalo (eds), *Policing Pop* (Philadelphia: Temple University Press, 2003), 107 (his emphasis). Dave Randall, guitarist with Faithless, recalls the pressure he was put under by his manager and others when he argued that the band should not perform in Israel. See Dave Randall, *Sound System: The Political Power of Music* (London: Pluto Press, 2017), 142–7.

15 Keith Negus, *Music Genres and Corporate Cultures* (London: Routledge, 1999).

16 Steve Knopper, *Appetite for Self-destruction: The Spectacular Crash of the Record industry in the Digital Age* (London: Simon & Schuster, 2009); Alex Sayf Cummings, *Democracy of Sound: Music Piracy and the Remaking of American Copyright in the Twentieth Century* (New York: Oxford University Press, 2013). The Our Subversive Voice project has been restricted in quoting lyrics of contemporary protest songs that are still in copyright, although the disruptive force of the digital has made it possible to provide video/audio via third parties. The historic printed songs, such as those in the database, are also subject to highly contested copyrights, which are interpreted differently by holding archives (who charge) and libraries (who don't), though thanks to public funding, many recordings have been made on a copyright-free basis.

17 David Hesmondhalgh, 'Streaming's Effects on Music Culture: Old Anxieties and New Simplifications', *Cultural Sociology* 16, no. 1 (2022): 3–24.

18 Sabine Jacques, Krzysztof Garstka, Morten Hviid, and John Street, 'An Empirical Study of the Use of Automated Anti-piracy Systems and Their Consequences for Cultural Diversity', *Scripted* 15, no. 1 (2018).

19 Unfortunately, no central records survive by which we can assess the nature or number of licences awarded. Occasional references appear in local records. We could assume that depositions featuring people whose trade is described as a 'ballad singer' did, in fact, have some sort of official licence.

20 Oskar Cox Jensen, *The Ballad-Singer in Georgian and Victorian London* (Cambridge: Cambridge University Press, 2021), 83–91.

21 Oskar Cox Jensen, *Napoleon and British Song, 1797–1822* (Basingstoke: Palgrave Macmillan, 2015), 30, 32.

22 James Winter, *London's Teeming Streets, 1830–1914* (London: Routledge, 1993); Tim Hitchcock and Heather Shore (eds), *The Streets of London: From the Great Fire to the Great Stink* (London: River Orams Press, 2003); Cox Jensen, *The Ballad-Singer*, 236–7.

23 Paul F. Rice, *British Music and the French Revolution* (Newcastle: Cambridge Scholars, 2010).

24 Derek B. Scott, 'Music Hall: Regulations and Behaviour in a British Cultural Institution', *The Victorian Web*, at https://victorianweb.org/mt/musichall/scott.html.

25 See https://www.gov.uk/guidance/entertainment-licensing-changes-under-the-live-music-act ; https://www.royalgreenwich.gov.uk/info/200299/alcohol_and_entertainment_licences/723/regulated_entertainment https://www.ppluk.com/about-us/our-history/ https://www.prsformusic.com/about-us/history#F843083B-D04E-4546-98B3-5BD1013AA3DD. For laws and debates over individual performance in the 1790s, 1827, and 1864, see Cox Jensen, *The Ballad-Singer*, chapter 2.

26 https://commonslibrary.parliament.uk/constituency-casework-playing-music-in-public-places/.

27 John Street, 'From *Gigs* to Giggs: Politics, Law and Live Music', *Social Semiotics* 22, no. 5 (2012): 575–85.

28 Not all restrictions on musical performance are necessarily acts of censorship, but they may create the opportunity or excuse for them. The advent of broadcast music performances on radio saw the introduction of a new licensing system emerged, following negotations between the BBC and the Musicians' Union over the amount of live vs recorded music that could be played, creating the 'needle time agreements'. This restricted how much recorded music could be broadcast. This cannot be seen as direct censorship, but it might be viewed as limiting what could be played and heard. See John Williamson and Martin Cloonan, *Players' Work Time: A History of the British Musicians' Union, 1893–2013* (Manchester: Manchester University Press, 2016). Similarly, in 2023, during a performance of the Libertines at the Royal Albert Hall, as a deliberate challenge to fussy policing by music venues, the lead singer invited the audience to join the band on the stage. This was seen by the stewards as a potential health and safety breach that could damage the hall's entertainment licence, and so they brought the show to an end, ejected the band, and sent the entire audience home. For the band, this was a protest thwarted; for the venue, a licence protected (personal communication from an audience and a staff member, 2023).

29 Simpson, 304–6; Frith and Marshall (eds), *Music and Copyright*; David Hunter, 'Music Copyright in Britain to 1800', *Music and Letters* 67 (1986): 269–82.

30 On this, see Ruth Towse, 'Copyright and Economics', in Frith and Marshall (eds), *Music and Copyright*, 54–69.

31 Alastair Bellany, 'Singing Libel in Early Stuart England: The Case of the Staines Fiddlers, 1627', *Huntington Library Quarterly* 69.1 (2006): 177–93; Clegg, *Press Censorship in Jacobean England*; Clegg, *Press Censorship in Caroline England*; John Barrell, *Imagining the King's Death: Figurative Treason, Fantasies of Regicide, 1793–1796* (Oxford: Oxford University Press, 2000).

32 Philip A. Hamburger, 'The Development of the Law of Seditious Libel and the Control of the Press', *Stanford Law Review* 661 (1985): 661–765. *The Sale of Esau's Birthright*, discussed above, in part satirizes a burgess who became victim of this law; see McShane, *Ballad Trade and Its Politics*, chapter 10. For current use of the law, see 'Scandalum Magnatum', *Guardian*, 31 January 2000: www.theguardian.com/world/2000/jan/31/law.theguardian.

33 See, for example, the case of James Dover, printer of 'The Belgick Boar': https://oursubversivevoice.com/song/12041/; for his trial report see: *Old Bailey Proceedings Online* (www.oldbaileyonline.org, version 8.0, 27 October 2023), April 1695, trial of J - D - (t16950403-22).

34 Paul Slack, *From Reformation to Improvement: Public Welfare in Early Modern England* (Oxford: Clarendon Press, 1999); Audrey Eccles, *Vagrancy in Law and Practice under the Old Poor Law* (Farnham: Ashgate, 2012). On the repeal of the law, see: *The Big Issue*, 28 June 2022: www.bigissue.com/news/housing/what-is-the-vagrancy-act/#:~:text=The%20Vagrancy%20Act%20makes%20it,homelessness%20in%20present%2Dday%20UK. See also www.libertyhumanrights.org.uk/advice_information/pcsc-policing-act-protest-rights/.

35 Melissa Bradshaw, 'Anti-Sus Soundsystems: An Interview with Dennis Bovell', *The Quietus*, 2 February 2011; available at: https://thequietus.com/articles/05630-dennis-bovell-interview.

36 The scope of Henry V's censorship is overstated in Martin Cloonan, *Banned!: Censorship of Popular Music in Britain, 1967–1992* (Aldershot: Ashgate, 1996), 11. See Sir Richard Baker, *A Chronicle of the Kings of England, from the Time of the Romans Goverment [sic] unto the Raigne of Our Soveraigne Lord, King Charles* (London: D. Frere, 1643), 123: 'Yet king Henry, to make his enemies the better contented with their overthrow, and to take away the envy of his Victory; at his returne into England with his Prisoners, which was on the sixt of November following, he presently gave straight order, that no Ballad or Song should be made or sung, more then of Thanksgiving to God for his happy Victory and safe Returne; but without words of either disgracing the French, or extolling the English'.

37 McShane, *The Ballad Trade and Its Politics*, chapter 6.

38 G. Thompson, '"A Day in the Life": The Beatles and the BBC, May 1967', in Patricia Hall (ed), *The Oxford Handbook of Music Censorship* (Oxford: Oxford University Press, 2018), 535–55.

39 'British Folk Singers Denied Visas for US', 29 September 1964; available at: www.nytimes.com/1964/09/29/archives/british-folk-singers-denied-visas-for-us.html; Jon Wiener, *Come Together: John Lennon in His Time* (New York: Random House, 1984).

40 Quoted in Lynskey, *33 Revolutions Per Minute*, 461.

41 Ibid., 454, 464, 465.

42 Communications were limited to letters carried by messengers on horses, boats, or canals until the 1830s; were accomplished by trains and the telegraph until the 1920s; and relied upon motor transport and radio signals until the 1990s brought the Internet, mobile phones, and satellites.

43 See the OSV Website Case Study: https://oursubversivevoice.com/case-study/the-subversive-voice-of-early-modern-hunger-1596-1774-songs-as-weapons-of-the-weak-or-ballading-the-badgers-in-times-of-dearth/.

44 See, for example, John Walter (ed), *Crowds and Popular Politics in Early Modern England* (Manchester: Manchester University Press, 2006); Tim Harris, *London Crowds in the Reign of Charles II. Propaganda and Politics from the Restoration until the Exclusion Crisis* (Cambridge: Cambridge University Press 1987); Nicholas Rogers, *Crowds, Culture, and Politics in Georgian Britain* (Oxford: Clarendon Press, 1998). For relevant OSV songs, see https://oursubversivevoice.com/song/11956/; https://oursubversivevoice.com/song/11982/; https://oursubversivevoice.com/song/12019/.

45 '1643 The Womens Tumult at the House of Commons, Aug. 7.', John Rushworth (ed), *Historical Collections of Private Passages of State ... Third Part*, vol. 2 1640–1644 (London: R. Chiswell and T. Cockerill, 1692), 357–8.

46 For the song, see: https://oursubversivevoice.com/song/12047/.

47 See 'Riotous Petition of the Shoemakers'; 'Order against Tumultuous Assemblies'; and 'Act for Laying Additional Duties … and for Allowances of Exporting Made Wares, of Leather, Sheep-Skins, and Lamb-Skins', "Fourth Parliament of Great Britain: First session (3 of 3) – begins 17/4/1714." *The History and Proceedings of the House of Commons: Volume 5, 1713–1714*. (London: Chandler, 1742), 106–54.

48 For this case, see www.parliament.uk/about/living-heritage/transformingsociety/electionsvoting/newport-rising/1839-newp-ris/riot-act-1714/.

49 See the OSV Case Study: https://oursubversivevoice.com/case-study/the-subversive-voice-of-early-modern-hunger-1596-1774-songs-as-weapons-of-the-weak-or-ballading-the-badgers-in-times-of-dearth/.

50 For 'The Powte's Complaint', see: https://oursubversivevoice.com/song/11933/; and Todd A. Borlik and Clare, 'Angling for the "Powte": A Jacobean Environmental Protest Poem', *English Literary Renaissance* 48, no.2 (2018): 256–89. For 'The Newgate Street Petition', see: https://oursubversivevoice.com/song/12179/. For the story behind Extinction Rebellion's rewriting of 'A Nightingale Sang in Berkeley Square', see: https://extinctionrebellion.uk/2019/04/29/from-6pm-today-london-a-nightingale-sang-in-berkeley-square/; last accessed on 26 April 2024.

51 See the Petitioning Project: https://petitioning.history.ac.uk/; David Zaret, *Origins of Democratic Culture: Printing, Petitions, and the Public Sphere in Early-Modern England* (Princeton, NJ: Princeton University Press, 2000); Edward Vallance, *Loyalty, Memory and Public Opinion in England, 1658–1727* (Manchester: Manchester University Press, 2019); Daniel P. Carpenter, *Democracy by Petition: Popular Politics in Transformation, 1790–1870* (Cambridge, MA: Harvard University Press, 2021).

52 Bamford, *Life of a Radical*, 150–60.

53 Eleven are included in the Our Subversive Voice website; see also Alison Morgan, *Ballads and Songs of Peterloo* (Manchester: Manchester University Press, 2019).

54 Michael Clarke, *The Politics of Pop Festivals* (London: Junction Books, 1982); George McKay, *Senseless Acts of Beauty: Cultural Resistance since the Sixties* (London: Verso, 1996).

55 John Street, Matthew Worley, and David Wilkinson, '"Does It Threaten the Status Quo?" Elite Responses to British Punk, 1976–1978,' *Popular Music* 37, no. 2 (2018): 283.

56 Ibid., 281–2.

57 Tim Jonze, 'Rapper Giggs's Cancelled after Police Warning', *Guardian unlimited*, 23 February 2010; Street, 'From *Gigs* to Giggs'.

58 Lambros Fatsis, 'Policing the Beats: The Criminalisation of UK Drill and Grime Music by the London Metropolitan Police', *Sociological Review* 67, no. 6 (2019): 1300–16.

59 The rapper Digga D was subject to a Criminal Behaviour Order, under the terms of which he was restricted in what his songs could say. His lyrics had to be submitted to the Met in advance (see Ciaran Thapar, 'I'm Banned from Areas I Don't Even Know', *Guardian* G2, 30 June 2023, 4–5).

60 Keir Monteith, 'Ban Rap and Drill Lyrics in the Courtroom', *Popular Music* 41, no. 4 (2022): 556; see also Fatsis, 'Policing the Beats'.

61 See Our Subversive Voice website: https://oursubversivevoice.com/case-study/from-come-all-you-farmers-out-of-the-countrey-to-question-time-critique-contempt-and-ruling-classes-in-english-protest-songs-since-1603/. See also https://thehistoryofparliament.wordpress.com/2019/08/20/the-six-acts-and-censorship-of-the-press/.

62 Alastair Bellany, 'Singing Libel in Early Stuart England: The Case of the Staines Fiddlers, 1627', *Huntington Library Quarterly* 69, no. 1 (March 2006): 177–94.

63 Ibid., 181.

64 Ibid., 182.

65 See, for example, https://oursubversivevoice.com/song/12470/; https://oursubversivevoice.com/song/12435/.

66 Available at: https://oursubversivevoice.com/song/12373/; see also Our Subversive Voice website: https://oursubversivevoice.com/case-study/paul-mccartney-the-protest-singer/.

67 Tom Doyle, *Man on the Run: Paul McCartney in the 1970s* (New York: Ballantine Books, 2013), 62.

68 *The Moderate Messenger* 14 (23–30 July 1649): 93.

69 From Frank Peel, *The Risings of the Luddites, Chartists and Plug-drawers* (New York: N.p., 1880), 333–4; quoted in Kate Bowan and Paul Pickering, *Sounds of Liberty: Music, Radicalism and Reform in the Anglophone World, 1790–1914* (Manchester: Manchester University Press, 2017), 193–4.

70 Tim Harris, *London Crowds in the Reign of Charles II* (Cambridge: Cambridge University Press, 1987), chapter 6; and for a catalogued list of ballad titles, see McShane, *Political Broadside Ballads of Seventeenth-Century England: A Critical Bibliography* (London: Pickering and Chatto, 2011), 275–387.

71 Margaret L. Laware, 'Circling the Missiles and Staining Them Red: Feminist Rhetorical Invention and Strategies of Resistance at the Women's Peace Camp at Greenham Common', *NWSA Journal* 16, no. 3 (2004): 18–41.

72 For the songs, see: https://oursubversivevoice.com/song/12447/; https://oursubversivevoice.com/song/12448/; for the event, see the Our Subversive Voice

website: https://oursubversivevoice.com/voice/osv-the-carnival-band-at-cecil-sharp-house/.

73 David Nash, *Acts against God: A Short History of Blasphemy* (Chicago: University of Chicago Press, 2020).

74 John Street, *Rebel Rock: The Politics of Popular Music* (Oxford: Basil Blackwell, 1986), 17; quoted in McShane, *The Ballad Trade and Its Politics*, chapter 1.

75 Available at: https://oursubversivevoice.com/song/11969/.

76 Hansard (26/10/82).

77 Robert Walser, 'Professing Censorship: Academic Attacks on Heavy Metal', *Journal of Popular Music Studies* 5 (1993): 68–78; see also the *Guardian*'s list of 'The 10 Best Banned Songs', 15 December 2019 – no. 1: Frankie's 'Relax'; 6. Billie Holliday's 'Strange Fruit'. Available at: www.theguardian.com/music/2019/feb/14/the-greatest-banned-songs-of-all-time-ranked. The DJ who provoked the ban of 'Relax' would, some thirty years later, produce an obscenely racist protest song of his own ('UKIP Calypso' (2014), discussed in chapter 3).

78 See https://oursubversivevoice.com/case-study/this-is-religion-a-case-study-of-pils-religion-and-crass-asylum/.

79 Lynskey, *33 Revolutions Per Minute*, 353–4.

80 Jim McGuigan, *Cultural Populism* (London: Routledge, 1992); Martin Scherzinger, 'Double Voices of Musical Censorship after 9/11', in Jonathan Ritter and J. Martin Daughtry (eds), *Music in the Post-9/11 World* (London: Routledge, 2007), 91–122.

81 McShane, *The Ballad Trade and Its Politics*, chapter 6; *Sounds*, 7 June 1980: 10. See also *New Musical Express*, 14 June 1980.

82 McShane, *Ballad Trade and Its Politics*, chapter 1.

83 Ibid., chapter 9.

84 This was also the case with the military protest song 'McCafferty' (1862). See Roy Palmer (ed), *The Rambling Soldier*, 2nd ed. (Gloucester: Alan Sutton, 1985), 119–26.

85 'The Lord Mayor of London to Lord Burghley, 26 July 1596', Burghley Papers, BL, Lansdowne MS 81/30, f. 76. Discussed in Walter, *Crowds and Popular Politics in Early Modern England*, 196–222.

86 Lynskey, *33 Revolutions Per Minute*, 500.

87 Theodor Adorno, 'On Popular Music', *Essays on Music*, edited by Richard Leppert (Berkeley: University of California Press, 2002), 437–69; see also Adorno on music and protest: https://www.youtube.com/watch?v=-njxKF8CkoU.

88 McShane, *The Ballad Trade and Its Politics*, chapter 1.

89 Mark Fisher, *Capitalist Realism* (London: Zone Books, 2009).

90 As in the case of James Dover, printer of 'The Belgick Boar' (noted above), see the 100 Ballads Website No. 118.

91 The song was illustrated with a detailed satirical cartoon engraved in wood: two 'states' survive suggesting this too was discussed and improved, see B.J. Rahn, 'A Ra-ree Show – a Rare Cartoon: Revolutionary Propaganda in the Treason Trial of Stephen College', in Paul J. Korshin (ed), *Studies in Change and Revolution: Aspects of English Intellectual History 1640–1800* (Menston, Yorkshire: The Scolar Press, 1972), 77–98.

92 See Jane Wessel, 'Performing "A Ra-ree Show": Political Spectacle and the Treason Trial of Stephen College', *Restoration: Studies in English Literary Culture, 1660–1700* 38.1 (2014): 3–17.

93 OED: 'an exhibition, show, or spectacle of any kind, esp. one regarded as lurid, vulgar, or populist'.

94 Gary S. De Krey, 'College [Colledge], Stephen (*c.*1635–1681), poet and political activist.' *Oxford Dictionary of National Biography*; available at: www.oxforddnb.com/display/10.1093/ref:odnb/9780198614128.001.0001/odnb-9780198614128-e-5906.

95 Ibid.

96 Ibid.

97 Available at: https://oursubversivevoice.com/song/12106/.

98 For more details, see Kate Horgan, *The Politics of Songs in Eighteenth-Century Britain, 1723–1795* (London: Pickering and Chatto, 2014), 129–70; see also James Montgomery, *The Trial of James Montgomery for a Libel on the War ... at Doncaster Sessions, January 22, 1795* (Sheffield, 1795), *passim*, and James Montgomery, *The Poetical Works of James Montgomery, Collected by Himself* (London: N.p., 1854), 134–40.

99 Horgan, *The Politics of Songs*, 156–7.

100 John Thelwall, *The Tribune, A Periodical Publication, Consisting Chiefly of the Political Lectures of J. Thelwall. Taken in Short-hand by W. Ramsey and Revised by the Lecturer*, 7 (London: N.p., 25 April 1795).

101 Ibid.

102 John-Erik Hansson, 'The Genre of Radical Thought and the Practices of Equality: The Trajectories of William Godwin and John Thelwall in the Mid-1790s', *History of European Ideas* 43 (2017): 776–90.

103 The last of these is on our list, and the lyrics of all three are at The Best of the OLL #69, available at: https://oll-resources.s3.us-east-2.amazonaws.com/oll3/store/titles/2671/Thelwall_PoliticalSongs1795.pdf.

104 Michael Scrivener, 'John Thelwall and Popular Jacobin Allegory, 1793–95', *ELH* 67 (2000): 951–71, 951.

105 Jon Mee, *Print, Publicity, and Popular Radicalism in the 1790s: The Laurel of Liberty* (Cambridge: Cambridge University Press, 2016), 78–84; Ian Newman, *The Romantic Tavern: Literature and Conviviality in the Age of Revolution* (Cambridge: Cambridge University Press, 2019), 182–5.

106 Colin Jones, private communication to Oskar Cox Jensen, 2022.

107 Mee, *Print, Publicity, and Popular Radicalism*, 83.

108 Philip Schofield, 'Reeves, John, 1752–1829', *Oxford Dictionary of National Biography* (2008), at https://doi.org/10.1093/ref:odnb/23306.

109 Donald E. Ginter, 'The Loyalist Association Movement of 1792–3 and British Public Opinion', *Historical Journal* 9 (1966): 179–90.

110 Thomas Holcroft, *A Narrative of Facts, Relating to a Prosecution for High Treason* (London: H. D. Symonds, 1795), 11.

111 *'A Friend to Church and State' to John Reeves' Association for the Preservation of Liberty and Property against Republicans and Levellers, 12 December 1792*, British Library Add. MSS 16922, fol. 43.

112 Cited in Mark Philp, *Reforming Ideas in Britain* (Cambridge: Cambridge University Press, 2014), 233–4.

113 Holcroft, *A Narrative of Facts*, 11.

114 See Cox Jensen, *Napoleon and British Song*, for a full account and further references.

115 See also Mark Philp, 'Music and Movement in Britain, 1793–1815', *Journal of British Studies* 60 (2021): 403–15.

116 Peter Lewis and Jerry Booth, *The Invisible Medium: Public, Commercial and Community Radio* (Basingstoke: Palgrave Macmillan, 1989).

117 Asa Briggs, *The BBC: A Short Story of the First Fifty Years* (Oxford: Oxford University Press, 1985).

118 Graham Abraham (gramophone director), memo, 24 September 1943. Note: All material from the BBC is copyrighted and is quoted with permission.

119 *This Record Is Not to Be Broadcast: 75 Records Banned by the BBC 1931–1957* (Acrobat Records, 2008).

120 Donald MacLean (assistant head of popular music), memo, 16 July 1969.

121 Assistant director of sound broadcasting, memo, 25 June 1961.

122 Kenneth Baynes (head of popular music), memo, 23 June 1966.

123 Ray Kinsella, 'The Bebop Scene in London's Soho, 1945–1950' (Houndmills: Palgrave Macmillan, 2022), 187ff.; and George McKay, '"Crippled with Nerves": Popular Music and Polio, with Particular Reference to Ian Dury', *Popular Music* 28, no. 3 (2009): 341–65.

124 McKay, 'Crippled with Nerves'.

125 BBC's Central Music Advisory Committee.

126 Assistant head of gramophone programmes, memo, 3 November 1961.

127 Cecil Madden (producer of live programmes of variety, ballets, and drama), memo, 13 November 1947.

128 Robert MacDermot, memo, 21 November 1944.

129 Chief assistant, productions, popular music (sound), memo, 9 April 1964.

130 Graeme Thompson, '"A Day in The Life": The Beatles and the BBC, May 1967', in Patricia Hall (ed), *The Oxford Handbook of Music Censorship* (Oxford: Oxford University Press, 2018), 535–55.

131 Controllers of BBC TV and of Radios 1 and 2, memo, 2 June 1971.

132 Secretary to Douglas Lawrence (assistant head of gramophone programmes), memo, 3 November 1965.

133 Spencer Leigh, Sleeve notes for *This Record Is Not to Be Broadcast: 75 Records Banned by the BBC 1931–1957*, Acrobat Records, 2008.

134 Director general, memo, 19 July 1943.

135 The men allowed to sing 'Don't Let's …' included Edward Cooper and Ronald Frankan.

136 Assistant controller (progammes), memo, 28 July 1943; see also memo, 27 July 1943.

137 Leigh, Sleeve notes for *This Record Is Not to Be Broadcast.*

138 Assistant director of sound broadcasting, memo, 28 April 1964.

139 Letter from Pye Records, 6 April 1962.

140 Music organiser, light entertainment (sound), memos, 9 and 17 October 1962, and 10 January 1963.

141 Donald MacLean (head of popular music), memo, 18 July 1962.

142 Ibid.

143 Head of gramophone programmes, memo, 14 April 1964.

144 H.W. McMullan, memo, 5 October 1962.

145 Pat Hillyard (head of sound light entertainment), memo, 29 December 1961.

146 In the same year, John Lennon and Yoko Ono's album *Sometime in New York City* (1972) was reportedly censored for public display because its cover contained an

image of the naked President Nixon dancing with the naked Chairman Mao (https://faroutmagazine.co.uk/john-lennon-album-was-censored/). The songs themselves were poorly reviewed and received relatively little media attention or airplay, but John and Yoko did perform three of them on ITV's *David Frost Show*.

147 https://oursubversivevoice.com/song/11973/; https://oursubversivevoice.com/song/12316/; https://oursubversivevoice.com/song/12173/; https://oursubversivevoice.com/song/12068/; https://oursubversivevoice.com/song/12001/; https://oursubversivevoice.com/song/12333/; https://oursubversivevoice.com/song/12050/.

148 Lynskey, *33 Revolutions Per Minute*, 485, 681–3.

149 Quoted in Lynskey, *33 Revolutions Per Minute*, 524.

Conclusion

1 Greil Marcus, *Folk Music: A Bob Dylan Biography in Seven Songs* (New Haven: Yale University Press, 2022), 85.

2 See 'Song Suggestions' at https://oursubversivevoice.com/voice/song-suggestions-the-people-have-spoken/.

3 *Last Word*, BBC Radio 4, 27 October 2023; available at: www.bbc.co.uk/sounds/play/m001rqzo.

4 John Hasted, *Alternative Memoirs* (Shipton Green, Sussex: Greengates Press, 1992), 45.

5 Quoted in Dave Simpson, 'Johnny Marr on the Smiths, Morrissey and Putting Politics Back in Pop', *Guardian*, 11 January 2013; available at: www.theguardian.com/music/2013/jan/11/johnny-marr-smiths-morrissey-politics-pop.

6 See https://oursubversivevoice.com/song/12471/ and https://oursubversivevoice.com/song/12443/.

7 Available at: https://oursubversivevoice.com/song/12262/.

8 Benedict Anderson, *Imagined Communities: Reflections on the Origins and Spread of Nationalism* (London: Verso, 1983).

9 Steve Connor, 'Choralities', *Twentieth-Century Music* 13, no. 1 (2016): 6.

10 Christian Lahusen writes of how the anti-apartheid song 'I Ain't Going to Play Sun City', 'with its sing-along tune', became 'a metaphor for the collective sanction' of South Africa's political system. Christian Lahusen, *The Rhetoric of Moral Protest: Public Campaigns, Celebrity Endorsement and Political Mobilization* (Berlin: Walter de Gruyter, 1996), 215.

11 Rob Rosenthal and Richard Flacks, *Playing for Change: Music and Musicians in the Service of Social Movements* (Boulder: Paradigm Publishers, 2012).

12 See the interview with Kimwei of Extinction Rebellion: https://oursubversivevoice.com/interview/kimwei/.

13 James Garratt, *Music and Politics: A Critical Introduction* (Cambridge: Cambridge University Press, 2018), 13.

14 Chris Waters, *British Socialists and the Politics of Popular Culture, 1884–1914* (Manchester: Manchester University Press, 1990), 97.

15 Garratt, *Music and Politics*, 132.

16 Oskar Cox Jensen, *Napoleon and British Song* (Houndmills: Palgrave Macmillan, 2015).

17 Simon Frith, *Performing Rites: On the Value of Popular Music* (Oxford: Oxford University Press, 1996), 20 (his emphasis).

18 Waters, *British Socialists*, 103–4.

19 Georgina Boyes, *The Imagined Village: Culture, Ideology and the English Folk Revival*, (Manchester: Manchester University Press, 1993), 63.

20 Dave Harker, *One for the Money: Politics and Popular Song* (London: Hutchinson, 1980).

21 Oliver Anthony's success was, it seems, not the result of music industry support and marketing (he had no record label), but rather of the support of right-wing media and the Republican Party.

Index of Songs

General Index